Rethinking Water Management

Innovative Approaches to Contemporary Issues

EDITED BY

CAROLINE M FIGUÈRES,
CECILIA TORTAJADA AND
JOHAN ROCKSTRÖM

Earthscan Publications Ltd
London • Sterling, VA

First published in the UK and USA in 2003
by Earthscan Publications Ltd

ISBN: 1-85383-994-9 paperback
       1-85383-999-X hardback

Typesetting by MapSet Ltd, Gateshead, UK
Printed and bound in the UK by Creative Print and Design (Wales), Ebbw Vale
Cover design by Danny Gillespie

For a full list of publications please contact:

Earthscan Publications Ltd
120 Pentonville Road, London, N1 9JN, UK
Tel: +44 (0)20 7278 0433
Fax: +44 (0)20 7278 1142
Email: earthinfo@earthscan.co.uk
Web: **www.earthscan.co.uk**

22883 Quicksilver Drive, Sterling, VA 20166-2012, USA

Earthscan is an editorially independent subsidiary of Kogan Page Ltd and publishes in
association with WWF-UK and the International Institute for Environment and
Development

A catalogue record for this book is available from the British Library

Library of Congress Cataloging-in-Publication Data

Rethinking water management : innovative approaches to contemporary issues / [edited
by] Caroline Figuáeres, Johan Rockstrèom, Cecilia Tortajada.
    p. cm.
  Includes bibliographical references and index.
  ISBN 1-85383-994-9 (pbk.) — ISBN 1-85383-999-X (hardback)
    1. Water-supply—Management. 2. Water resources development—Government
policy. 3. Water-supply—Management—International cooperation. I. Figuáeres,
Caroline. II. Rockstrèom, Johan. III. Tortajada, Cecilia

TD345.R47 2003
333.91—dc21

                                                                        2003006474

Contents

List of figures, tables and boxes

FIGURES

TABLES

BOX

About the contributors

Zahir Uddin Ahmad, Advisor, Development Aid, Royal Netherlands Embassy, Dhaka, Bangladesh, *zu.ahmad@dha.minbuza.nl*

Odeh Al-Jayyousi, Associate Professor, Civil Engineering Department, College of Engineering, Applied Science University, Amman, 11931 Jordan, *jayousi@go.com.jo*

Naser Faruqui, Senior Specialist (Water), International Development Research Centre, PO Box 8500, 250 Albert Street, Ottawa, Canada K1G 3H9, *nfaruqui@idrc.ca*

Caroline M Figuères, Head, Urban Infrastructure Department, UNESCO-IHE Delft, PO Box 3015, 2601DA Delft, The Netherlands, *cfi@ihe.nl*

Karin E Kemper, Senior Water Resources Specialist, Water Resources Management Unit, The World Bank, 1818 H St, NW, Washington, DC 20034, USA, *kkemper@worldbank.org*

Johan Rockström, Water Resources Expert, UNESCO-IHE Water Education Institute, PO Box 3015, 2601 DA Delft, The Netherlands, *jro@ihe.nl*

Christopher A Scott, Director, India Regional Office, International Water Management Institute (IWMI), c/o ICRISAT, Patancheru, A P 502 324, India, *c.scott@cgiar.org*

Dajun Shen, Senior Water Engineer, China Institute of Water Resources and Hydropower Research (IWHR), Department of Water Resources, Beijing 100044, China, *shendj@iwhr.com*

Cecilia Tortajada, Vicepresident, Third World Centre for Water Management, Mexico, Av Manantial Oriente 27, Los Clubes, Atizapán, Estado de México, 52958, Mexico, *thirdworldcentre@att.net.mx*

Aaron T Wolf, Associate Professor, Department of Geosciences, Oregon State University, Oregon, USA, *wolfa@geo.orst.edu*

Foreword

Predicting the future is a hazardous business but one thing is certain: the world in 2020 will be vastly different from that of today, perhaps altered significantly more by comparison with the changes that have occurred during the past 20 years. Among the main driving forces likely to contribute to future changes are the demographic transitions in different parts of the world, technological advances, the extent of globalization, improvements in human capital and national government policies.

Of these main drivers, demographic prospects are the most predictable over the period to the year 2020. We can now predict with reasonable certainty that population growth, especially in Africa and parts of South Asia, would account for much of the increase in world population, from 5 billion in 1990 to about 8 billion in 2020. The urbanization process is likely to be very significant in developing countries as their economic structures become increasingly more oriented towards industry and services. Current estimates indicate that the urban population of developing countries may rise from 33 per cent in 1990 to over 50 per cent by 2020, with a dramatic rise of a large number of megacities, especially in Asia.

All the above factors, individually and collectively, would affect water management in a variety of significant ways. Water and wastewater planning and management is likely to become an increasingly complex process in the coming decades. The ability of water professionals to appreciate the magnitude and extent of the unprecedented pressures that water resources would be concurrently subjected to in the coming decades, at global, regional and local levels, and their capacity to steer the management practices correctly, cost-effectively and in a timely manner in the uncharted new areas, will dictate whether the profession can successfully rise to the profoundly new challenges that would undoubtedly confront us in the future. Within countries, as well as among countries, the emerging complex issues would necessitate a thorough re-examination of the roles played by the state and other public and private actors. Unquestionably, new balances will have to be found between the various stakeholders. Changes in mindsets at all levels will be essential to help the different societies realize their expectations in terms of quantities and qualities of water available, economic and social benefits that could accrue from rational water management, and the preservation and maintenance of associated ecosystems. Water-related institutions may have to be radically restructured, and some politically unpalatable decisions may have to be taken if the water problems of the future are to be solved rationally. The continuation of the 'business as usual' practice would undoubtedly contribute to the rapid destabilization of the earlier fragile equilibrium, in terms of water use and availability, water quantity and quality interrelationships, and concurrent satisfaction of human and ecosystem needs. This continuation of existing policies will unquestionably prove to be too high a price to pay, and thus may be an unacceptable management alternative to society as a whole.

Past experiences in water resources management have conclusively demonstrated that the future solutions of current and emerging water problems need to span across regions, disciplines and stakeholders, and should be viewed within an inter-generational framework. However, development of an acceptable inter-generational framework would require intensive and extensive interactions between potential leaders of the next generation and the leading world experts of today, as well as continuing dialogues and interdisciplinary work across a full range of technical, economic, social, environmental and developmental issues. To make significant and sustainable progress, it is essential to appreciate that close interrelationships are needed between the young and the experienced water professionals in terms of continued dialogues, sharing and review of inter-generational expectations and visions. Such an inter-generational interaction process, if well planned and properly executed, would also impart the best knowledge and experiences available to the potential water leaders of the next generation so that they could develop much faster than otherwise may have been possible. This would mean that the potential leaders would not only become real leaders faster but would also become better and more effective leaders than may otherwise have been possible.

Unfortunately, however, for a variety of reasons, the potential water leaders of the next generation are not receiving the type of support and encouragement they need to be able to successfully lead the water profession during the first quarter of the 21st century. This is in spite of the fact that the water problems the next generation of water leaders will face will be significantly more complex and difficult compared with what we are witnessing at present. In addition, except for the Stockholm Water Symposium, no international forums exist where the potential leaders can receive the types of information and interactions that would speed up their leadership development process. Equally, because of the lack of interactions, the current generation of water leaders are not even aware of the present concerns and the thinkings of our younger counterparts. Thus, even though the present leaders claim to speak for the future generations, they are not even aware of the issues that concern most the next generation, except in a somewhat general fashion.

Faced with this unsatisfactory situation, the Third World Centre for Water Management in Mexico made a determined attempt to foster speedy development of the next generation of water leaders. With support from the Nippon Foundation, and assistance from the Stockholm International Water Institute (SIWI) and the International Water Resources Association (IWRA), the centre embarked upon a three-year programme to identify and mentor potential water leaders. The programme's objectives were to:

- identify potential water leaders of the next generation from all over the world;
- facilitate interactions between the potential leaders, as well as between the potential leaders and the current leaders;
- involve the potential leaders in the discussions of important national and international water issues;
- encourage the young leaders to develop their visions and solutions for water management for the coming decades; and
- promote an informal but functional network between the young leaders, as well as with the currently established leaders.

Nominations were invited from all over the world to identify potential leaders who were below the age of 40 on 1 January 1999. Nearly 300 nominations were received, ranging from Australia to Zimbabwe, from which a committee of leading international water experts selected 14 potential leaders. The entire group first met during the Second World Water Forum in The Hague, The Netherlands, in March 2000.

At this meeting, the group agreed that each member would identify and prepare an in-depth review of an important water issue. The group met for the second time in The Hague in 2001 to consider and critique the 14 draft papers with a view to publishing them in a single volume. During this second meeting, the group entrusted Caroline Figuères, Johan Rockström and Cecilia Tortajada to be the editors of the resulting book. Following the meeting, the finalized contributions were peer reviewed and ten were selected for inclusion in this book.

The programme has attracted considerable international attention. For example, during the 11th Stockholm Water Symposium in August 2001, five members of the group had a lively discussion with five winners of the Stockholm Water Prize. By all accounts, the potential leaders not only held their own against the established leaders but also gave an excellent performance. The group also organized an inter-generational dialogue at the Third World Water Forum in Kyoto, Osaka and Shiga, Japan, in March 2003, which was supported by the Toyota Foundation.

On behalf of our centre, I would like to thank each member of the group, and especially Caroline Figuères, Johan Rockström and Cecilia Tortajada, for making the present book possible. The programme was supported by the Nippon Foundation. I would also to like express our appreciation to Mr Reizo Utagawa and Mr Masanori Tamazawa of the Nippon Foundation for their interest and support in the overall programme, without which neither the activities nor the book would have been possible.

Asit K Biswas, President
Third World Centre for Water Management
Los Clubes, Atizapan
Estado de México, 52958 Mexico
Email: akbiswas@att.net.mx

List of acronyms and abbreviations

ACC	Administrative Sub-committee on Coordination (United Nations)
ACT	African Conservation Tillage
ADR	alternative dispute resolution
ASAL	agricultural structural adjustment loan
BAMWSP	Bangladesh Arsenic Mitigation Water Supply Project
BCM	billion cubic metres
BOD	biochemical oxygen demand
BOO	build-own-operate
BOT	build-operate-transfer
CBC	Canadian Broadcasting Corporation
cm	centimetre
CO_2	carbon dioxide
CIDA	Canadian International Development Agency
CNA	Comisión Nacional del Agua (Mexico)
CT	conservation tillage
DAP	di-ammonium phosphate
ECLAC	Economic Commission for Latin America and the Caribbean
EIA	environmental impact assessment
EPA	Environmental Protection Agency (USA)
ESA	external support aid
ESCAP	Economic and Social Commission for Asia and the Pacific
ET	evapotranspiration
EU	European Union
FAO	Food and Agriculture Organization of the United Nations
FAOSTAT	FAO Statistical Databases
FDI	foreign direct investment
GAP	Southeastern Anatolia Project (Turkey)
GATT	General Agreement on Tariffs and Trade
GBM	Ganges-Brahmaputra-Meghna
GCC	Gulf Cooperation Council
GDP	gross domestic product
GEF	Global Environment Facility
GIS	geographic information system
GLOF	glacier lake outburst flood
GNP	gross national product

GTZ	German government agency for international cooperation
GUI	graphical user interface
GWP	Global Water Partnership
ha	hectare
HIPC	Highly Indebted Poor Countries
HRD	human resources development
IBRD	International Bank for Reconstruction and Development
IDRC	International Development Research Centre (Canada)
IFC	International Finance Corporation
IHE	International Institute for Infrastructural, Hydraulic and Environmental Engineering (The Netherlands)
IMF	International Monetary Fund
IWM	integrated water management
IWMI	International Water Management Institute
IWRM	integrated water resource management
ITN	International Training Network for Water and Waste Management
JICA	Japan International Cooperation Agency
kcal	kilocalorie
kg	kilogram
km	kilometre
LGEEPA	Ley General de Equilibrio Ecológico y Protección Ambiental (General Law of Ecological Balance and Environmental Protection, Mexico)
LPCD	litres per capita per day
m	metre
M$	Mexican peso
MAP	mono-ammonium phosphate
MENA	Middle East and North Africa
mg	milligram
mm	millimetre
MMS	modular modelling system
MMT	methylcyclopentadienyl manganese tricarbonyl
MW	megawatts
N	nitrogen
NAFTA	North American Free Trade Agreement
NGO	non-governmental organization
OECD	Organisation for Economic Co-operation and Development
OFWAT	Office of Water Services (UK)
P	phosphorus
PAP	project affected person
ppm	parts per million
PPP	public–private partnership
PRA	participatory rural appraisal

PROFEPA	Procuraduria Federal de Protección al Ambiente (Office of the Federal Attorney for Environmental Protection, Mexico)
PRSP	'Poverty Reduction Strategy Paper'
PUP	public–public partnership
RRA	rapid rural appraisal
RSD©	Rapid Spray Distillation©
SAARC	South Asian Association for Regional Cooperation
SADC	South African Development Community
SME	small- or medium-sized enterprise
T	transpiration
t	tonne
TDS	total dissolved solids
UFW	unaccounted for water
UK	United Kingdom
UN	United Nations
UNCED	United Nations Conference on Environment and Development (*known as the* Earth Summit)
UNCHS (Habitat)	United Nations Centre for Human Settlements (*now* UN-HABITAT)
UNDP	United Nations Development Programme
UNEP	United Nations Environment Programme
UNESCO	United Nations Educational, Scientific and Cultural Organization
UNGA	United Nations General Assembly
UN-HABITAT	United Nations Human Settlements Programme (*formerly* UNCHS (Habitat))
USA	United States of America
USAID	United States Agency for International Development
WAPDA	Water and Power Development Authority (Pakistan)
WCED	World Commission on Environment and Development (*known as the* Brundtland Commission)
WHC	water holding capacity
WHO	World Health Organization
WSSD	World Summit on Sustainable Development
WTO	World Trade Organization

Chapter 1

Introduction

CECILIA TORTAJADA, JOHAN ROCKSTRÖM AND
CAROLINE FIGUÈRES

At the dawn of a new century, we are at a critical juncture in the area of water management. According to the report of the World Commission on Water for the 21st Century (World Water Commission, 2000), renewable blue water flows will be insufficient to meet all industrial, domestic and agricultural needs by 2020, primarily due to growing water pollution, population growth, urbanization and inappropriate management practices. Many countries are already facing water crises, particularly those in arid and semi-arid regions. A new generation of water managers is needed, with new mindsets that can develop and implement innovative policies and practices. In brief, water management in the 21st century must change: business as usual is no longer a viable option. Yet, throughout human history, change is almost always resisted, especially when it is revolutionary.

Future water management at global, regional and local scales is an area of increasing concern among water professionals, policy-makers and the public in general. This is because the current trends indicate that water scarcity is likely to threaten up to 50 per cent of the world population within the next generation, and continued mismanagement of water will result in significant local and regional water quality deteriorations. Many governments, international institutions and experts have started to address the urgent need to establish a new development agenda in the field of water management. Awareness of water crisis is well underway now, but mental switch has yet to happen.

During the last three decades, a wide range of economic, environmental and social reforms have been put in place in the water sector of both developed and developing countries. Institutions have been established and/or strengthened, legislations have been passed and instruments have been formulated. Inter-sectoral approaches and water quality management are receiving increasing attention, and the general public is becoming increasingly aware of the importance of water to economic development, improvements in the lifestyles of the people and environmental conservation.

Global gatherings on water resources have also been organized for the last three decades. The most important one at high policy-making level was the United Nations Water Conference held in Mar del Plata, Argentina, in 1977. Some 15 years later, the United Nations Conference on Environment and Development (UNCED, known as the Earth Summit) discussed many aspects of water in Rio de Janeiro, Brazil, 1992. A prelude to the Earth Summit was the International Conference on Water and Environment in Dublin, Ireland, in 1992. In 2001, the International Conference on Freshwater was organized in Bonn, Germany, as a preparatory meeting for the World Summit on Sustainable Development (WSSD) in Johannesburg, South Africa, in 2002. In addition to these gatherings, the First, Second and Third World Water Forums met in Marrakesh, Morocco, The Hague, The Netherlands, and in Kyoto, Osaka and Shiga, Japan, in 1997, 2000 and 2003 respectively.

Past experiences in water resources management have conclusively demonstrated that the future solutions of current and emerging water problems need to span across regions, disciplines and stakeholders, and should be viewed within an inter-generational framework. However, development of an acceptable inter-generational framework would require intensive and extensive interactions between potential leaders of the next generation and the present leading world experts, as well as continuing dialogues and interdisciplinary work across a full range of technical, economic, social, environmental and developmental issues. To make significant and sustainable progress, it is essential to appreciate that close interrelationships are needed between the young and the experienced water professionals in terms of continued dialogues, sharing and review of inter-generational expectations and visions. Such an inter-generational interaction process, if well planned and properly executed, would also impart the best knowledge and experiences available to the potential water leadership of the next generation so that they could develop much faster than otherwise may have been possible. This would mean that the potential leaders would not only become leaders faster, but would also become more effective.

Thus, it is essential to blend mature concepts with new approaches, which in many instances the next generation of water managers may be better able to address and implement. This book looks to contribute to the effort of influencing the mindset of the various water actors so that they can comprehensibly face the increasingly alarming water crisis.

The contributors to this book often challenge the current wisdoms in terms of paradigm changes; global and local agendas; globalization and its impact on equity issues; transboundary water management and groundwater management; water rights; water for agriculture as well as recycling and reuse of wastewater for agriculture; financing of water management; etc. The present and future challenges of social and environmental issues are addressed in all of the chapters.

Chapter 2 points out that one main constraint to an efficient water planning and management strategy is that most developing countries face fundamental problems that relate to issues as basic as the definition of goals and objectives regarding policy formulation and implementation, as well as institutional arrangements. Concepts such as sustainable development and river-basin management are appealing, and have received widespread global acceptance from national and international institutions in recent years. However, while concepts such as integrated water resources management or sustainable development have become popular and are extensively mentioned in national and/or regional policies, their effective incorporation and implementation have proved to be extremely difficult, irrespective of the country concerned. Thus, there is an increasing urgency to move from concept to implementation, and from vision to action. This means that to follow the global agenda, countries have to overcome shortcomings, such as inadequate institutional and legal frameworks for integrating environment and development-related issues, highly centralized decision-making, absence of political will to change the status quo, lack of an adequate number of qualified and trained personnel, and non-availability of financial resources on a timely basis. Chapter 2 analyses some of the current conceptual frameworks and theories on development as they relate to water resources. It concludes that the present frameworks should be carefully analysed and, if necessary, reconsidered, the final objective being to contribute to increasingly more efficient water management.

Chapter 3 focuses on the fact that it is precisely the convergence or divergence in the global and local agendas in water management that results in the gaps of communication between those who look at the big picture as represented in the World Water Vision developed by the World Water Council (Cosgrove and Rijsberman, 2000), and those who focus on day-to-day water issues. It argues that, in essence, this dialogue represents the divergence in development paradigms and means of linking theory to practice between the North and the South. For example, 'think global, act local' is a well-known saying that still needs to be formalized and operationalized. This concept dates back to *The Ecologist*'s *Blueprint for Survival* (1972), Schumacher's *Small is Beautiful* (1973) and the Brundtland Commission report, *Our Common Future* (1987). However, the implementation of community-based water resources development projects has frequently fallen short of expectations. Chapter 3 intends to shed light on the linkages and divergences in the global and local agendas in water management. A review of the goals and visions of water at the global level is assessed in terms of action at the local level. Special emphasis is given to the balance between sustainable development and economic growth. A case study is presented on global and local agendas regarding water management, with specific reference to the Middle East and North Africa (MENA) region.

Another topic related to the global agenda is economic globalization and its impact on water management, including the principle of treating water as an economic good and the resulting controversy. Chapter 4 argues that with globalization come new ideas and approaches that offer opportunities and pose some risks to water management. The discussion takes an even-handed look at water and globalization – a very complex topic where debate and research are in its infancy. Rather than examining any one topic in great depth, the analysis covers the range of issues related to water in order to provide a general framework for further discussion, debate and research. It challenges some of the common arguments against full-cost pricing and public–private partnerships, while also identifying some of the potential negative impacts of economic globalization on water management. It argues that neither private nor public utilities are the sole means for achieving sustainable and equitable water management. It concludes by examining the impact of international trade on water management.

Regarding water for food, Chapter 5 introduces the fact that, over the next generation, humankind will be confronted with an enormous challenge of securing water resources to feed 80 million new persons per year, without jeopardizing water requirements for natural ecosystems. The challenge is not normally distributed on Earth, as 95 per cent of the population growth occurs in developing countries that are located in tropical and subtropical environments, of which a large proportion is in semi-arid, drought-prone landscapes. Chapter 5 addresses strategies for improved rural livelihoods through water and soil productivity in agriculture in smallholder farming systems. It focuses on the region on Earth where the poverty–water–food–environment challenge is largest, namely in semi-arid rural watersheds in sub-Saharan Africa. A future-oriented approach is taken, beginning with a critical assessment of the past approach to water resources management. The analysis shows that applying a more pragmatic development paradigm that blends top-down and bottom-up approaches, while integrating innovations with indigenous capacities, will generate larger opportunities for significantly improved crop yields in semi-arid rain-fed farming systems. It demonstrates the urgent need for a shift in hydrological thinking from a blue water bias towards a blended green–blue approach, which naturally leads to the abandonment of the inappropriate distinction between irrigated and rain-fed farming. The discussion focuses on the opportunities lost as long as a business-as-usual approach to rural development in so-called dry lands is applied. It shows that semi-arid savannah agro-ecosystems present large inherent development potential that, if properly identified and developed in partnership with local stakeholders, could result in a prosperous 21st century for agriculture in the hot semi-arid tropics.

One main issue at present is the scarcity of water in many regions of the world, and the rapidly growing dependency on non-conventional 'derivative' water sources, mainly in regions facing water scarcity. Chapter 6 shows that the approach of the present 'peer' generation to water management has largely been supply driven, based on major capital investment and centralized, bureaucratic management institutions that grapple with environmental and social issues associated with water resources development. It notes that that there is recent, welcome recognition of demand-side options, and that a significant attraction of derivative water is that its very use helps to overcome the demand–supply debacle. As options that impose high access costs (social, institutional, financial and environmental), derivative sources internalize the need for conservation. Chapter 6 aims to open the debate on the use of non-conventional water sources by addressing how relevant they are compared to primary water sources, as well as a range of questions related to access. Cross-sectoral linkages have confounded conventional management approaches and water multipliers despite the fact that water used for human purposes follows cycles, as in its natural state. While water recycling and reuse may not currently appeal to increasingly consumer-oriented societies, they will inevitably become central to water management. There are a variety of reasons for this, including the need to internalize the changes and costs associated with particular uses of water, and the growing scarcity of water worldwide, particularly in arid and semi-arid regions with moderate to high demand for water.

The very important topic of groundwater management is also analysed. Given the importance of groundwater – its increasing role in domestic, municipal, industrial and irrigation supply, and the socio-economic, environmental and health problems related to current trends – Chapter 7 highlights the importance of providing groundwater users with adequate incentives to begin a more sustainable era of groundwater management. These include both economic incentives as well as the power for the different groundwater users to make decisions about their resource. The focus of Chapter 7 is primarily on developing countries, as well as issues related to the need for groundwater management due to aquifer overexploitation and, to a certain extent, pollution. Worldwide, a situation has developed where some countries are regionally suffering from overdraft of their aquifers, such as Mexico, Yemen, the USA, China, Jordan and India, while other countries are more known for groundwater quality problems, such as Argentina, The Netherlands, Germany and Bangladesh. A neglected aspect is that countries that are traditionally more concerned with groundwater overexploitation are also subject to water pollution. The analysis does not attempt to provide a sole solution to groundwater management. However, it proposes that it is important to think about the underlying issues that prevent effective groundwater management and how to tackle those issues. Addressing groundwater issues from a technical perspective alone, as has been unsuccessfully tried in a number of cases, is clearly not sufficient.

The issue of water rights is highly debated at the national and international levels. Chapter 8 mentions that, in the resources allocation process, the right to property is the most critical issue due to its impact on water management. While there is a series of concerns regarding water rights (price, transfer, priority uses, third-party effects), one potential advantage of the market mechanisms approach is that it can improve the efficiency of water resources allocation. One important issue that is mentioned is that perfect market operation is based on private ownership rights, while water is a life-supporting resource and cannot be fully assigned to private property rights. This is a dilemma. It is necessary to achieve a balance between the assignment of rights and the development of the market in order to meet the social and environmental objectives, as well as to allocate water resources efficiently. That is the critical issue facing water rights management in the water sector. Case studies are analysed, China being one of them.

Regarding development on water bodies that cross political boundaries, Chapter 9 analyses the disparities between riparian nations (in terms of economic development, infrastructure capacity or political orientation) that add further complications to water resources development, institutions and management. The fortunate corollary of water as an inducement to conflict is that water, by its very nature, tends to induce even hostile co-riparians to cooperate, even as disputes rage over other issues. At present, there are 261 watersheds that cross the political boundaries of two or more countries, covering 45.3 per cent of the land surface of the Earth, affecting about 40 per cent of the world's population, and accounting for approximately 80 per cent of global river flow. These basins have certain characteristics that make their management especially difficult, most notably the tendency for regional politics to regularly exacerbate the already difficult task of understanding and managing complex natural systems. As a consequence, development, treaties and institutions are regularly seen as inefficient and ineffective, and, occasionally, as new sources of tensions themselves. Despite the tensions inherent in the international setting, riparians have shown tremendous creativity in approaching regional development, often through preventative diplomacy and the creation of 'baskets of benefits' that allow for positive-sum, integrative allocations of joint gains. It is argued that development on waters crossing political boundaries has complexities brought about by strains in riparian relations and institutional limitations.

Along the same line, water development potentials are discussed in depth in Chapter 10 on the Ganges-Brahmaputra-Meghna (GBM) region, beyond the limit of its political boundary to derive a win–win scenario. The GBM region river systems constitute the second largest hydrologic region in the world. The total drainage area is about 1.75 million square kilometres, stretching across five countries: Bangladesh, Bhutan, China, India and Nepal. While Bangladesh and India share all three rivers, China shares the Brahmaputra and the Ganges, Nepal only the Ganges, and Bhutan only the Brahmaputra. The region is rich in natural resources, including water; but the irony is that over 600 million people who live in this region are still struck by endemic poverty: one tenth the population of the world. The development and utilization of the region's water resources had never been sought in an integrated manner by the countries concerned because of past differences, legacies of mistrust and lack of goodwill. An integrated and holistic approach to the development of the region, considering water resources as a point of departure, is desperately needed for this region. The abundance of water in the GBM region as a shared resource can serve as a principal agent of development for millions of people living in the region, thus achieving a win–win scenario. A number of options and opportunities exist for collaborative efforts in sectors such as hydropower development; flood management; dry season flow augmentation and water sharing; water quality improvement; navigation; and catchment/watershed management.

Regarding water sector investment, the World Water Vision and the associated Framework for Action developed during the Second World Water

Forum in The Hague in 2000 estimate the cost of required water services for developing countries in the period between 2000 and 2025 at around US$180 billion per year. And this estimate is only for new works. It does not account for the costs of maintenance, rehabilitation and replacement. The sectoral breakdown is about US$30 billion for agriculture, US$75 billion for environment and industry, and US$75 billion for water supply and sanitation. At present, the largest investor in water services in developing countries is government (the traditional public sector), which contributes about US$50 billion. The domestic private sector contributes US$15 billion. International donors contribute a further US$9 billion (the World Bank, for example, accounts for about US$3 billion), and the international private sector contributes around US$4 billion. The total is therefore only US$78 billion per annum. The annual shortfall between demand and present resources is unimaginably huge: US$102 billion per year for new works alone. Chapter 11 analyses the present situation and tries to explain why it is so difficult to meet the financial challenge in developing countries. The main challenges include how to channel money into the water sector; how to use available money in a more efficient way; and how to change the perception of risk in relation to water infrastructure. The analysis also suggests some concrete actions to complement the proposals contained in the World Water Vision, and examines their feasibility. Chapter 11 has a second purpose. The financial shortfall must be made up as soon as possible. It is necessary to speed up progress towards the set targets and find new ways of pumping money into the water sector. Hence, this chapter is written to improve communication between financial specialists and users of financial services in the water sector. It aims to increase understanding on both sides and to facilitate the decision-making process.

Despite the increased attention to future water problems and challenges, a major constraint continues to be how to establish an enabling environment that could accommodate the necessary shift from the present unacceptable state of affairs to a more sustained future. Surprisingly, alarming reports on water quantity and quality deterioration have not translated into the paradigm shifts and institutional set-ups necessary to deal with the problems. It is still business as usual in most water sectors of the world. Advances continue to be incremental in nature.

Overall, the book deals with essential paradigm shifts while addressing some major water sector 'hot spots', all within a new and fresh framework proposed by a new kind of water manager.

REFERENCES

World Water Commission (2000) *World Water Vision: Commission Report – A Water Secure World: Visions for Water, Life and the Environment*, World Water Council, Marseille

Cosgrove, W J and Rijsberman, F R (2000) *World Water Vision: Making Water Everybody's Business*, World Water Council, Earthscan, London

Chapter 2

Rethinking development paradigms for the water sector

CECILIA TORTAJADA

INTRODUCTION

The development landscape has evolved during the second half of the last century, mainly because the practices of development have not produced the expected results. The inclination has been to consider the development goals equal to the more narrowly conceived objective of economic growth as measured by the rise in gross national product (GNP).

While in the 1970s the debate was about environment versus economic growth, during the 1990s it was about growth and development, where development was seen as improvement on the quality of life of the populations (Pearce et al, 1999). During both decades, attempts were made to articulate alternatives to an almost exclusive reliance on conventional indicators, such as economic growth, in terms of GNP, balance of payments, employment, index of inflation, etc. Among other catchwords, 'qualitative growth' was one of the first to signal a new direction in societal interest. It was argued that growth exclusively in terms of GNP for some activities is incompatible with environmental goals, while growth in other activities (with related goods and services) is beneficial (Soderbaum, 1998).

At present, it is usually recognized that high economic growth does not itself guarantee the easing of urgent social and human problems (Gillespie, 2001; Easterly, 2001; Soderbaum, 2000). In fact, many countries with high growth rates have also experienced increasing unemployment, rising income disparities both between groups and between regions, and deteriorating social, cultural and environmental conditions (Easterly, 2001). Policy-makers have realized that development should go well beyond economic growth to encompass social goals, focusing not only on income distribution per se, but also on issues such as increased employment generation and the provision of better social services such as education and health facilities. The end objectives of development are to improve quality of life and to create a better environment.

Regarding water policy formulation and implementation, as well as institutional arrangements, most of the developing countries face fundamental problems relating to issues as basic as the definition of goals and objectives (ECLAC, 1998). Both the planning and management of natural resources, water included, are plagued by concepts that often cannot be implemented because they are not properly defined and operationalized. However, despite these shortcomings, the governments often insist on using certain paradigms, such as sustainable development, simply because they are part of the current global thinking – even though they represent more of a concept than a reality that can be implemented (Dragun and Jakobsson, 1997; Meppem and Bourke, 1999; Meppem and Gill, 1998). Thus, it is somewhat unlikely that any government pursuing sustainable development, as it is defined at present, will develop feasible plans that can be implemented properly.

There is an urgent need for water professionals to move from concept to implementation. Global paradigms such as sustainable development and integrated water resources management are conceptually attractive, but their actual implementation in operational terms has much to be desired. It is important, then, to objectively analyse their applicability – conceptual attractiveness alone is not a solution. Rather than ignoring the need for alternative conceptual frameworks that can be implemented, individuals and institutions should collectively welcome constructive analyses and criticisms of the existing mainstream approaches. Some of the current conceptual frameworks and theories on water development should be carefully analysed and, if necessary, reconsidered. Such analyses and open discussions can only be beneficial to the water profession, and may also contribute to increasingly more efficient water management.

The objective of this chapter is to analyse the effectiveness of some global paradigms in the field of water, as well as the necessity to move from concept to implementation in terms of water management. Many concepts are used extensively at present, such as sustainable development, environmental sustainability, integrated water resources management or integrated river basin management. However, this chapter will only analyse the concepts of sustainable development and environmental sustainability of water projects. Since the origin of 'sustainable development' is not well known, a brief review of its evolution is included. A case study shows that, even though some of our developing countries have adopted the global views in theory, they still need to strengthen their institutions, implement legislation, develop long-term policies, and build management capacity to ensure that the theory is translated into effective practices.

SUSTAINABLE DEVELOPMENT

Evolution of the concept

Even though the concept of sustainability has been used extensively since the mid 1980s, the idea is not new. For example, the term 'sustainability' has been widely used in fisheries and forestry for nearly a century to define long-term management techniques for harvesting reproducible natural resources. Thus, terminology such as 'maximum safe yield' has been common for decades in the fishery and forestry fields.

Contrary to the popular view, the concept of sustainable development did not start with the publication of the report by the World Commission on Environment and Development (WCED, known as the Brundtland Commission) in 1987. In fact, by the mid 1980s, well before this report was published, the concept of sustainable development had been popularized, initially through the work of the United Nations Environment Programme (UNEP), and later by the activities of the World Bank.

The earliest reference to the concept of sustainable development, as well as the use of this terminology, goes back at least half a century. It is possible that other authors may have used this terminology before 1948, even though no such reference was found during the course of research for this chapter.

In 1948, Fairfield Osborne, the founder and the then president of the Conservation Foundation, wrote in his book *Our Plundered Planet* that:

> *We are rushing forward unthinkingly through days of incredible accomplishment...and we have forgotten the earth, forgotten it in the sense that we are failing to regard it as the source of our life.*

Osborne was concerned with the 'accumulated velocity with which [man] is destroying his own life sources'. He insisted that the only kind of development that makes sense is 'development that can be sustained'.

In 1962, the United Nations General Assembly (UNGA) recognized that 'to be effective, measures to preserve natural resources should be taken at the earliest possible moment simultaneously with economic development' (UNGA, 1962). Later, both during the African Convention on the Conservation of Nature and Natural Resources in 1968 (UNTS, 1968) and the United Nations Second Development Decade in 1970 (UNGA, 1970), it was mentioned again that economic development should consider the preservation of natural resources. In 1971, the Founex Report stated that 'the recognition of environmental issues is an aspect of this widening of the development concept' (UNEP, 1981). During the United Nations Conference on the Human Environment in Stockholm in June 1972, there was a realization that 'States should adopt an integrated and coordinated approach to their development planning so as to ensure that development is compatible with the need to protect and improve the human environment for the benefit of their population' (Stockholm Declaration, 1972, Principle 11 in UNEP, 1981; Gillespie, 2001).

Intellectually, however, the concept of sustainable development was promoted by UNEP, which was established in Nairobi, Kenya, as a direct result of the Stockholm Conference. A small group of environmental scientists meeting in Nairobi in 1975, under the aegis of UNEP, extended the concept of sustainability from fisheries and forestry to the development process itself.

Shortly after this meeting, Mostafa Kamal Tolba, then executive director of UNEP, in an address in London, pointed out (Tolba, 1982):

> *A new kind of development is needed because it is essential to relate development to the limitations and opportunities created by the natural resource base to all human activities. It is also required because it is now clear that past patterns of development in both developed and developing countries have been characterized by such serious environmental damage that they are simply not sustainable.*

Tolba then went on to argue:

> *The most pressing objective of environmental management is to meet basic human needs within the potentials and constraints of environmental systems, including natural resources. Environmental management brings two new dimensions to the development process: it broadens the concept to include environmental quality, and it expands it in time to include development over the long term on a sustainable basis.*

Tolba's eloquent arguments for a new form of development process that is sustainable over the long term touched a chord in the environment movement. In 1981, A W Clausen, then president of the World Bank, gave a major statement on 'Sustainable development: The global imperative' (Clausen, 1981). A year later, during the commemoration of the tenth anniversary of the Stockholm Conference in Nairobi during 10–18 May 1982, the world community of states unanimously recommended 'sustainable socio-economic development'. The Nairobi Declaration, resulting from the commemorative meeting, concluded by urging (Tolba, 1988):

> *...all Governments and peoples of the world to discharge their historical responsibility, collectively and individually, to ensure that our small planet is passed over to future generations in a condition which guarantees a life in human dignity for all.*

In its report entitled *Our Common Future*, the WCED (1987) recommended the concept of sustainable development, which it loosely defined as 'development that meets the needs of the present without compromising the ability of the future generations to meet their own needs'.

Even though the WCED report made continual references to sustainable development, it was totally silent on how the concept could be operationalized. Sustainable development was to be achieved in an unspecified and undetermined way some time in the future. Nor did the definition include the realization of an equitably distributed level of economic well-being, without which no development can be sustained over the long term, especially in developing countries (Biswas, 1997).

The UNGA considered both the WCED report and a UNEP report called *Environmental Perspective to the Year 2000 and Beyond*. In Resolution 42/186, UNGA (1987) noted that 'different views exist on some aspects' of the WCED and UNEP reports but it also welcomed:

> *...as the overall aspirational goal for the world community the achievement of sustainable development on the basis of prudent management of available global resources and environmental capacities and the rehabilitation of the environment previously subjected to degradation and misuse.*

Following the work of UNEP and the WCED, and the passing of the UNGA Resolution 42/186, sustainable development became *the* development paradigm. The various United Nations (UN) agencies, all of the development banks and the bilateral aid agencies, and nearly all of the governments embraced the paradigm of sustainable development, even though its definition was broad and general. Additionally, no serious discussion ever took place about how the concept could be operationalized in the real world so that a development process could be managed from the very beginning to ensure that it becomes inherently sustainable.

The discourse

As mentioned before, in response to the perceived threat of impending ecological crisis during the post-1970 period, a dominant environmental discourse was constructed. Certain words were favoured for their ability to evoke images of consensus, unity and common purpose, such as sustainability, diversity, democracy, community, globalization and environment. An important consideration within this overall environmental discourse has been the concept of sustainable development and mechanisms to address it. But so far there has been no agreement on the meaning or definition of sustainable development. Thus, it is not surprising that little consensus exists regarding the formulation of sustainable development policies, except in broad and general terms (Bourke and Meppem, 2000; Meppem, 2000; Meppem and Bourke, 1999; Dragun and Jacobsson, 1997; Goodland, 1997; Biswas, 1996).

The ongoing debate about sustainable development and its various meanings is very much ideological (Soderbaum, 2000). The diversity of discourses on sustainable development does not reflect conflict over content. Instead, it reflects a conflict over interests and opinions that results from different sectors of society ensuring that their own needs and interests are represented in the decision-making process. Thus, sustainable development may not refer to a quantifiable goal that can be achieved at any specific moment in time. Instead, it may refer to the possibility of establishing a balance between environmental, social and economic interactions. This process, at least in theory, should improve quality of life and, simultaneously, maintain the integrity of the environment.

Sustainable development may benefit future human development, while constraining present development. It may guarantee certain life opportunities in the future, but at the cost of present life opportunities. At first glance, sustainable development may appear easy; in reality, it is quite complex. A series of decisions must be made by several generations of people throughout the world and at different levels of government. There are changing socio-economic conditions, differing cultural values, uncertainties and socio-economic goals that are seldom shared by everyone. This is because people tend to work at the individual level (Dourojeanni, 1999). In addition, nation states have their own interests that may change over time. This complexity could result in a permanent gap between the current understanding and the one necessary to comprehensively address evolving economic, social and environmental planning and management issues.

Working with the concept of sustainable development means embracing ambiguity. If conflicts in interpretations over sustainable development reflect the diversity of concerns, then we must learn how to accommodate these divergent claims. Additionally, if relations among citizens and public and private sectors are increasingly interdependent, necessary processes and policies should be developed in order to approach the various interests from an integral viewpoint (Meppem, 2000; Meppem and Gill, 1998).

Bottlenecks for its implementation

In order to design appropriate policies for sustainable development, goals must have specific indicators. However, these choices are subjective by nature and dependent on the cultural preferences of an individual, a community or a country. This implies that different societies with differing social, economic and cultural conditions may choose different sustainability criteria, and may even select different paths to sustainability (Raskin et al, 1998). Thus, one of the greatest difficulties for achieving sustainable development is the lack of indicators to properly measure it. This is because none of the three objectives of sustainable development (economic, environmental and social objectives) are currently measured using compatible parameters. The indicators used to quantify the economic, social and environmental objectives do not have a common denominator, nor do universal conversion formulae exist – economic growth is measured using economic indicators, social equity is determined on the basis of social parameters, and environmental protection is measured in physical and biological terms. Given the absence of suitable indicators, it is not possible to link the three objectives (Dourojeanni, 1997).

At the same time, sustainable development cannot be achieved if emphasis is placed solely on one of the economic, social or environmental objectives at the expense of the others. Thus, stakeholders must contribute simultaneously to economic growth, social equity and environmental protection, most likely through trade-offs, negotiations and by modifying everyday practices. The agreements between various stakeholders are likely to be more productive and equitable if there is an understanding of the actual value of the specific resources and products (Dourojeanni, 1997). However, values are often subjective. Therefore, a comparison of subjective values can be difficult under the best of circumstances (see Chapter 11).

Another major issue confronting sustainable development comprises the risks and uncertainties inherently associated with complex systems. For example, it is universally accepted that food production must be maximized to feed an expanding population base in developing countries. Accordingly, resources such as land and water must be used intensively to maximize food production. A fundamental question for which there is no clear-cut answer is, then, up to what level can the food production system be intensified without sacrificing sustainability (see Chapter 5)? There are other difficult questions, as well. For example, in the area of water, what early warnings could indicate the beginning of a transition process from sustainability to unsustainability? What parameters should be monitored to indicate that such a transition is about to occur or, indeed, is occurring? Existing knowledge bases and databases are inadequate for identifying all of the relevant parameters that could indicate passage from one stage to another. Thus, it is not possible to accurately detect, much less predict, the transition of a sustainable system to an unsustainable one and vice versa (Biswas, 1996; see Chapter 7).

In order to formulate sustainable water development policies, developing countries require more knowledge, expertise, data and information than they currently possess. One of the first priorities should be to broaden their knowledge in the technical, economic, social and environmental fields. Research, training and capacity building, both for individuals and institutions, should be developed, keeping in mind the kinds of environmental problems that they are likely to face during the process of water development over the next several decades. Developing nations should base their development agendas on their own administrative, technical, scientific and economic capacities. For water development to be more effective, those being educated must approach their disciplines from a broader perspective, and develop knowledge that will be useful to decision-makers outside the academic and research fields (Serageldin, et al, 1998; see Chapters 11 and 12).

In terms of technology, we must remember that while it may have a major impact on the global development process, technology may not necessarily solve demographic, social and environmental problems. The level of technological impact often depends on the social context and – more specifically – on how, when and whether it is used. Technological innovations may have important economic effects, lowering costs through improved efficiency, making alternatives possible, and accelerating economic growth. However, the development of new technology is often less important than its appropriate use (see Chapter 6). Whether technology will solve all or most water-related problems remains to be seen. Social factors have the definitive say in its implementation, and it may take decades before new technology is adopted, and even longer for societies to reap the benefits (Hammond, 1998).

Integrating environmental concerns with development planning requires action at the national level. Some of the major policy areas may include location (or relocation) of industries, land-use policies, and community development. Proper planning of infrastructures is important in order to ensure that individual development projects are integrated within an overall framework of regional development planning and management. The social benefits and costs of projects, including their favourable and unfavourable impact on the environment, should be fully reflected in these policies. Too often the negative impacts of projects have been ignored in the initial planning stage, and societal awareness of the environmental disruptions resulting from these projects has come late when construction is already finished and the adverse impacts have begun to surface. Cost-effective alternatives available at such late stages to take ameliorative measures are limited. Accordingly, it is important to analyse comprehensively both the favourable and unfavourable social and environmental impacts before implementing development projects. This way, society is able to compare the impacts against the economic and social benefits that are expected from the project. Feasible alternatives can then be considered (Modak and Biswas, 2001; Tortajada, 2000).

ENVIRONMENTAL SUSTAINABILITY OF WATER PROJECTS

The interest in environmental management at the global level resulted from the establishment of legal and institutional frameworks in both developed and developing countries, as well as from economic, social and environmental policies and instruments that have promoted simultaneous economic development, social welfare and environmental protection. Regarding water development projects, sustainability may depend on how economic, social and environmental issues are approached during the planning, construction and operation of the projects.

It still has not been easy to know when water projects should be considered sustainable or unsustainable, mainly due to the difficulty of defining sustainability in operational and quantitative terms. One hypothesis is that identifying and estimating a project's environmental and social costs, through a comprehensive assessment process, can show whether it is sustainable or unsustainable. However, at present no technique exists that can reliably identify and price all of the environmental and social costs. According to Mikesell (1994), for a project to be sustainable, the following conditions must be met: depleted renewable natural resources must be restored; compensation to future generations for depleted non-renewable natural resource capital must be included in the social cost of the project; and damage to life-supporting natural resources and environmental assets must be avoided. The compensation included in the social cost of the project may take the form of either a contribution to the quantity and/or quality of natural resource assets equivalent to what has been depleted or damaged, or the accumulation of a fund sufficient to offset the loss of income to future generations resulting from the depletion of natural resource capital. Mikesell (1994), however, agrees that there are limits to compensation levels. It may be impossible to find a substitute for environmental assets damaged beyond a certain absorptive capacity of the environment, and it would be unrealistic to assume that, in economic terms, real loss from the depletion of natural resources can be replaced. It can be concluded that, as attractive as the economic instruments are, practical techniques to identify and estimate all of the environmental and the social costs within the framework of environmental management are not currently available. And the methodologies and implementation strategies for economic instruments, in general, have not proven themselves in practice. Therefore, at least methodologically, the degree by which compensation in the form of financial capital can substitute the loss of certain kinds of natural capital is severely limited.

Even though there are no blueprints for a transition to environmental sustainability, there are policy reforms that could reduce environmental degradation. As mentioned before, to guarantee environmental protection, including the protection of humans, most countries have developed legal and institutional frameworks, including a series of environmental regulations. One of the most frequently used instruments for environmental policy and decision-making in both developed and developing countries is the environmental impact assessment (EIA), which makes it possible to assess the social, economic and environmental impacts of development projects.

EIA, when properly conducted, provides a range of alternatives for development processes, since it can be used to review policies, programmes and project proposals. It also has the potential to integrate these proposals with other instruments available for environmental planning, such as land-use planning, economic instruments, environmental regulations, environmental auditing, public participation and access to information. One of the important aspects of EIA is that, at least in theory, economic, social and environmental considerations are given the same weight, within the same time frame for decision-making purposes (Tortajada, 1999a, 1999b).

One important issue that requires special attention is whether environmental sustainability (as 'assessed' with the help of EIA) should be approached differently in developed and developing countries, or if a unique process should be developed and implemented in general. To answer these questions, it is important to remember that the conditions prevalent for environmental management in developing countries may be different from those in developed countries. Availability of funds and expertise may be limited in developing countries (see Chapter 11). Additionally, the data necessary to identify and estimate the various environmental impacts may not be readily available, and, if available, the quality of the data may be uncertain (see Chapter 10). However, many developed and developing countries share the same concerns regarding environmental management, including post-development auditing; process implementation costs; process development and support costs; estimation of cumulative impacts; availability of adequate funding and time for conducting environmental studies; accessibility of information; and the timing of studies during project or programme development and its implementation process (Modak and Biswas, 2001; Canter, 1997; Ortalano, 1997).

It is clear that there are no universal solutions. Therefore, it would be difficult for developed and developing countries to approach environmental sustainability in a similar fashion. Each country would rather develop the most appropriate methodology for assessing water projects and programmes, as well as establish its own priorities in accordance with prevailing conditions, needs, national plans, policies and programmes, and social expectations. In other words, developing countries should not automatically accept solutions that may have been formulated specifically for use in developed countries. These alternatives should be carefully reviewed and, if necessary, adapted to suit the conditions prevalent in developing countries.

Institutional acceptability of the EIA procedures is an important factor. For example, in many developing countries, water ministries are not convinced that EIA is an essential procedure (Tortajada, 2000). Thus, even if legal requirements mandate that such assessments are necessary – and even if external funding agencies insist that conducting EIA is a pre-condition for receiving funds – as long as water ministries are not convinced of its necessity, EIA will be a mechanical process with virtually no impact on the actual sustainability of proposed water development projects. For example, analyses of the environmental sustainability of water projects in Mexico (Tortajada, 1999a, 1999b, 2000) indicate that even though EIA studies are carried out because of legal requirements and donor insistence, they have had little impact on improving water project planning and management. Many problems still have to be resolved, including poor implementation of the proposed mitigation measures, environmental monitoring, compliance control, and lack of coordination among the several governmental ministries – particularly in the implementation of mitigation measures (Tortajada, 2001).

Environmental management is not enough to achieve the environmental sustainability of water projects. Public participation is required. In this regard, it is well known that stakeholders should be aware of the social, economic and environmental impacts that proposed projects will have on the surrounding environment. However, if information is only presented for review, or the outputs are not integrated within the studies, public consultation will differ very little from no consultation at all. There are, then, many important issues to be considered for an effective public participation, such as who should be consulted, by what process or criteria should they be selected, at what stage of the process should they be consulted, and which methods will be used. Public participation, when properly conducted, should improve the project planning and implementation processes, as well as the overall acceptability of the projects. The process must be consultative and transparent, otherwise the impacts are likely to be minimal.

It is true that there is an increasing need for public participation in water resources planning and policy-making processes where the main objective is to satisfy certain social needs. However, formulating planning and policy-making frameworks that are flexible enough to handle changing long-term attitudes and/or requirements has been difficult. Methodologies to forecast future public attitudes still need substantial improvement. This is an important issue because the gestation period of large water development projects often exceeds ten years, during which public attitudes and opinions may change. It is important to stress that increasing public participation in the water resources planning process is still no panacea. It could even raise difficult philosophical concerns. For example, the public may be more interested in achieving short-term goals rather than long-term objectives. What, then, should be the role of the water resources planners when the public prefers a course of action that may not be beneficial in the long term? Do the planners go along with the public preference even when they disagree with it, or do they suggest what they feel is best for the region? If planners follow the first alternative and ten years later are proven right, can they escape the charge of abdicating their professional responsibilities? If they wish to follow the second alternative, do they have the moral authority to do so? The conviction and sincerity of the water planners may be unquestioned; but what if they are wrong? These are difficult questions that have not been properly addressed

CASE STUDY OF MEXICO

The following is an analysis of the situation in Mexico in terms of environmental management of water projects. In order to ensure that the environment would be protected during the construction and operation of current and future water projects, legislation and procedures have made EIA procedures mandatory in Mexico since 1988. Currently, the General Law of Ecological Balance and Environmental Protection (Ley General de Equilibrio Ecológico y Protección Ambiental, LGEEPA) and its regulation (SEMARNAT, 2002) have established the evaluation procedure for the environmental assessment of different projects and activities as an instrument to reduce their negative impacts on the environment.

An EIA report must be produced before a project is carried out. The report should evaluate negative impacts and proposed alternatives, from site selection to the general approaches for their management. However, there is no legislative requirement stipulating that once the assessment report is prepared, evaluated and approved, it should actually be implemented. This is a major gap in the legislation which water authorities have taken full advantage of in the past. The environmental assessment procedure is basically a paper exercise, neither improving the environmental and social impacts of the water project, nor being a useful tool for environmental management. It has simply become a legal formality that is necessary to clear a project, irrespective of the EIA findings. Once the approval process, which is automatic, is completed, the report is filed and never again consulted.

The implementation of the LGEEPA has been consistently poor. In general, the EIA reports of water projects are descriptive, superficial and mechanical, rather than analytical, predictive and comprehensive. Accordingly, they are of questionable value for rational environmental project management. Mitigation measures that are proposed are based on generalized principles and are not supported by specific facts, analyses or findings. The studies do not include any consideration of a monitoring programme to test predictions and facilitate impact management. They also lack any serious social or environmental analyses. Participation and involvement of the public, for all practical purposes, is non-existent. The unsatisfactory quality of the EIA studies of water projects in the country represents a serious limitation for developing any post-project evaluation.

The mitigation measures proposed are so vague that it is impossible to seriously consider them. The reports do not contribute to any in-depth discussion of how to mitigate adverse impacts, even when they are identified, or how to enhance project benefits. The institutional arrangements necessary for implementing the proposed general measures are never defined, and the costs of implementing the recommendations are never estimated. Mitigation measures are characterized by their generality, scarcity and superficiality. Predictive techniques are used with unknown margins of error, and numerous tables of data are presented without any reference to their usefulness or reliability. The data listed are seldom analysed properly. Evaluation methods that assess and present information are concerned primarily with the approval of the project. Little or no attention is paid to environmental management during the post-approval stage.

The LGEEPA promotes public participation while EIA studies are conducted. Before the amendments to this regulation, public participation meant that the general public could read the assessment studies prepared on the projects and activities. However, the only problem was that the public had no access to such reports, irrespective of the legal requirements. With the new modifications, the Ministry of the Environment has to publish the requests that it receives for clearance of EIA every week, both in its magazine and electronically. Additionally, any person, association or non-governmental organization (NGO) can lodge objections to the Office of the Federal Attorney for Environmental Protection (Procuraduria Federal de Protección al Ambiente, PROFEPA), particularly with respect to those activities or omissions that do not comply with the law, that could result in ecological deterioration, or that could threaten the environment. Legally, the promoters or institutions responsible for the project can be taken to court. However, irrespective of the legal requirements, the opinion of the general public is still largely ignored. They continue to have no real role to play in the construction or operation of new projects.

The comprehensiveness, objectivity and accuracy of EIA studies as they are currently carried out in Mexico are matters of concern because many of the reports do not meet the minimum regulatory requirements, much less provide adequate information and analysis from which to base necessary decisions. Proponents of the projects need to monitor the quality of their assessment studies and to review them critically before submitting them for approval to the appropriate authority. Furthermore, the authority must reject all assessment reports, unless certain minimum standards are maintained. At present, neither of these two actions is likely to occur.

Therefore, despite legal and institutional requirements for rational environmental management of water development projects, only limited progress has been made thus far in Mexico. Laws have been systematically ignored and/or circumvented. Accordingly, two important conclusions can be drawn. Firstly, the legal and institutional processes that currently exist in the country do not contribute to the environmental management of water development projects. Secondly, even when EIA studies are carried out, they have no impact on the actual planning and management of water projects (for the specific case of groundwater, see Chapter 7; for derivative water, see Chapter 6).

EIA water project studies are an important requirement to ensure that economic and social benefits accrue as planned, and that environmental costs are kept to an acceptable level. While conducting objective environmental assessments is an important first step, such studies alone will not guarantee long-term management of the projects. Unless the senior decision-makers in water ministries believe that environmental and social considerations are important issues, real progress is likely to be minimal and slow. In addition, regular monitoring and evaluation at appropriate intervals during the operational phase of a project by the decision-making levels are absolutely essential in order to safeguard sound, long-term management of water projects.

Unfortunately, in Mexico there are many examples of political correctness that have not improved the poor management of water resources, contributing, instead, to negative social, economic and environmental impacts. One concrete example is the Chapala Lake in Mexico – the largest natural lake in the country and the third largest in Latin America. Chapala Lake provides roughly 60 per cent of the water supply for the country's second largest city, Guadalajara, and it supports the socio-economic development of a large region, mainly through fishing, agriculture and tourism. The lake is also an important refuge for migratory birds in North America. However, water demand for domestic, industrial and agricultural uses upstream have increased so much that during the 1990s, the volume of the lake decreased by almost 30 per cent. Water pollution has increased exponentially because nearly 20 per cent of all municipal, industrial and agricultural wastewater discharged in the Lerma-Chapala basin ends up in the Chapala Lake. It is estimated that more than 12 kilograms (kg) of chromium and more than 4kg of zinc are deposited every day in the lake as a result of the industrial wastewater discharges. Fish production is less than 70 per cent of what it used to be a decade ago.

While the lake's importance to the regional economy is recognized by everyone, no viable action has been taken by any of the governments in power over the last 30 years. On 9 May 1971, the president made a firm commitment to protect the lake. Since then, there have been at least 24 presidential statements assuring that specific actions would be taken to improve the environmental conditions of the lake. Despite these statements, the health of the lake continues to deteriorate, with the current situation significantly worse than 30 years ago. There has been no shortage of political rhetoric from the highest level of government. Making politically correct statements will not improve the conditions of the lake; there has to be a viable long-term plan that must be implemented. Surprisingly, even with such records, the Organisation for Economic Co-operation and Development (OECD) has given Mexico its seal of approval for achieving the goals set by *Agenda 21*, the plan of action agreed at the United Nations Conference on Environment and Development (UNCED or Earth Summit) in Rio de Janeiro in 1992. The OECD apparently took the political statements at face value without verifying the facts.

CONCLUSIONS

Without question, in the international political forums sustainable development has become a powerful and all-embracing slogan over the last 15 years. Every government supports it, as does every major international organization and environmental NGO. This is despite the fact that there is no agreement about what is meant by sustainable development, whether it works and under what conditions, and whether it has a positive, negative or neutral impact on humanity.

In addition, the world is heterogeneous, with different cultures, social norms, physical attributes and a skewed availability of renewable and non-renewable resources, investment funds, management capacities and institutional arrangements. The systems of governance, legal frameworks, decision-making processes and effectiveness of institutions often differ significantly from one country to another. Countries are also at different stages of development, with different needs. These needs vary with time. Accordingly, and under such diverse conditions, another fundamental question must be asked: is it possible that a single paradigm (sustainable development) can encompass all countries, or even regions, with diverse physical, economic, social and cultural conditions? Can a single paradigm such as sustainable development be equally valid for technological giants such as the USA and Japan, for the world's most populous countries such as China and India, and for countries as diverse as Burkina Faso and Vanuatu? Can a single concept be equally applicable for Asian values, African traditions, Japanese culture and Western civilization?

The point of departure for the development process is different from one country to the next for technical, economic, historical, cultural and other associated reasons. In terms of water resources, it is clear that each country needs to formulate its own water development strategies based on its specific conditions, requirements and expectations. However, in many parts of the world, practices, processes and legislation are being copied from other countries, without adapting them specifically to their own conditions. Institutional frameworks are being structured that often respond to the latest international thinking without any detailed review of their applicability in the national context.

Regarding environmental sustainability of water resources, although most developing countries have tried to protect their image at the international level, poor management of water resources will continue to have serious social, economic and environmental implications at the local and national levels over the short and the long term. Often, such mismanagement has contributed to increasing poverty and the deterioration of quality of life, especially in terms of health. Many developing countries have claimed that the main constraint to fulfilling their commitments of *Agenda 21* has been the lack of financial support. While insufficient funding is certainly a constraint, even bigger constraints have been the absence of leadership and managerial and technical capacities, an almost exclusive top-down centralized approach, an absence of stakeholder participation, and a lack of any long-term vision in the water development field. Not surprisingly, progress towards improving water management practices has been limited during the last 30 years in the developing world. In fact, much more could have been accomplished with the budgets that were available if the leadership had a clear vision of what should be accomplished. Not surprisingly, water problems in developing countries have increased significantly, especially in terms of water pollution.

Regardless of the sustainable development and environmental sustainability rhetoric, even after 15 years of use it has been impossible to define a development process that could be planned and implemented in such a way that, from the very beginning, it could become inherently sustainable. Nor has it been possible to identify the parameters that should be monitored and evaluated to indicate the beginning of a transition process from sustainability to unsustainability and vice versa. After 15 years of rhetoric, we still do not known how sustainability can be measured, analysed, judged or implemented.

Any development expert intuitively knows that no single pattern of development is the most appropriate for all countries of the world at any specific point in history. There is simply no one single path to development. The fundamental question that must be asked and unambiguously answered, then, is can it be possible that one single paradigm (sustainable development) is valid for the entire world?

REFERENCES

Biswas, A K (1996) 'Water development and environment in water resources' in Biswas, A K (ed) *Environmental Planning, Management and Development*, McGraw Hill, New York

Biswas, A K (1997) *Sustainable Water Development from the Perspective of the South: Issues and Constraints in River Basin Planning and Management*, Abu-Zeid, M and Biswas, A K (eds), Oxford University Press, New Delhi

Bourke, S and Meppem, T (2000) 'Privileged narratives and fictions of consent in environmental discourse', *Local Environment*, vol 5, no 3, pp299–310

Canter, L W (1997) *Environmental Impact Assessment*, 2nd edition, McGraw-Hill, New York

Clausen, A W (1981) 'Sustainable development: The global imperative', *Mazingira*, vol 5, no 4, pp2–13

Dourojeanni, A (1997) *Management Procedures for Sustainable Development (Applicable to Municipalities, Micro-regions and River Basins)*, Economic Commission for Latin America and the Caribbean, United Nations, Santiago

Dourojeanni, A (1999) *La Dinámica del Desarrollo Sustentable y Sostenible*, Comisión Económica para América Latina y el Caribe, Naciones Unidas, Santiago

Dragun, A and Jakobsson, K (1997) 'Introduction' in Dragun, A K and Jakobsson, K M (eds) *Sustainability and Global Environmental Policy: New Perspectives*, Swedish University of Agricultural Sciences, Edward Elgar, Cheltenham

Easterly, W (2001) *The Elusive Quest for Growth: Economist's Adventures and Misadventures in the Tropics*, MIT Press, Cambridge and London

ECLAC (1998) *Reflections on Territorial Strategies for Sustainable Development*, Economic Commission for Latin America and the Caribbean, United Nations, Santiago

Gillespie, A (2001) *The Illusion of Progress: Unsustainable Development in International Law and Policy*, Earthscan, London

Goodland, R (1997) 'Biophysical and objective environmental sustainability' in Dragun, A K and Jacobsson, K M (eds) *Sustainability and Global Environmental Policy: New Perspectives*, Edward Elgar, Cheltenham

Hammond, A (1998) *Which World? Scenarios for the 21st Century, Global Destinies and Regional Choices*, Island Press and Shearwater Books, Washington, DC, and Covelo, CA

Meppem, T (2000) 'The discursive community: Evolving institutional structures for planning sustainability', *Ecological Economics*, vol 34, pp47–61

Meppem, T and Bourke, S (1999) 'Different ways of knowing: A communicative turn toward sustainability', *Ecological Economics*, vol 30, pp389–403

Meppem, T and Gill, R (1998) 'Planning for sustainability as a learning concept', *Ecological Economics*, vol 26, pp121–137

Mikesell, R F (1994) 'Environmental assessment and sustainability at the project and programme level' in Goodland, R and Edmundson, V (eds) *Environmental Assessment and Development: An IAIA-World Bank Symposium*, World Bank, Washington, DC

Modak, P and Biswas, A K (2001) *Conducting Environmental Impact Assessment for Developing Countries*, Oxford, India

Osborne, F (1948) *Our Plundered Planet*, The Conservation Foundation, New York

Ortalano, L (1997) *Environmental Regulation and Impact Assessment*, John Wiley and Sons, New York

Pearce, D, Markandya, A and Barbier, E (1999) *Blueprint for a Green Economy*, Earthscan, London

Raskin, P et al (1998) *Bending the Curve: Toward Global Sustainability*, A Report of the Global Scenario Group, Stockholm Environment Institute, PoleStar Series Report No 8, Stockholm

SEMARNAT (2002) 'Ley general del equilibrio ecológico y la protección al ambiente y su reglamento en materia de evaluación del impacto ambiental', www.semarnat. gob.mx

Serageldin, I et al (eds) (1998) *Organising Knowledge for Environmentally and Socially Sustainable Development*, Proceedings for a Concurrent Meeting of the Fifth Annual World Bank Conference on Environmentally and Socially Sustainable Development, Co-sponsored by UNESCO and the World Bank, World Bank, Washington, DC

Soderbaum, P (1998) 'Economics and ecological sustainability: An actor–network approach to evaluation', in *Evaluation Planning*, Kluwer Academic Publisher, The Netherlands

Soderbaum, P (2000) *Ecological Economics: A Political Economics Approach to Environment and Development*, Earthscan, London

Tolba, M K (1982) 'Development without destruction', Address to Chelsea College in 1976, in *Development without Destruction: Evolving Environmental Perceptions*, Tycooly International, Dublin

Tolba, M K (ed) (1988) *Evolving Environmental Perceptions: From Stockholm to Nairobi*, United Nations Environment Programme, Butterworths, London

Tortajada, C (1999a) *Environmental Sustainability of Water Management in Mexico*, Third World Centre for Water Management, Mexico

Tortajada, C (1999b) *Approaches to Environmental Sustainability for Water Resources Management: The Case Study of Mexico*, Licentiate thesis, Division of Hydraulic Engineering, Department of Civil and Environmental Engineering, Royal Institute of Technology, Stockholm

Tortajada, C (2000) 'Environmental impact assessment of water projects', *Water Resources Development*, vol 16, no 1, pp73–78

Tortajada, C (2001) 'Evaluaciones Ambientales en el Sector Hidráulico en México', *XI Jornadas de Derecho del Agua*, Zaragoza, España

United Nations Environment Programme (UNEP) (1981) *In Defence of the Earth: The Basic Texts on Environment, Founex, Stockholm, Cocoyoc*, United Nations Environment Programme, Executive Series 1, Nairobi

United Nations General Assembly (UNGA) (1962) Resolution 1831 XVII, UNGA Official Records, 17th Session, Supplement No 17, p21

United Nations General Assembly (UNGA) (1970) Resolution 2626, at 39, UN Document A/8028

United Nations General Assembly (UNGA) (1987) Resolution 42/186, Environmental Perspective to the Year 2000 and Beyond, 11 December

United Nations Treaty Series (UNTS) (1968) 'African Convention on the Conservation of Nature and Natural Resources', *United Nations Treaty Series*, vol 1001, no 14689, pp3–33

WCED (1987) *Our Common Future*, Report of the World Commission on Environment and Development, Oxford University Press, Oxford

Chapter 3

Global and local agendas in water management: From vision to action

Odeh Al-Jayyousi

INTRODUCTION

The convergence or divergence between the global and local agendas in water management represents the level of communication between those who look at the big picture, as represented in the World Water Vision developed by the World Water Council (Cosgrove and Rijsberman, 2000), and those who focus on day-to-day water issues. The global and local agendas stimulate dialogue and debate by offering different views of how to translate a global water vision into action. In essence, this debate represents the divergence between development paradigms and the means of linking theory to practice between the North and the South. This chapter will shed some light on global and local agendas in water management with specific reference to the Middle East and North Africa (MENA) region.

It is evident that water management brings with it the reality that the world has become a global village. Insight into water management might be gained by looking at three different levels: the local level, where operations are carried out; the regional level, where policies are made; and the global level, where funding and external support are generated. It is also crucial to identify the *enabling factors*, such as sound water institutions and laws, and the *change agents*, such as non-governmental organizations (NGOs) who build the bridges between water stakeholders at global, regional and local arenas (Al-Jayyousi, 2001).

However, there is evidence that global water institutions such as the United Nations (UN) have experienced some constraints while implementing global water goals. Mageed and White (1995) documented that international efforts in water management – from the United Nations Water Conference in Mar del Plata in 1977 to the International Conference on Water and Environment in Dublin and the United Nations Conference on Environment and Development (UNCED or Earth Summit) in Rio de Janeiro, both in 1992, and later the World Water Vision – may be described as converging activities without unifying organization. Before Mar del Plata, international cooperation in the field of water resources as part of the UN system was limited to coordination through the Committee on Natural Resources at the inter-governmental level, and by the Administrative Sub-committee on Coordination (ACC) at the secretarial level. However, the effectiveness of the ACC was limited because it was merely a consultative body, lacking implementation mechanisms.

Understanding the global and local water agendas is vital to conveying the 'water knowledge' between the North and the South. Building an 'institutional water memory' is a necessary condition for transferring 'water knowledge' between the global and local arenas. The experience of the last three decades, as formulated in the Mar del Plata Action Plan, the Dublin Principles and the Earth Summit's *Agenda 21*, emphasized the need for integrated water management. All of these initiatives call for a comprehensive vision of the water sector, which combines both sanitation and irrigation in the water sector (Solanes and Villarreal, 1999). The last two decades have taught us two major lessons in water management. Firstly, water was recognized as only one of a number of natural resource elements that needs to be managed in a sustainable manner. Secondly, we realized that water resources development is not attained by only supplying physical infrastructure. A new shift in thinking took place by changing infrastructure from supply oriented – supply of facilities to communities who will, one day, become consumers – to demand oriented by focusing more on adequate assistance and the development of local capacity (Al-Jayyousi and Shatanawi, 1995; Al-Jayyousi and Mohsen, 1999). Disseminating these lessons of sustainable water management may be achieved through dialogue and partnerships between the North and the South. This, in turn, is an important factor in enhancing the adaptive capacity of the people in the South.

It is interesting that combining the global water vision with action at the local level was evident in the Earth Summit and *Agenda 21*. Both of these global initiatives advocate solutions in water management that are characterized by a combination of government decentralization, devolution of local communities in terms of responsibility for natural resources, and community participation. Duda and El-Ashry (2000) argued for strengthening linkages among the United Nations Framework Convention on Climate Change, the Convention on Biological Diversity and the Convention to Combat Desertification, to create new global driving forces for actions and to address the crises holistically in the context of a country's national sustainable development strategy. Moreover, they state that the three global environment conventions provide a framework that countries can use for testing opportunities to address both global and local concerns.

This chapter's aim is to shed some light on the linkages and divergences between global and local water management agendas. It intends to present 'regionalism' as the unit of water management analysis by focusing on the role of virtual water in the global–local interactions in the Middle East.

GLOBAL–LOCAL AGENDAS IN WATER MANAGEMENT: THEORY AND PRACTICE

The global and local agendas in water management may be understood from various dimensions, including *impact, benefits and externalities*. These three factors are explained below.

'Think global, act local' is a well-known saying that must be formalized and put to work. Local and community-based water resource management models were proposed by Ghai and Vivian (1992; Ghai, 1994). This concept dates back to *The Ecologist*'s *Blueprint for Survival* (1972), Schumacher's *Small is Beautiful* (1973) and, more recently, the Brundtland Commission's *Our Common Future* (WCED, 1987).

However, the implementation of community-based water resource development projects has frequently fallen short of expectations. A number of reasons have been identified. These include:

- a lack of direct economic benefit to the poor (Al-Jayyousi, 2001);
- a tendency for the intended beneficiaries to be treated as passive recipients of project activities (Pimbert and Pretty, 1995);
- a tendency for projects to be short term in nature and over-reliant on expatriate expertise; and
- a lack of clear criteria by which to judge sustainability or success in meeting development goals (Western et al, 1994).

Others suggest that the interests of certain social groups have been consistently marginalized (Sarin, 1995).

Establishing a shared vision on integrated water management (IWM) between the North and the South may be attained through participatory approaches and communicative action. Gaining local people's acceptance of a plan associated with an outside agency requires informal and formal communication, and the nurturing of relationships with all groups of relevant local, regional and global interests early in the process. The importance of developing and nurturing trustful relationships by means of open and honest negotiations with all stakeholder groups seems to be the most critical factor in successful planning. This process is viewed as one of 'mutual learning', where planners at the global/regional level learn about the values and language of clients at the local level, and clients learn from planners. Berger and Luckmann (1967) call this the 'construction of a joint reality'. This means that global- and local-level visions are being unified. Carroll and Hendrix (1992) argued for effective local involvement in river planning. They proposed a new paradigm in water planning called 'transactive planning'. Friedman (1973) described transactive planning as follows:

Transactive planning changes knowledge into actions through an unbroken sequence of interpersonal relations. Transactive planning is a response to the widening gulf in communication between technical planners (at global level) and their clients (at local level).

Resource professionals realize the need to develop and use new approaches to planning and management that incorporate local values and worldviews more effectively than in the past. Such approaches should combine the strengths of transactive planning with the rational comprehensive tradition.

In the global–local dialogue, public participation is vital to ensuring sustainability and equity. At the global level, the water vision was formulated through a participatory approach from various stakeholders in the North and the South. However, living in a globalized world brings with it the fear that people become more likely to think and conceptualize various 'water issues' in a globalized mind – thinking within the box. To transfer the 'water knowledge' from the North at the global level to the South at the regional or local level, an 'outsider–insider' model was proposed by Allan (2000). In this model, Allan argued that the process of knowledge transfer from global to local is incremental and slow. For example, the notion of water productivity and water pricing in the MENA region took more than a decade before becoming an accepted policy. Allan outlined the interactions between the technical and political discourses in water management and the evolution of different paradigms (hydraulic mission, environmental, economic, social and governance).

In theory, globalization may be characterized by two competing salient forces – the *integration* and *marginalization* forces. Takahashi and colleagues (2002) argued that there are two different types of globalization – *market-based globalization* and *civil-society globalization*. This chapter argues that the marginalization of the poor in the South due to privatization of the water services may be minimized if we consider the 'region' rather than the 'nation state' as the unit of analysis for IWM. Simply stated, the region provides the critical mass for achieving water and food security in the MENA region. The region also provides a reasonable framework for trading food (especially wheat) at the global level since most water is being used for irrigation in the developing world (see Chapter 4).

Implementing the global agenda in water and environment may have externalities on national or local levels. For example, the policies imposed by the International Monetary Fund (IMF) and the World Bank, through the agricultural structural adjustment loan (ASAL), shifted the economic incentives away from small farms toward large estates producing for export. As a result, many small farmers are at risk of poverty. In addition, the global agenda addressed the need for river basin planning and IWM rather than sectorial planning. However, implementation of IWM at the national/local level clashes with issues of equity and sovereignty.

The evaluation of the global/international experience in river basin planning reveals that growth-related problems regarding environmental protection blur the distinction between regional and local responsibilities, and create overlapping and potentially conflicting state and local constituencies (Zimmerman, 1983; Wright, 1988). Mismatches frequently appear between the common level of growth regulation (municipal) and the level of impact (regional) of many development proposals. Such mismatches occur when there are solely local benefits but primarily regional or global costs, or when overdevelopments have primarily global or regional benefits but primarily local costs (see Chapters 9 and 10).

The implications of growth-oriented policies are of crucial significance to sustainable water management in a river basin. In some cases, the fragmentation of local growth management efforts encourages policy-makers at the local level to ignore the harmful global/regional effects, such as environmental degradation. Therefore, reliance on local growth controls may lead to environmental deterioration as negative externalities escape policy attention (Barrows, 1982). State intervention in this case seeks to incorporate the consideration of negative externalities within the decision-making process and thus tends to be environmentally focused and growth restrictive.

Building a common vision for water and environment through public participation among stakeholders at both the global and local levels is crucial for conceptualizing the notions of equity, distributional benefits and costs.

RESEARCH QUESTIONS

The three main research questions in this chapter are summarized as follows:

1   How can we manage the human dimension in water management at the local level?
2   Is it possible to apply the global water agenda to local or regional needs?
3   How can we address water equity and ethics in the global–local dialogue?

The following is an attempt to address these questions in the global–local interactions.

The human dimension in water management

In the global vision, water has been linked recently to many attributes such as gender, poverty alleviation and ethics. However, it is interesting to note that at the local scene, the work of many anthropologists reveals interesting dimensions of how local people in the developing world perceive life and happiness. Norberg-Hodge (1993) documented her observations on the local people of Ladakh in Kashmir before and after the intrusion of Western-style development. She stated:

> *In traditional Ladakh, to link happiness to income or possessions*
> *would have been unthinkable. A deep-rooted respect for each*
> *other's fundamental human needs and an acceptance of the*
> *natural limitations of the environment kept the Ladakhi people*

free from misplacing values of worth. Happiness was simply experienced.

However, it was documented by Norberg-Hodge that the Western-style development models created inferiority in the local people's self-perception and a greed for material wealth.

From colonialism to development to structural adjustment, people in the South have been integrated within the global economy. As a result, aid agencies and global banks have dictated the economic and water policies of the developing countries, increasing the dependence of local people on foreign money. This section argues that there was no significant 'development' of the social capital in many developing countries in the South due to foreign aid. The following are some reflections on the notion of the human dimension and 'development'.

Korten (1990) argued that development is a process by which people increase their human, institutional and technical capacities to produce the goods and services needed in order to achieve sustainable improvements in their quality of life using the resources available to them. It is referred to as 'people-centred' development not only because it benefits people, but also because it is centred on people. It is especially important to involve the poor and the excluded, allowing them to meet their own needs through their productive efforts.

Korten (1995) argued that a small amount of help from abroad can be very useful in a people-centred development process; but too much foreign funding can prevent real development and even break down the existing capabilities of a people to sustain themselves. Debates about import substitution versus export-led development rarely acknowledge the people-centred alternative. Poor people seldom buy imported goods. Simple locally produced goods meet their needs. Therefore, localized small-scale and low-cost water solutions should be encouraged to address water scarcity and poverty.

Korten (1990) argues that poverty is generally defined as a lack of adequate money. However, lack of money is not an issue. It is the deprivation associated with a lack of money that is the problem – for example, the lack of access to adequate water, food, clothing and shelter. This simple fact suggests a people-centred alternative to both the import-substitution and export-led development models. This implies pursuing policies that create opportunities to produce the things that people who are experiencing deprivation need in order to have a better life.

In the current globalized money markets where the institutions of money rule the world, it is inevitable that the interests of money will take precedence over the interests of people (see Chapter 4). Hence, the global financial institutions and donor agencies largely determine the global water agenda. Local agendas, focusing on what the poor really need, are the interpretations and reflections of the North on the global scene.

The evolution of global–local interactions may be traced back to the era of colonialism. There was always mutual interdependence between the rich export-based countries and the poor countries. In terms of the current state of global environmental degradation, both industrialized rich countries and developing poor countries are contributors. The North produces the industrial waste, and the mismanagement of resources is attributed to the South. Many schools of thought addressed this interaction, each adopting a different paradigm.

Economic growth and environmental protection, some argue, are inherently incompatible (Schnaiberg and Gould, 1994). Others argue that sustained economic development to relieve the multitudes in poor countries is an essential pre-condition for the long-term protection of the global environment (WCED, 1987). Some counter that poor countries are the major threat to the global environment (Caldwell, 1990), and the long-term protection of the global environment depends on the advanced industrial societies (Frankland and Schoonmaker, 1992). Others argue that environmental policy is inevitably a 'distributive policy' within individual countries, but especially between rich and poor countries (Goodman and Redclift, 1991). The fate of the global environment, they argue, depends on making the world more equitable and just. They believe environmental protection, especially in the developing world, rests on one word: justice (Hencht and Cockburn, 1989). Nevertheless, all seem to agree that environmental protection is inseparable from economic well-being (see Chapter 2).

On the other hand, Schnaiberg and Gould (1994) argue that the environment is in an enduring conflict with the model of growth. Economic growth requires the exploitation of natural resources and the dumping of waste products. In rich countries, mass production and consumption are major causes of environmental degradation and the destruction of natural resources. In poor countries, value creation and access to subsistence are typically linked to sacrificing environmental quality for short-term economic gain (Goodman and Redclift, 1991). A dominant current of thought addresses this paradox by stressing scientific knowledge and technological innovation as the key to reducing poverty. The end result is economic growth without environmental degradation. This way of thinking places faith in human technological ingenuity and rational planning, enabling people to escape the environmental costs of economic growth. In this perspective, the environmental crisis is a 'crisis of will and rationality' (Caldwell, 1990).

Equity considerations, it is argued, are vital to environmental protection, especially in the poor countries. There are two types of equity considerations. One deals with the assessment of how environmental pollution and hazards are distributed, both within and among the global, regional, national and local levels. The other type of equity deals with the distribution of the benefits and costs of growth. Equity considerations at the global level – the distribution of the resources and benefits of economic growth among nations – are equally critical in protecting global ecology. In terms of biological diversity, most economic benefits flow to the rich countries while local, often poor, people bear the bulk of the costs (Goodman and Redclift, 1991).

Some constraints to effective water and environmental management include the notion of national sovereignty (see Chapter 9). Activities in one country that are detrimental to the environment of neighbouring countries constitute 'an international security issue'. Presumably, such a situation would justify an affected country taking action to defend its 'national security' by all necessary means. Many people in poor countries see the environment as an excuse for political intervention by rich countries. In fact, a great many of the US government's objections to the Rio Earth Summit agreements were grounded in an unwillingness to agree to anything that even remotely appeared to impinge on its sovereignty.

In sum, the perception and value of water differ between people living in the North and the South. The human dimension that is part of the global and local water management agendas is a dialogue about access to water resources and equity, and it is a question of how to provide clean water for the poor.

From global vision to local action

Translating a global water vision into action is a significant indicator of the performance of global–local agendas. One crucial condition to implementing a global agenda at a local level is to build, and strengthen, the capacity of the local people through three major elements – institutions and legislation, human resource development, and information dissemination. The effectiveness of sound water institutions lies in their capacity to create an *enabling environment*.

The importance of capacity building is evident due to changes in water technology, private sector and consumer involvement in water management, as well as innovations in institutional arrangements (Al-Jayyousi, 2001). Moreover, rainfall fluctuations, water pollution and the impact of global warming have raised the value of water. Urbanization and economic development impose another stress on water demand.

The World Water Vision recognizes that water management requires the involvement of government, civil society and the private sector, and that the principle of subsidiarity must be respected (Cosgrove and Rijsberman, 2000). A Framework of Action for the World Water Vision was developed by the Global Water Partnership (GWP, 2000). The challenge, however, is to operationalize the global-level concepts and principles, and to implement them at the local level. This goal can be attained by assessing the local community's adaptive capacity.

The social adaptive capacity refers to the set of norms and attitudes people have to cope with water deficit. This includes a local community's ability to harness technology, to accept institutional changes and to adapt to new consumption patterns. Ohlsson and Turton (1999) argued:

> *Bringing the adaptive capacity of a society in the equation means transcending the trap of absolute scarcity. Absolute scarcity of water is turned into a relative scarcity in a sense that how societies will succeed to live with less water now depends on how well they handle the challenges of adapting to another social usage of water.*

Attaining this notion of adaptive capacity is the core of capacity building and sustainable water management at the local level. The concept of capacity building has a correlation with many types of sustainability. These types of sustainability include *technical sustainability, environmental sustainability, financial sustainability, social sustainability and institutional sustainability* (Alaerts et al, 1991). All of these types of sustainability should be linked to the national policy, as well as to economic development plans, in order to reflect the global vision of sustainability (see Chapter 2).

There is evidence that, at the local level in many developing countries, failures to achieve effective water management are not the result of technology or the availability of funds. Some projects were not sustained after external support aid (ESA) ended. This highlights the value of capacity building for sustainable water management. The role of sound policy formulation in developing countries is vital to ensure that ESA (at the global level) is linked to long-term capacity building at the local level (Alaerts et al, 1991).

The limitations to an effective, efficient and reliable water management system exist in the institutional framework to manage loans and funds, and to convert those loans into sustainable projects at the national/local level. The crucial question to be addressed is how can capacity building be translated into projects?

From a global perspective, capacity building calls for the development of long-term effective strategies at the national/local level. At the national/local level, projects (two to four years) or programmes (five to ten years) can be formulated to strengthen the institutional performance of organizations. Moreover, local communities, water-user associations, the private sector and NGOs should benefit from capacity-building projects or programmes. For capacity building in the water sector to be effective, it requires a new 'contractual approach' between donor agencies, at the global level, and communities, at the local level (Alaerts et al, 1991).

Capacity building relies on the concept of learning by doing through stakeholder participation. The impact of many projects and programmes can be greatly improved if they could help the local counterpart be self-sufficient. This requires a new approach to project formulation and implementation. Projects need to become *change agents* directed toward building the local people's capacity (Alaerts et al, 1991).

Many capacity-building models were applied to the developing world with the aim of translating the global vision to action (Al-Jayyousi, 2001). ESA, public institutions, the private sector or NGOs supports these models. These include:

- The United Nations Educational, Scientific and Cultural Organization–IHE Water Education Institute (UNESCO-IHE) model that addresses the education and training of water professionals through regional networks of water resources training centres.
- Training projects as change agents, putting the emphasis on human resources development (HRD) – for example, the International Training

Network for Water and Waste Management (ITN) is a joint bilateral and multilateral development agency in support of providing capacity building to low-income and rural areas; this model helped to institutionalize the training capabilities of the water sector.
• Building Agents Model that advocates the concept of institutional development and restructuring; the rationale is that when institutions are developed or strengthened, they are likely to become capacity-building agents at the local level.

In sum, capacity building serves as the vehicle that moves the global vision towards action. Creating enabling environments and change agents is vital for implementing this vision.

Water equity and ethics

Equity may be judged in terms of demand for, and access to, a resource. The basic policy question of who gets what and how has both equitable and ethical dimensions. Global and local interpretations of what is equitable and ethical in water management may be understood in terms of each one's frame of reference. Establishing a shared vision of water management among the global and local stakeholders helps address water equity and ethics (see Chapters 4 and 7).

The crucial issue in terms of local-level implementation is that survival and poverty reduction take precedence over environmental concerns. In the developing countries, at the local level, questions of environmental quality are unlikely to receive careful hearing amid the overwhelming problems of poverty. This is evident in the resistance of semi-industrialized countries, such as Malaysia, India and Brazil preceding the UN Conference on the Human Environment at Stockholm in 1972, to industrialized countries' focus on global environmental protection (Korten, 1995). Kolars (2000) advocates a new water ethic with respect to river basin management. He argues that a river should be viewed in terms of spatial, temporal and socio-economic perspectives.

The insistence on the part of poor countries that poverty reduction should be the first goal of local-level water management has been the catalyst for developing approaches to reconcile economy and environment. The idea of 'sustainable development' is the most accepted approach to reconcile economy and environment in a global context. The World Commission on Environment and Development (WCED, known as the Brundtland Commission), in its report *Our Common Future* (1987), developed a framework for the future of global human society. It considers economic growth to be essential in relieving the deepening poverty in much of the developing world, and declares that environment and development are not separable; they are inexorably linked.

Equity and the equitable distribution of resources among people are closely related to sustainability. Water and environmental problems affect the poor the most, yet they are the least equipped to solve these problems. Moreover, social inequity usually promotes unsustainable consumption patterns. Studies show that a preference for local solutions is justified only by the notion of equity, interpreted as the need to prevent shifting problems to others or elsewhere. Shifting problems to other places is not equitable for the part of the generation given the problem (from an intra-generational equity point of view). Ignoring problems is not equitable for the following generation (from an inter-generational point of view).

The indicators of success in implementing the global agenda are judged on impact, benefit and outcomes at global, regional, national and local levels. For example, the Brundtland Commission's proposed answer to global poverty and environmental problems was an annual 3 per cent increase in the per-capita income. If we apply this global goal to the national/local level, it will yield interesting results. There would be a first year annual per-capita increase of US\$633 for the USA, US\$3.60 for Ethiopia, US\$5.40 for Bangladesh, US\$7.50 for Nigeria, US\$10.80 for China and US\$10.50 for India. After ten years, such growth will have raised Ethiopia's per capita income by US\$41, while the USA's will have risen by US\$7257 (Goodland et al, 1992).

At both the global and local levels, the future of water management will be shaped by raising the 'civic intelligence' concerning how water should be valued and managed (see Chapters 4 and 11). Promoting the notion that water is a human right is vital to providing water for the poor. An interdisciplinary approach to formulating a water ethics code is also needed.

RECOMMENDED ACTIONS: NEW REGIONALISM FOR WATER MANAGEMENT IN THE MIDDLE EAST

For nearly two decades, the worldwide amount of irrigated land per person has been declining because of the rise of economic, social and environmental costs of large new projects. While grain yields rose an average of 2.1 per cent a year between 1950 and 1990, that annual increase dropped to 1 per cent between 1990 and 1998. Water scarcity is now the single biggest threat to global food production. More than 1 billion people live in regions where there is insufficient water to meet modest food needs per person (Postel, 1999). Population growth in developing countries raises the prospect of greatly increased food import needs. However, poverty levels raise doubts about the ability of these nations to import enough grain to fill their food gaps.

In this chapter the concept of *new regionalism* is introduced as a vehicle for achieving integrated water management and food security in the MENA region (see also Chapter 10). Linkages between trade, water and agricultural policies are of crucial significance to achieving food security. How irrigation water is valued and managed in the MENA region offers challenges and opportunities for sustainable water management. For the MENA region, it is evident that the region depends on both global and regional waters. It is likely that the region will become more dependent on global water in the future. That the major indicator of an economy's water deficit level is the extent of its food imports is interesting to note (see Chapter 10).

The concept of virtual water – water embedded in food – proposed by Allan (2000) reflects the interdependencies between the global and the local water management agendas. The production of every tonne of a food commodity such as wheat requires a water input of about 1000 cubic metres. The trend in cereal imports reflects a reasonable approximation of the capacity of an economy to meet its strategic food needs. The change in water and agricultural policies in major countries such as Egypt and Saudi Arabia is evidence of the role of virtual water. For example, in 1986 Egypt changed its cotton-favouring subsidies policies so that wheat production could become a sound financial option for its farmers. Furthermore, by 1986 Saudi Arabia's irrigation projects had begun to produce sufficient wheat for most of its needs, and it was about to become a significant wheat exporter in the world market. Later, Saudi Arabia reduced its wheat production because it was unsustainable to use fossil water.

Water scarcity is evident at the national level in most MENA countries. However, most water is depleted during food production, which consumes nearly 90 per cent of a community's water. Since 1970, the predicament faced by the Middle East was a lack of sufficient water. As a result, water was imported in the form of food. In practice, more water flows into the Middle East each year in this 'virtual form', embedded in cereal imports used for annual crop production in Egypt. Usually, regional and global markets can overcome water deficit by importing food from the global markets. McCalla (1997) argued that global players, especially in the water-intense food sector, can provide virtual water solutions to local water deficits through the water, food and trade nexus. The global–local virtual-water dialogue is an interesting example of the type of water management partnerships, collaborations and convergence in the MENA region.

The rationale for rethinking the conventional way (water balance per country) of water management comes from the emergence of a globalized economy. The crucial challenge for future water professionals is how to induce a paradigm shift in the conventional modes of water-sector planning towards new modes of thinking that take into account global and regional perspectives as units of analysis rather than the nation state perspective. This shift in thinking brings about interesting findings. Simply said, we do not have a water crisis at the global and regional arenas. Water for food (virtual water), which is the leading consumer of water, can be substituted by trade. Thinking out of the box brings new options in a globalized economy.

The European Community's water management experience is an interesting example of 'water knowledge' sharing between the North and the South from which lessons can be learned. Regionalism is thus one way of coping with global transformation, since most states lack the capacity to manage such a task on the 'national' level. The new regionalism is a more comprehensive, multidimensional process. This process includes not only trade and economic development, but also environmental policy, water policy, social policy and security. The regions themselves constitute arenas for sometimes competing, sometimes converging, 'national interests'.

The following are seven arguments in favour of a more comprehensive development regionalism, presented by Acharya (1992):

- *The 'sufficient size' argument:* Although the question of territorial size might be of lesser importance in a highly interdependent world, regional cooperation is, nevertheless, imperative, particularly in the case of micro states, such as the MENA region, which either have to cooperate to solve common problems or become client states of the 'core countries'.
- *The 'viable economy' argument:* Self-reliance, rarely viable on the national level, may yet be a feasible development strategy at the regional level if defined as the coordination of production, the improvement of infrastructure and the making use of interdependencies.
- *The 'credibility' argument:* Economic policies may remain more stable and consistent if underpinned by regional arrangements that cannot be broken by a participant country without provoking some kind of sanction from the others.
- *The 'effective articulation' argument:* Collective bargaining on the regional level could improve the economic position of marginalized countries in the world system, or protect the structural position and market access of emerging export countries.
- *The 'social stability' argument:* Regionalism can reinforce societal viability by including social security issues and an element of redistribution (through regional funds or specialized banks) in the regionalist project.
- *The 'resource management' argument:* Ecological and political borders rarely coincide. Few serious environmental problems can be solved within the framework of the nation state. Some problems are bilateral, some are global, while quite a few are regional; the latter are often related to coastal waters, rivers and groundwater. The fact that regional management programmes exist and persist, in spite of nationalist rivalries, shows the imperative need for environmental cooperation.
- *The 'peace dividend' argument:* Regional conflict resolution, if successful and durable, eliminates distorted investment patterns since the 'security fund' (military expenditures) can be tapped for more productive use.

In sum, development regionalism contains the traditional arguments for regional cooperation such as territorial size and economies of scale, but, more significantly, adds some arguments that express new concerns and uncertainties about climate change and its impact on water resources.

CONCLUSIONS

Bilgin (1997), in his work on the making of regions through security discourses, argues that parallel to globalization is another process at work: *regionalization*. It is often argued that peoples of a globalizing world, in search of some degree of control over their external environments, have started taking action within their own milieu in cooperation with other actors sharing similar problems. Regionalization, in this sense, is seen as an attempt to come to terms with the forces of globalization. Regionalization and globalization, then, may be viewed as two mutually reinforcing processes.

A shift in thinking is needed in the new global economy. Instead of adopting the saying 'think global, act local', we must adhere to a motto of 'globalize consciousness, regionalize vision and localize benefits'. People-centred development must be adopted as a model for achieving sustainable development. A regional water vision in the MENA countries may provide a fresh way of looking at the region's water crisis.

REFERENCES

Acharya, A (1992) 'Regional military-security cooperation in the Third World: A conceptual analysis of the relevance and limitations of ASEAN', *Journal of Peace Research*, vol 29, no 1, pp7–21

Alaerts, G J et al (1991) 'Procedures and partners for capacity building in the water sector', Proceedings of the UNDP Symposium, 3–5 June, Delft, The Netherlands

Allan, T (2000) *The Middle East Water Question: Hydropolitics and the Global Economy*, I B Tauris Publishers, London

Al-Jayyousi, O (2001) 'Capacity building for desalination in Jordan', *Desalination*, vol 1, no 141, pp169–179

Al-Jayyousi, O and Mohsen, M (1999) 'Evaluation of fog collection in Jordan', *Journal of Water and Environmental Management*, vol 12, no 3, pp195–199

Al-Jayyousi, O and Shatanawi, M (1995) 'An analysis of future water policies in Jordan using decision support systems', *International Journal of Water Resources Development*, vol 11, no 3, pp315–330

'A strategy for water sector capacity building in Palestine', Proceedings of the Symposium Birzeit Agenda, Birzeit University, 6–7 September, 1995

Barrows, R L (1982) 'The roles of federal, state and local government in land-use planning', National Planning Conference, Washington, DC

Berger, P L and Luckmann, T (1967) *The Social Construction of Reality: A Treatise in the Sociology of Knowledge*, Anchor Books, Garden City, NY

Bilgin, P (1997) 'Inventing Middle Easts? The making of a region through security discourse: A critical security studies perspective,' Paper presented at CRIPT Workshop, University of Bristol, 8 November

Caldwell, L K (1990) *International Environmental Policy: Emergence and Dimensions*, 2nd edition, Duke University Press, Durham, NC

Carroll, M S and Hendrix, W G (1992) 'Federally protected rivers: The need for effective local involvement', *American Planning Association Journal*, vol 58, no 3, pp346–352

Cosgrove, W J and Rijsberman, F R (2000) *World Water Vision: Making Water Everybody's Business*, World Water Council, Earthscan, London

Duda, A M and El-Ashry, M T (2000) 'Addressing the global water and environment crisis through integrated approaches to the management of land, water, and ecological resources', *Water International*, vol 25, no 1, pp115–126

Frankland, E G and Schoonmaker, D (1992) *Between Protest and Power: The Green Party in Germany*, Westview Press, Boulder, CO

Friedman, J (1973) *Retracking America: A Theory of Transactive Planning*, Anchor Books, Garden City, NY

Ghai, D (ed) (1994) 'Development and environment: Sustaining people and nature', (special issue) *Development and Change*, vol 25, no 1

Ghai, D and Vivian, J (eds) (1992) *Grassroots Environmental Action: People's Participation in Sustainable Development*, Routledge for UNRISD, London

Global Environment Facility (GEF) (1996) 'Operational strategy', GEF, Washington, DC

Global Water Partnership (GWP) (2000) *Towards Water Security: A Framework for Action*, GWP, Stockholm, Sweden

Goodland, R, Daly, H E and El-Serafy, S (eds) (1992) *Population, Technology, and Lifestyle: The Transition to Sustainability*, Island Press, Washington, DC

Goodman, D and Redclift, M (eds) (1991) *Environment and Development in Latin America: The Politics and Sustainability*, Manchester University Press, Manchester

Grub, M, Koch, M, Munson, A, Sullivan, F and Thompson, K (1993) *The Earth Summit Agreements: A Guide and Assessments*, Earthscan, London

Hencht, S and Cockburn, A (1989) *The Fate of the Forest*, Verson, London

Kolars, J (2000) 'The spatial attributes of water negotiations: The need for a river ethics and river advocacy in the Middle East' in Amrey, H and Wolf, A (eds) *Water in the Middle East*, The University of Texas Press, Austin, TX

Korten, D C (1990) *Getting to the 21st Century: Voluntary Action and the Global Agenda*, Kumarian Press, West Hartford, CT

Korten, D C (1995) *When Corporations Rule the World*, Earthscan, London/Kumarian Press, West Hartford, CT

McCalla A (1997) 'Diversification and international trade', International Conference of Agricultural Economics, Sacramento, CA

Mageed, Y A and White, G F (1995) 'Critical analysis of existing institutional arrangements', *Water Resources Development*, vol 11, no 2, pp103–111

Mohsen, M and Al-Jayyousi, O (1999) 'Brackish water desalination: An alternative for water supply enhancement in Jordan', *International Journal of Desalination*, vol 124, pp163–174

Norberg-Hodge, H (1993) 'The psychological road to development', *PCD Forum*, Column, no 62, 8 October

Ohlsson, L and Turton, A R (1999) 'The turning of the screw: Social resource scarcity as a bottleneck in adaptation to water scarcity', Proceedings of the Stockholm Water Symposium, Stockholm, 9–12 August

Pimbert, M and Pretty, J (1995) 'Parks, people and professionals: Putting participation into protected area management', UNRISD Discussion paper, no 57, UNRISD, Geneva

Postel S (1999) *Pillar of Sand: Can the Irrigation Miracle Last?*, Environmental Alert Series, WW Norton, New York

Sarin, M (1995) 'Regenerating India's forests: Reconciling gender equity with forest management', *IDS Bulletin*, vol 26, no 1, pp83–91

Schnaiberg, A and K Gould (1994) *Environment and Society: The Enduring Conflict*, St Martin's Press, New York

Schumacher, E F (1973) *Small is Beautiful: A Study of Economics as if People Mattered*, Blond and Briggs Ltd, London

Shatanawi, M and Al-Jayyousi, O (1995) 'Evaluating market-oriented water policies in Jordan: A comparative study', *Water International*, vol 20, no 2, pp88–97

Solanes, M and Villarreal, F G (1999) 'The Dublin Principles for Water as reflected in a comparative assessment of institutional and legal arrangement for integrated water resources management', Global Water Partnership, Technical Advisory Committee (TAC), TAC Background Papers, no 3, June

Takahashi K et al (2002) 'Driving forces and incentives for change: Towards sustainable water development', *Water Science and Technology*, vol 45, no 8, pp141–144

WCED (1987) *Our Common Future*, Report of the World Commission on Environment and Development, Oxford University Press, Oxford

Wells M, Ganapin, D and Trempe, F (1998) 'Second independent evaluation of the GEF/SGP: The transition to an operational phase', Main Report, vol 1, UNDP, NY, 8 May

Western, D, Wright, M and Strum, S (eds) (1994) *Natural Connections: Perspectives in Community-Based Conservation*, Island Press, Washington, DC

Wright, DS (1988) *Understanding Intergovernmental Relations*, Brooks-Cole, Pacific Grove, CA

Zimmerman, J F (1983) *State–Local Relations: A Partnership Approach*, Praeger, New York

Chapter 4

Balancing between the eternal yesterday and the eternal tomorrow: Economic globalization, water and equity

NASER FARUQUI

INTRODUCTION

At the dawn of a new century, we are at a critical juncture in the relationship of water and development. According to the World Water Vision, renewable blue water flows will be insufficient to meet all industrial, domestic and agricultural needs by 2020 (Cosgrove and Rijsberman, 2000).[1] This is because of increasing water pollution, population growth and urbanization. Many countries are already in a state of water crisis, particularly those in arid regions. We need to develop a new way of thinking and acting on water management. We need to use new ideas or implement neglected ideas, and we need to adopt new attitudes. In brief, we need to change. Yet, throughout human history, change, particularly revolutionary change, is almost always resisted.

The world is going through an unprecedented period of integration in trade, finance, technology and communications, a process that is commonly referred to as globalization. With changes come new ideas and approaches that offer opportunities, and also pose some risks, for water management. However, two features characterize our typical response to globalization. First, the process itself, which is complex and not well understood, is presented in simplistic terms. Second, the reaction to it is very polarized: globalization is presented as either humanity's saviour or its downfall.

For instance, the growing integration of economies between countries has engendered a sharp response from a coalition of diverse groups, including environmentalists, advocates for the poor, unions and anarchists. Recent meetings of the World Trade Organization (WTO) Ministerial Conference in Seattle in 1999, the Summit of the Americas in Quebec City in 2001, and the July 2001 G8 Summit meeting in Genoa, Italy, resulted in riots, violence and tear gas. This forceful rejection of economic globalization and the absolute belief in its detrimental effects on the environment, employment, culture and the poor is not unlike the reaction of British textile workers in 1811. Led by Ned Lud, they rebelled against upgrading the industry's technology and began smashing machinery (Britannica.com, 2001).

A number of social activists believe that many aspects of economic globalization, such as deregulation, privatization and free trade, will cause 'the destruction of our water systems' (Barlow, 2000, p79). In contrast, free market advocates such as Francis Fukuyama maintain that the free market will solve all of our problems (Burchill and Linklater, 1996). Neither is correct. Moreover, both analyses are superficial, polarized and dangerous. We must change. However, we must do it carefully by examining the opportunities offered by globalization, while at the same time recognizing its risks. As stated by Farhang Rajaee (2000), 'Civilizations continue to flourish as long as they can respond to challenges, which come either from the past or from the future.' Rajaee argues that creativity and productivity occur at the intersection of the past and future, which requires balancing between Max Weber's concept of 'the eternal yesterday' (Gerth and Mills, 1958, p78) and 'the eternal tomorrow'.

The 'eternal yesterday' is a romanticized perception of the past. It reflects a natural human tendency, with the passage of time, to remember only the positive aspects of a day, a society or a relationship. Meanwhile, the negative aspects, which we wish to forget, slowly fade from memory. According to the old saying, it is as if we are looking at the past through rose-coloured glasses. Thus, the past often seems more just and equitable than today, even if it was not. As well, values, such as close family ties, good manners and respect for one's fellow humans, are seen to be traditional values and associated with the past, even if they are actually more prevalent today.

The 'eternal tomorrow' is a misnomer because Weber was really thinking about the present, not the future. Although it is the opposite of the 'eternal yesterday', it is no less utopian an ideal. The 'eternal tomorrow' is based on a belief in the superiority of current ideas over older ones, and the ability of today's newer approaches, such as innovative technology and free trade, to improve efficiency, productivity and our lives. This view assumes that to retain legitimacy, older ideas or philosophies must be harmonized with contemporary ideas.

The problem with much of what has been written or said about the challenge of globalization is that it does not strike a balance between the 'eternal yesterday' and the 'eternal tomorrow' – it represents either one flawed view or the other. Such polarized and superficial analyses either rely too much on a glorified vision of the past, and a rejection of technology and modernity, or express too much faith in the economic tool currently in vogue. However, balance is essential between the two extremes, both of which contain some truth. This also applies to how civilizations address the challenge of water and equity.

This chapter will take an even-handed look at water and globalization, which is a very complex topic whose debate and research are in their infancy. Rather than examining any one topic in great depth, the chapter covers the range of issues related to water to provide a general framework for further discussion, debate and research. Because economic globalization cannot be discussed in the context of water management without a basic understanding of the globalization process itself, the chapter begins by outlining the interconnected aspects of globalization, and then challenges common perceptions. With a better appreciation of the complexities of globalization, the chapter then focuses on economic globalization and its impact on water management, including the principle of treating water as an economic good and the resulting controversy. It challenges some of the common arguments against full-cost pricing and public–private partnerships, while also identifying some of the potential negative impacts of economic globalization on water management. The chapter argues that the focus should be to enhance equity – whether utility operation is public or private is less important. It concludes by examining the impact of international trade on water management, specifically looking at the questions of bulk water exports and transforming economies.

THE DIFFERENT ASPECTS OF GLOBALIZATION

Globalization, a complex phenomenon, has political, cultural, social, economic and environmental aspects. There are both positive and negative elements to each aspect. For example, politically, a common criticism of economic globalization is that nation states lose their power to regulate and to set domestic trade and economic policies to international corporations and organizations such as the WTO. On the other hand, international trade deals guarantee access for small countries into the markets of larger ones. Developing countries have commonly expressed the view of 'fair trade, not aid' (Trade Aid, 1998; Canadian International Development Agency, 1995). Culturally, it is generally believed that globalization means national and indigenous cultures will be obliterated by the dominant Western, and particularly American, culture. However, according to the World Values Survey, a study of 65 societies containing 85 per cent of the world's population, 'traditional cultural values have a surprising resilience and persistence that will keep most countries from becoming clones of the United States' (Inglehart, 2001, p1). Socially, many activists worry that, due to growing economic interdependence, social issues will become subordinate to economic ones and that the market will become more important than human rights. Yet, with some exceptions, the more powerful Western cultures promoting globalization prize not only the market but also the rule of law, participatory government and human rights.[2] The World Values Survey indicates that the process of modernization drives cultural change, which encourages major transformations such as the rise of women in public life and the development of democratic institutions (Inglehart, 2001). However, of all the aspects of globalization, the most relevant to water management are economic and environmental issues.

Economic aspects

Economic globalization is the integration of individual economies through regional trade deals such as the European Union (EU) Trade Agreement and the North American Free Trade Agreement (NAFTA), or global deals such as the General Agreement on Tariffs and Trade (GATT) implemented by the WTO. With the gradual elimination of tariffs and the eroding of state boundaries for trade, the world's economy is becoming increasingly interdependent. Proponents of economic globalization maintain that increased trade means increased growth and increased wealth. For example, according to a study by Harvard Professors Sachs and Warner, poor countries with open economies grew by an average of 4.5 per cent during the 1970s and 1980s, while those with closed economies grew by 0.7 per cent (as cited in the *Globe and Mail*, 13 April 2001). In fact, many claim that economic globalization is the best weapon the world has ever seen for fighting poverty, pointing to countries that have embraced trade, such as Singapore or South Korea; the latter was as poor as Ghana three decades ago (*Globe and Mail*, 13 April 2001). In China, 160 million people left the ranks of the poor as that country joined the global economy, and average incomes quadrupled in just 20 years (*Globe and Mail*, 13 April 2001).

While it may be true that economic globalization leads to greater overall growth and greater wealth, ultra neo-liberals tend to ignore the fact that the benefits of that increased wealth are unevenly distributed, both internationally and within countries. While globalization has generally been good for both rich and poor in developed countries, as well as in East and South-East Asia, it has been mixed or bad for many other developing countries, and especially bad for Africa (Streeten, 1998). Overall, the developing countries' share of global wealth shrank from 20 per cent in 1960 to 18 per cent in 1994 (Streeten, 1998). It remains to be seen whether this trend will change with accelerating globalization. Furthermore, within countries, both poverty and the gap between rich and poor have increased, especially in Africa and South Asia, because 'international competition for markets and jobs has forced governments to reduce taxation and with it the social services, particularly food subsidies, that had protected the poor' (Streeten, 1998, p22). So, while economic globalization can increase the absolute wealth in a society, it does not help the poor unless that wealth gain or the incremental wealth is redistributed through taxes or other means.

Environmental aspects

The general perception is that globalization is bad for the environment. As will be discussed below, industries that are generally associated with globalization, such as those in the high-technology sector, are not as 'clean' as commonly believed. Furthermore, increased growth spurred on by economic globalization will lead to a higher consumption of resources and the increased potential for pollution. In general, however, it is industrialization that causes pollution, not globalization. Countries that industrialize without much trade or foreign investment are likely to have worse environmental records than those that are more open. For example, it only became obvious how contaminated the air and water in the former Eastern Bloc was after their borders opened (*Globe and Mail*, 14 April 2001). Furthermore, despite having similar populations and number of vehicles, Delhi's air pollution is far worse than Karachi's. This is due to the policy of import substitution followed so long by India. This policy led to the prevalence of ancient Maruti automobiles (based upon an even older Fiat design) that spew at least ten times as many pollutants into the air per car as do the newer vehicles in Karachi. Moreover, as people grow richer they demand a cleaner environment, and because they are richer they can afford it. A 1994 study showed that pollution levels in developing countries started to fall when per-capita income levels reached US$8000 (Kruger and Grossman, 1994).

Activists worry about the 'race to the bottom' – that nations will lower their environmental standards to compete with other states for investment. However, 'there is no evidence that any relatively affluent nation has lowered its existing environmental standards in order to increase the competitiveness of domestic producers' (Vogel, 1999). The reason that there is no 'race to the bottom' is that for most industries environmental compliance adds up to less than 2 per cent of total production costs (Vogel, 1999). Thus, relative to other costs, such as labour, pollution-control expenses alone are too small to make it worth relocating because of higher environmental standards in one region compared to another. In fact, the 'California effect' illustrates how automobile emission standards in developed nations around the world have risen to meet the most stringent in the world, which are those of California. This mainly happened because German and Japanese auto-makers, having upgraded their standards to access the California market, encouraged their home markets to strengthen their own standards because their exports were already meeting them (Vogel, 1999).

Economic globalization is inevitable

In summary, globalization is a far more complicated process than commonly presented and offers both benefits and costs. Proponents of globalization celebrate the former, while discounting the latter. Opponents focus on the costs, often missing the crucial point that globalization is inevitable and likely to accelerate. Furthermore, while globalization does have negative impacts, as more and more nations enter into regional and global trade deals, not participating is likely to have worse effects than participating, especially for developing countries. Even some economists who identify the negative aspects of globalization acknowledge this. For example, Bhalla (1998) indicates that because most countries have already liberalized, 'any [country] that does not, does so at its own peril'. Streeten adds that 'It does not follow that developing countries would have been better off if they had closed themselves off from the process of globalization... As Joan Robinson once said, there is only one thing that is worse than being exploited by the capitalists, and that is not being exploited by them' (Streeten, cited in Bhalla, 1998). However, this does not mean that the 'losers' should be abandoned and left to buffet in globalization's wild gales. There are ways to protect these people, and, as we shall see in the following sections, this applies to their access to water as much as anything else.

ECONOMIC GLOBALIZATION AND WATER

This section outlines both the rationale for considering water as an economic good and the resulting controversy surrounding full-cost pricing and public–private partnerships. It then examines the arguments advanced by those who are opposed to a greater role for the market in water management and challenges some of these arguments, while validating others dismissed by proponents of a market approach. Using case studies from both public and private water operations, the chapter takes a more nuanced look at the privatization debate by suggesting that different models are appropriate for different contexts. Following this, the concept of public–public partnerships is introduced. Finally, the chapter examines the issues of bulk water, international trade and exports.

The rationale for considering water as an economic good

The International Conference on Water and Environment held in Dublin in 1992 described water as a social good, and then in the next breath also described it as an economic good. This was recently confirmed in the World Water Vision, which calls for full-cost pricing to encourage water conservation, to ensure more water is available to go around, and to pay for the proper operation and maintenance of infrastructure, including sewage treatment to prevent water pollution (Cosgrove and Rijsberman, 2000). Full-cost pricing will also ensure that additional investments in water infrastructure can be made so that coverage is extended to the unserved poor. At present, the World Bank reports that subsidies inherent in low water prices go primarily to the non-poor (Bosch et al, 2000).

Another increasingly common issue associated with economic globalization is the privatization of water services. The four different privatization models are described in Table 4.1, ranging from the most to the least degree of public control. Most current privatizations are some form of the first three public–private partnerships (Yaron, 2000). In the remainder of the document, the term 'privatization' implies these types of public–private partnerships and does not imply divestiture.

Table 4.1 *Privatization models*

Privatization models	Responsibilities
Operations and lease contracts	Governments will outsource specific tasks to private firms. Investment funds are often provided by development bank loans to the government.
Build-operate-transfer (BOT) contracts	The private partner must build and operate the system and transfer all assets to the government immediately or following the contract term.
Concessions	Full operational responsibility and commercial and investment risk are placed on the private sector.
Divestitures	Ownership is completely transferred to private interests, as happened during the Thatcher administration in the UK. These are now rare.

The World Bank states that 'public water and sanitation services are often plagued by inefficiency' (Bosch et al, 2000). Several reasons are given why private-sector involvement in water service is likely to be beneficial, including the following:

- Private utilities are likely to work under greater scrutiny than public systems because of the controversy surrounding privatization.
- The government itself is more likely to criticize and act against a private operator than a government corporation.
- A private utility has a greater incentive to reduce losses because lost water means lost profits.
- Private operators are more likely to draw upon international experience and know-how than are government utilities.

The controversy

For several reasons, the idea that water is an economic good is controversial. Many social activists feel that because water is a vital social need, governments should provide water free, or greatly discounted, to the poor. Furthermore, they see an inherent contradiction between the idea that water is a fundamental human right and social good and that it could potentially be allocated like any other commodity – only to those who can afford it.

For example, Barlow (1999) argues that considering water as an economic good leads to the 'commodification' of the world's water supply. Driven by economic globalization, this is pushing us down a slippery slope that will lead to greater inequities and to water that flows only to the highest bidder. Activists fear that economic globalization, as envisaged by transnational corporations that are pressuring national governments to privatize, deregulate and relinquish state controls, is pushing us into a single global economy. They say that in this global economy, corporations and financial markets will set the rules and the entire food chain. According to Shiva (1999), this includes seeds and water, which will be controlled by private companies.

Like ultra neo-liberals, advocates of full government control over all aspects of water management tend to have a lopsided view of reality. While some of their concerns are valid, they have an idealized memory of the 'eternal yesterday'. This is so much the case that in their well-intentioned attempts to combat the increasing use of market forces in water management, they may make statements backed by little proof and list causes without proving their effects. Two common concerns that can be challenged are that the market approach will result in the poor being cut off from water supplies and that their health will suffer.

High prices and being cut off

The strongest and most emotional criticism of the activists is the least likely to be correct:

> *When water is privatized, prices are set on the open market. As a result, millions of poor people have been cut off* (Barlow, 1999, p16).

While this may apply to water for farming, as will be explored below, it is unlikely that it applies to water for drinking, even in rural areas. Activists often suggest that private–public partnerships, followed by steep increases in water prices, are the cause of high prices for the poor. In fact, the very high prices the poor often pay for water rarely have anything to do with privatization. The unserved poor pay 10 to 20 times the price that the served non-poor pay per unit for water (Serageldin, 2000) precisely because subsidized water prices mean that public utilities do not generate adequate funds to serve the poor. To quote Serageldin: 'It is the perversity of defending subsidized water prices in cities in the name of the poor, when they have no access to the piped water in their shanties, and end up paying 10 to 20 times as much to unregulated water vendors' (Serageldin, 2000, p33).

Prices do usually rise following the establishment of public–private partnerships. Activists tend to perceive such rate hikes solely as a cash grab by private operators seeking to improve their profit margins. For example, 'following a privatization scheme in Bolivia, residents faced a doubling or more of the water rates' (Shulk, 2000, p1). What is ignored by such activists is that regardless of whether the service is provided by a private or public operator, if the prices are less than the full cost of provision, then they must be increased and accompanied by targeted subsidies to the poor if necessary (see the following subsection).

As stated by the World Water Vision, prices in urban areas must increase until they reach the point of fully covering the cost of paying for capital infrastructure, proper treatment, sewage treatment and providing service to the poor (Cosgrove and Rijsberman, 2000). Yet, urban water rates in lesser developed countries are typically less than one sixth the full cost of water provision (Bronso, 1998). Governments can no longer afford such large subsidies and are turning to the private sector. In some municipalities, this may mean tariff increases as high as 600 per cent. While this may seem exorbitant, it does not appear so high when consumers' willingness to pay is considered. The full cost of water provision, including sewage treatment, varies with the quality of the raw water and the nature of the distribution system. The average, however, is typically about US$1 per cubic metre ($m^3$) (0.10 US cents per litre).[3] In other words, while the non-poor may be paying prices as low as US$0.20 per m^3, the unserved poor typically pay about US$2–US$4 per m^3 when the same, and frequently better quality, water could be purchased for US$1 per m^3 from the municipality.[4]

Protecting the extreme poor from market prices: Subsidies and tariffs

While not all the unserved urban poor pay 10 to 20 times as much as those who receive water service, most of the poor should still be able to afford to pay efficient market prices, even if this includes a reasonable profit. Consider the average full-cost price of 0.10 US cents per litre. Using this price, Lundqvist and Gleick's (1997) basic water requirement – the amount of water necessary to meet all domestic needs, including drinking, washing and cooking, which is 50 litres per capita per day (LPCD) – will cost 5 US cents per person per day, US$1.50 per month and US$18 per year. A 15 per cent profit would increase the price to US$21 per year. Almost everyone who has access to water at this price can afford it. For the poorest families who cannot afford this price, regulators can mandate a lifeline tariff that requires utilities, privatized or not, to deliver basic water requirements to all of its customers for a minimal cost or for free.[5] For example, South Africa's water law guarantees the first 25 LPCD free as a right for all of its citizens.[6] Another alternative is to consider World Water Vision's recommendation to offer targeted and transparent subsidies to the poor (Cosgrove and Rijsberman, 2000).

Public–private partnerships and public health

A common concern of those opposing a greater role of the market in water management is the risk of placing water, vital for public health, in the hands of the private sector whose first concern is profit. For instance, Yaron (2000) notes that the post-privatization drinking water of Manila was contaminated, implying the contamination occurred because of privatization. This may or may not have been the case. It could well have occurred under the former public utility. All over the developing world and some parts of the developed world, public utilities routinely deliver drinking water that compromises public health. In fact, with increasing pollution and large livestock operations coming closer to urban areas, outbreaks of contamination from bacteria, viruses or parasites, such as cryptosporidium in Milwaukee that resulted in the death of over 100 people and the sickness of over 400,000 (Euronature, 2001), are becoming increasingly common in public water supplies.

The tragic case of the small Ontario, Canada, town of Walkerton, where in 2000, after drinking municipal water contaminated with *E. coli* bacteria, seven people died, illustrates the danger of too quickly linking public health concerns with privatization. In this case, the town's water utility was not privatized. Outsourcing water testing to a privatized laboratory that did not notify the town's chief medical officer about the bacterial analysis was possibly one factor in the deaths. However, it was only one factor among several including:

- the presence of an exceptionally virulent form of *E. coli* in the water;
- extreme rainfall;
- improperly operating chlorinators; and
- an incompetent plant operator (www.alertontario.org).[7]

Factors more important than privatization in this case were budget cuts at the provincial Ministry of the Environment. Had irregularities in the quality of the water and the operation of the plant been caught and acted upon earlier by inspectors, the deaths might have been prevented. A key lesson is that increasing source-water pollution requires increased, not decreased, government regulation. This is the case whether or not service delivery is privatized.

Impact of privatization on labour

It is essential for employees to be paid fairly and have safe working conditions, regardless of whether they work in a privatized or a public utility. Maintaining excessive staff levels may or may not be in the broader interest of society. However, a key issue motivating the activists' battle with public–private partnerships is protecting union jobs at almost any cost. Unfortunately, this moves the debate away from equitable water management into the realm of labour–business conflicts. For example, Yaron indicates that 'protections [for employees] should be entrenched before communities permit privatization' (Yaron, 2000, p49). Yet, excessive staff levels and very low service characterize many water utilities in developing countries. Protecting poor consumers and protecting jobs at utilities may be mutually exclusive objectives; therefore, on their own, job losses are an insufficient reason to condemn privatization because performance, prices and efficiency may actually improve for poor consumers. As well, almost all successfully reformed public utilities also cut jobs, as we shall see below.

Troubling aspects of economic globalization and water

While some of the concerns raised by activists have little basis, issues relating to industry concentration, industrial water rates, transparency, lack of incentive to promote conservation and corruption are legitimate. However, privatization proponents often dismiss these concerns – demonstrating that holding a lopsided view of reality is not restricted to activists. This section examines some of these concerns.

Industry concentration and company size

In recent years, there has been a dramatic growth in privatization (see Chapter 11). Between 1984 and 1990, only eight new private water and sewerage contracts were signed in developing countries, compared with 97 between 1990 and 1997 (Silva et al, 1997). This is a very lucrative business. For example, the private water sector in the USA generates more than US$80 billion a year in revenue, four times the sales of Microsoft Corporation (Glassman, 1999). The growing supply of contracts has attracted the attention of a very small number of very large transnational corporations. Ten large firms control the global water market and have consolidated their hold through mergers and acquisitions.[8] Between 1994 and 1998, there were 139 water-related mergers and acquisitions, with a total market value of nearly US$15 billion. The two largest firms, both French, Suez Lyonnaise (now Ondeo) and Vivendi, comprise almost 70 per cent of the existing world water market (Yaron, 2000). Each has a total annual revenue of about US$30 billion, and they are respectively ranked 69th and 70th on the Fortune 500 list of companies. Water comprises only part of the operations of these giants: included are units in water-related sectors, in addition to electricity, construction and telecommunications. For instance, Vivendi owns the high-tech company Alcatel, which in turn recently purchased Canada's Newbridge Networks, a telecom company.

Controlled by a few large firms, the global water services market has become an oligopoly, characterized by serious barriers to entry and the potential for anti-competitive behaviour. As stated by Yaron (2000, p82), 'as water corporations grow in size, governments and regulators may likely find it challenging to control these giants, given their impact on the economy and employment'. This statement applies not only to core water operations as discussed below, but also to the telecommunications subsidiaries and clients of such companies, as discussed in the section on 'International trade'.

However, most industrialized countries have legislation, such as antitrust laws in the USA, that gives government the right to block mergers or acquisitions if it feels that the resulting industry concentration gives too much market power to a small number of firms. A government must demonstrate the leadership to use such legislation when it feels that firms are engaging in anti-competitive behaviour; for example, when the US Department of Justice ordered the break up of the telecommunications behemoth Bell into 'Baby Bells', or ordered the break up of Microsoft Corporation. While such rules are harder to enforce with transnational corporations, it is not impossible. Beginning in 1990, the European Commission's rules officially took precedence over the antitrust legislation of member countries in those cases where the merger involved activities in more than one member state (Colander, 2001). For example, in 2001 the European Commission blocked a US$42 billion General Electric and Honeywell merger because it felt that the concentration would result in limited competition. Although General Electric and Honeywell are American, mergers between companies that each do more than US$250 million of business within the EU can be blocked by the European Commission (Fraser, 2001/2002).

Lack of transparency

Private companies argue that making contract documents public hurts their competitiveness. Large water companies have had the clout to insist on confidentiality. For example, in Fort Beaufort, South Africa, the public's access to information about the contract is restricted by Suez Lyonnaise des Eaux subsidiary WSSA (Lobina and Hall, 2001). In the UK, residents, councillors and the government condemned Yorkshire Water for refusing to disclose local drainage information following several incidents of raw sewage discharges (Yaron, 2000). Given the importance of water to public health and the environment, agreements must be transparent and must require privatized water entities to disclose this kind of information.

Lack of incentive to pursue conservation strategies

The World Bank suggests that privatized utilities will cut leakage rates because lost water means lost profits. Yet, the UK's water companies did not take significant steps to repair leaking water pipes until 1999, when the regulator, Office of Water Services (OFWAT), imposed requirements to conserve water and to repair infrastructure. In 1996, the UK government chastised Yorkshire Water for not fixing leaking pipes over the past 12 years (Yaron, 2000).

Furthermore, because the ultimate aim of a private company is to maximize its profits, once the water has been sold, the company has no natural incentive to promote water conservation. For a well-run company operating below capacity, the more water it sells, the more profit it makes. Thus, the privatization of water is not in the long-term interest of society unless the contract includes performance requirements for reducing unaccounted water to acceptable levels, and for objectives relating to long-term water conservation.

Corruption

It is not suggested that most of the staff at the big ten water companies are anything but honest. And, certainly, corruption is not uncommon in public utilities, especially in developing countries where powerful customers often do not pay their bills. Nevertheless, even the World Bank, a strong supporter of public–private partnerships, indicates that 'the privatization process itself can create corrupt incentives. A firm may pay...to be favoured in the selection process [and] to obtain...subsidies, monopoly benefits and regulatory laxness in the future' (Rose-Ackerman, 1996). Activists point to several cases of corruption involving some of the big ten water companies. For instance, in Indonesia, local residents and contractors have taken legal action to revoke the water management contracts of both Suez Lyonnaise and Thames Water and to ensure that the companies pay compensation. Furthermore, residents allege that the Indonesian government broke the law granting water concessions without subjecting them to competitive tender (Lobina and Hall, 2001). In Grenoble, France, in 1996, a government minister and an executive of Suez Lyonnaise received prison sentences for receiving and giving bribes to award a water contract to a subsidiary of Suez Lyonnaise des Eaux (PSI, 2000). One way to combat and reduce the potential for corruption is if a government designs and implements a transparent regulatory and contractor selection process, and if the regulator is independent from the government.

A balanced approach to public–private partnerships

Privatization proponents such as the UK's Margaret Thatcher maintain that the private sector is always more efficient than the government, while activists such as Yaron feel that privatization threatens equity, and that only the public sector can be accountable to the people. Neither is correct. In most cases in developing countries, switching to private water operations will likely enhance equity, provided that the private sector is regulated to address accountability and equity. However, this is not true in every case. In this section, the issue is examined in more depth in order to search for facts to replace the rhetoric and for options ignored by both sides.

Public–private partnerships

As noted in the World Water Vision: 'In many countries the supply of water services has been entrusted to public agencies, which in most developing countries (and many developed ones) have become inefficient, unregulated, and unaccountable' (Cosgrove and Rijsberman, 2000). Except for a few cases, such as Chile, experiments in formal private–public partnerships are relatively recent. As a result, little data is available to assess their impact on the poor. What few studies do exist come primarily from the World Bank. The following cases provide information from which to draw some conclusions.

In the Ivory Coast during 1974, only 30 per cent of the urban population and 10 per cent of the rural population had access to safe water. By 1989, 72 per cent of the urban population and 80 per cent of the rural population had access to safe water. This occurred because the privatized Société de Distribution d'Eau de la Côte d'Ivoire was allowed to increase urban water tariffs above the level of long-term marginal costs, especially for industrial customers (Bhattia et al, 1995).

A similar transition accompanied by an innovative use of subsidies occurred in Conakry, Guinea. During the late 1980s, the performance of the public utility was very poor. Water was available only a few hours per day, and the poor were at the end of the line. Service was poor, people were unwilling to pay, revenues were inadequate, and so service became worse, which created a vicious circle. The government then leased the assets to a private operator who was paid a fee that reflected the full operating costs. However, consumers were initially only charged about a quarter of the full-cost tariff. Tariffs gradually rose, but only as service improved. The shortfall was covered by donor aid during the transition period. Although some problems still remain, this innovative approach worked well and coverage increased by 300 per cent in the first five years of the contract (World Water Commission, 2000).

Results in Bolivia are also promising. Prior to 1997, the public utility in La Paz–El Alto provided water and sanitation to city-centre residents, but was unable to serve poor residents in outlying areas that relied on alternative high-cost water and sanitation services. In 1997, a 25-year concession was granted to a consortium including Suez Lyonnaise des Eaux and Aguas de Illimani, a domestic company. The concession's primary objective was to expand service to the poor by increasing efficiency and holding down costs. To date, the concessionaire has met its service expansion obligations and 'took many steps to facilitate the expansion of in-house connections in low-income areas' (Komives and Brook Cowen, 1999). However, the project is not without problems. According to Komives and Brook Cowen (1999), the project objectives are not clear or easily measurable, the requirement for customers to hold property titles discriminates against the poor, and the initial mapping of service boundaries excluded some poor neighbourhoods. It is too early to assess whether the current gains are sustainable or to state how privatization will, ultimately, affect the poor in La Paz and El Alto (Komives and Brook Cowen, 1999).

Finally, one of the world's largest concession contracts for water and sanitation services was signed for Buenos Aires in 1992. The contract was very controversial in Argentina and attracted worldwide attention. According to Bosch et al (2000), the winning bid immediately resulted in reducing water system tariffs by 27 per cent, which was only partly reversed by subsequent changes in the tariff structure. Consumers benefited from the system's expansion. However, a contract that may allow the concessionaire to act opportunistically, and by a weak, politicized and non-transparent regulatory system, threatens the concession's sustainability. Public confidence in the process has evaporated because of arbitrary and politicized decision-making by the regulator.

Activists opposing public–private partnerships often associate such schemes only with large transnational water companies. However, a private operator can be small and local rather than large and global. Furthermore, the aim of the entity may be to serve as much of the community as possible, instead of maximizing profits. For instance, since 1987, small groups of villagers in Kerala, India, have been organizing and establishing small water supply schemes instead of depending upon the state government for their water. With the facilitation, rather than the financial support, of the state government, the households have formed 26 private cooperative societies, with six more planned. The villagers who share the profits, and who return the profits to the society, own the societies. The private societies have paid 100 per cent of the capital and operation and maintenance cost of the schemes, demonstrating a high willingness to pay. For the most part, poorer families are not excluded. Their contributions to the society are accepted in instalments, and, in some cases, the poor pay their capital costs by providing labour to help construct the water systems (Water and Sanitation Program, 2001).

The above-noted results demonstrate that public–private partnerships for water services can be promising for the poor, although it is too early to draw definitive conclusions. To date, little or no evidence of strong negative impacts can be found. On the whole, public–private partnerships appear to expand service to the urban poor. These benefits may not be as striking as proponents of privatization imply; but, on the other hand, the circumstance must be compared to the situation where the public utility was still providing water services, which in most cases meant a steady decline in service quality.

However, problems with public–private partnerships are also evident, most notably in:

- contracts that provide insufficient incentive for the concessionaire to provide services to the poor;
- contracts that discriminate against customers who do not hold property title; and
- governments that shirk their regulatory duty.

There have been an increasing number of public–private partnerships in recent years. These cases need to be carefully studied in order to identify how to structure contracts and policies to maximize benefits to the poor. Furthermore, a strong regulatory role by governments is essential.

Successful public utilities

Despite the rhetoric of privatization advocates, the best-run utilities in the world are public. Using unaccounted for water (UFW) as an indicator, which includes both physical losses (leakages) and commercial losses (meter under-registration and illegal connections), the best-run utility in the world in 1996 was Singapore with, UFW of 6 per cent. Tokyo was second, with UFW of 15 per cent (Yepes and Diandras, 1996). Both are public utilities, and both have even further improved their performance. Compare this to privatized utilities in the UK, where government data for the same year show that, through leakages only, Thames Water lost 38 per cent and Yorkshire Water lost 33 per cent (Turton, 1998).

According to the World Bank, the successful reforms of inefficient, publicly run water utilities in the developing world are rare, and failed reforms are much more common (Bosch et al, 2000). However, Lobina provides some successful examples. For instance, SANAA, the state-owned water company in Tegucigalpa, Honduras, was successfully restructured between 1994 and 1998. The restructuring, which greatly improved performance, included a significant increase in tariffs and a reduction in staffing levels. In Brazil, SABESP, the world's largest water utility, which serves Sao Paulo, has undergone extensive restructuring. In 1995 alone, the water supply coverage increased from 84 per cent to 91 per cent, and sewerage coverage increased from 64 per cent to 73 per cent. Operating costs were reduced by 45 per cent, partly due to outsourcing (Lobina and Hall, 2001).

Successful restructuring of most public utilities to improve service obviously requires increasing tariffs and cutting costs, including staff. These are the same measures for which activists criticize private water companies.

The point is that the best-performing utilities, and those that provide greater water coverage, are those that are run as self-sustaining commercial enterprises accountable to the people. This does not preclude the use of lifeline tariffs or targeted subsidies for the poor, as long as the utility is self-financing overall. Whether ownership is public or private is less important.

Public–public partnerships

An option often neglected by both proponents and opponents of privatization is public–public partnerships. In many developed countries, there are very efficient public utilities, such as in Singapore, Tokyo, Stockholm and in The Netherlands (Blokland et al, 1999). Therefore, there is no need to move to public–private partnerships. By contrast, in most cases, public utilities offer poor service and incomplete coverage in many transitional and developing countries because of a lack of resources and expertise, and weak institutions. Public–public partnerships (PUPs) and international twinning programmes are a means for transferring the institutional strength of the public sector in one country to another without involving the private sector. The stronger public partner helps the weaker one build capacity through consultation, training and management services (Lobina and Hall, 2001). This approach offers several advantages. Firstly, PUPs are often cheaper than private consulting services because public-sector employees' time is often offered at cost or may even be subsidized by their national governments or municipalities. Secondly, training under such programmes is usually very effective because it takes place in a utility and is run by the utility's staff. Spending time and learning on the job in a well-run public utility in another country, and then applying that knowledge at home, is invaluable for institutional strengthening.[9] PUPs are common between Scandinavia and Finland and former Soviet Republics such as Estonia and Latvia. The World Bank funded two successful capacity-building projects in Malawi, using a twinning approach between a public-sector partner from the UK (before British water was privatized) and the utility in Lilongwe. Access to water improved significantly. The UFW fell to 16 per cent and customer complaints decreased. In Ambon, Indonesia, a Dutch water company, WMD Drenthe, has created a joint venture water company with the Indonesian city of Ambon. With the technical support of WMD, Indonesian staff have already taken steps to increase water production, reduce leakage and make the company self-financing. In 2000, the governments of The Netherlands and Bangladesh developed a twinning arrangement, funded by both countries, to support policy development, instructional strengthening and planning for the water sector in Bangladesh (Lobina and Hall, 2001).

International trade

One of the main characteristics of globalization is increasing international trade. This section examines the impact of potential bulk trading of water, both on the environment and on national sovereignty, and the impact of transforming economies, including the high-technology industry, on water resources.

Bulk water exports

Globally, the water industry was worth about US$14 billion in 1995, with an annual growth rate estimated at 8 to 10 per cent (NRDC, 1998). Until recently, however, the bulk exports of water for sale across national borders and water basins have not been economically feasible for domestic purposes, especially due to dropping desalination costs. Because of the growing value, an issue of some concern is international bulk water exports (see Box 4.1 on the Canadian case study). International water markets for bottled water exports are already well established, and innovative means to transport water (for example, in large plastic bags, called medusa bags, towed behind barges) have been developed. Such schemes may now be profitable in some cases. For instance, Aquarius Water Trading and Transportation has already made deliveries between Piraeus and Aegina, Greece, and estimates that the market for transporting water to the Greek Islands exceeds 200 million tonnes per year (*Financial Times*, 1997, p80). Furthermore, globalization and two-way trade may make bulk water exports even more economically attractive. For example, one scheme proposes taking Alaskan water by tanker to China. The economic rationale is to use the abundant cheap labour available in China to assemble computer wafers, while importing the water necessary for this process (Barlow, 2000). Because computer wafers require ultra pure freshwater, which adds to the cost of desalination, such water export schemes, while not profitable for domestic purposes, may well be profitable for industrial purposes.

WTO yet to rule on bulk-water export issues While water has not yet been addressed directly by any WTO panels, according to Yaron, in each dispute brought before it, the WTO has always upheld the rights of commerce over the rights of environmental protection, which would limit a government's ability to 'turn off the tap' (Yaron, 2000). In contrast, trade advocates argue that it is untrue that the WTO is against 'Green' interests, and that two notable cases to date were about discrimination and not the environment.[10] In the successful challenge of a US ban on importing shrimp caught in nets that also trap sea turtles, while agreeing that protecting the turtles was necessary, the WTO panel disputed the extra-territorial application of American law. In the reformulated gasoline case, the Canadian government banned the cross-border sale of methylcyclopentadienyl manganese tricarbonyl (MMT), a gasoline additive, in June 1997. The Ethyl Corporation of Virginia argued that Canada was giving preferential treatment to Canadian gasoline producers and sued the Canadian government under NAFTA, Chapter 11. Although MMT is banned as a potential neurotoxin in some European countries and in California, the Canadian government feared that it would lose under a NAFTA panel because it could not prove that MMT poses a threat to human health or the environment (Canada, 1998). The government thus reversed its ban in July 1998 and paid Ethyl Corporation compensation (Schneiderman, 1999).

BOX 4.1 CASE STUDY: CANADA, NAFTA AND BULK WATER EXPORTS

The issue of bulk water exports has been controversial in Canada since the negotiation of the first free trade agreement with the USA. Many proposals have already been made to export bulk water, mostly from glaciers, lakes or rivers that flow directly into the sea, or for small amounts relative to the annual recharge of the water body. On the surface, such proposals, in the volumes proposed, may have minimal social and environmental impact, especially if the freshwater is running directly into the sea. However, Nova Scotia's Bedford Institute of Oceanography warns that 'massive reductions in freshwater discharge can alter, and in some cases destroy the existing ecosystem in the adjacent coastal region' (Drinkwater and Frank, 1994). Moreover, while under existing conditions initial proposals may have minimal social or environmental impact, this might change in the future or in a drought year. To date, none of these proposals have been approved in Canada. The federal government has also banned exports of transboundary water that comes under its jurisdiction. Most of the provinces have also passed legislation banning bulk water exports in their respective jurisdictions. However, Newfoundland has not banned exports and is currently holding public hearings on the issue.

Environmental activists maintain that according to the North American Free Trade Agreement (NAFTA), once any state or province allows water export for commercial purposes, water is considered a 'good', and all provisions of the agreement governing trade in goods would apply.[11] This would have three main effects under the NAFTA:

- Once bulk water is traded, no country can discriminate in favour of its own private sector, which means that foreign companies would have the same water trading rights as domestic ones. This is called 'national treatment'.
- NAFTA, Chapter 11, allows a corporation of one NAFTA country to sue the government of another for compensation if that country denies national treatment rights or expropriates the company's future profit.[12]
- Article 309, the 'proportionality' clause, means, among other things, that once trade has commenced, it is very difficult to stop trading in the future.[13]

However, the Canadian government's ban on water exports may be challenged under the WTO. According to Brutciski and Banicevic (1999, p15), an outright bulk-water export prohibition would 'likely run afoul of GATT Article XI, [Reduction of Quantitative Restrictions], unless it could be justified by an exception elsewhere in the GATT'. However, the Canadian government maintains that 'exports of water as a precedent do not preclude it from preventing exports of other waters' and points to exceptions in the NAFTA and the WTO that allow countries to ban trade practices that harm the environment (www.can-am.gc.ca).[14]

On the other hand, the WTO makes it clear that such measures can only be applied in a 'non-discriminatory' fashion in order to prevent 'the abuse of environmental policies and their use as protectionism in disguise'. This principle, known as a 'chapeau', fuels the debate between environmentalists and trade advocates.

Banning MMT may have been unfair discrimination by the Canadian government against a US gasoline supplier. However, the Canadian government's decision to drop the case out of fear that it would lose under a NAFTA panel is disturbing and relevant to bulk water exports. To successfully use Article XX of GATT (or NAFTA 2101), the onus is on the party seeking to stop trading to prove that the practice will harm the environment, rather than on the party who wishes to trade to prove that it will not harm the environment. This does not allow for the 'precautionary principle' of environmental management. This principle is based on the premise that if the effects of a particular practice are not well understood, it is prudent to avoid it until science catches up, even if, at present, negative effects cannot be proven. The history of water management includes many cases where not following the precautionary principle has resulted in unforeseen negative impacts, for example:

- releasing methyl mercury previously bound in the soil as a result of flooding land to make hydroelectric reservoirs (Heckey et al, 1991);
- the sheer scale of the toxic dust disaster from pesticide residues blown out from the dry seabed of the Aral Sea, dying from unwise river diversions (Postel, 1995); and
- the unexpectedly long cycle of melting permafrost and expanding lakes, with associated silting-up of reservoirs as a result of flooding in Arctic regions (Heckey et al, 1984).

Growing trend in USA to protect economy over environment   Concerns about bulk water exports are legitimate and timely. Although large water diversions across watersheds are likely to have very high environmental costs, the Bush administration has demonstrated a strong inclination to protect its economy at the expense of the environment and to favour a supply-side rather than a demand-side approach to environmental management. Examples include reneging on the American commitment to the Kyoto Protocol to cut greenhouse gas emissions, and reversing a prohibition to drill for oil in the Alaskan Wildlife Preserve. Furthermore, instead of encouraging energy conservation in California, the USA is pressing Canada to increase its energy exports (*Ottawa Citizen*, 19 May 2001). If various water export proposals receive similar support from the Bush administration, the effects of such trade precedents could extend much further than simply Canada and the USA.

Effect of lowering desalination costs   Whether or not pressure for large-scale bulk water exports will continue to mount depends largely on further advances in desalination. If the cost of desalination drops low enough, then it will be cheaper to generate freshwater from seawater or brackish sources near where it is needed, instead of importing freshwater in bulk from another country. The cost of desalination has already dropped to less than US$1 per m^3, even with the high current market energy prices, largely because energy input now represents less than 10 per cent of the total desalination cost. The World Water

Commission (2000) suggests that it is conceivable that desalination will become the favoured choice for drinking and industrial-use waters in coastal cities. However, for the foreseeable future, because of the purity of water required for particular industrial uses closely linked with globalization, such as making computer wafers, importing water may be more economic than desalination, thus maintaining the pressure for such exports.

Trade agreements and changing economies on water-use patterns

International trade driven by economic globalization is already having a significant impact on water-use patterns and sectorial water efficiency. This is likely to accelerate, accompanied by social repercussions. As noted by Biswas (2001): 'Water requirements of the border areas of Mexico with the United States have increased radically because of increased exports of manufactured goods to the USA and Canada.' People are migrating in large numbers to border cities in search of employment, boosting water demand significantly. For instance, over the past five years, water requirements for the Ciudad Juarez have increased at an average annual rate of 15 per cent (Biswas, 2001).

While there is little or no evidence to support claims that the urban or even the rural poor are being cut off from domestic water supplies as a result of economic globalization, the same is not true for poor farmers. During a drought in 1995, the Mexican government cut off supplies to poor farmers, while guaranteeing emergency supplies to industries in the same US–Mexican border zone referred to above (Barlow, 1999). What has happened in Mexico has also happened in almost every other developing country in the world experiencing water shortages. Whether or not water is privatized, informal or formal, water markets are transferring water out of agriculture (which typically uses 80 per cent of blue water flows) and into urban areas, because the economic value of water is at least ten times higher in urban areas than it is in rural areas (Gibbons, cited in Bhattia et al, 1995). In many cases, the farmers are not 'cut off'; rather, they willingly sell their water because they are making less money by farming. Economic globalization and the rising value of water will accelerate this process. Governments need to recognize this phenomenon, regulate these informal water markets to prevent negative impacts, and include plans in their industrialization policies for training and social safety nets for dislocated farmers.

Farmers are also losing supplies as a result of another feature of globalization – increased international tourism. In Puerto Rico, for example, during a drought, the government reduced water supplies to farmers while guaranteeing supplies to tourist resorts (Ruiz, 1999). This issue could be addressed in two ways. Firstly, resorts should always be charged full cost for their water because they can transfer these costs to tourists who are willing to pay. The full cost of water is negligible compared to other costs associated with tourism. Secondly, Puerto Rico's economy, like that of many other coastal islands, depends far more on tourism than on agriculture. Many of the farmers, who had their water cut off, have sons and daughters working in the resorts. Not only does tourism provide jobs; the government takes a direct cut from these revenues through room and food taxes. In brief, not providing the resorts with water might end up hurting the poor more than they suffer by having some water taken away from them. This is one of the attributes of an interconnected, globalized economy. It is not feasible to return to the 'eternal yesterday' memory of a utopian agricultural society. Of course, this does not mean that all farming must cease – world food security depends upon it. However, in arid areas, more and more blue water will be taken out of agriculture, and water managers will have to help farmers unlock the potential of green water flows (see Chapter 5).[15]

In fact, looking to the future, by 2020 or 2030 in arid regions such as the Middle East, only a small amount of existing renewable blue water flows, less than 20 per cent, will be used in agriculture, which will be reserved for high-value crops – mostly fresh vegetables. All cereal crops will have to be either imported, grown in improved rain-fed systems or irrigated by marginal waters, such as treated wastewater. In fact, every drop of domestic wastewater will have to be treated and reused (see Chapter 6) where it is generated, in and around cities, in urban and peri-urban agriculture.[16]

Another issue that will have to be raised in future international trade negotiations is the subsidization of irrigated agriculture. If countervailing duties can be applied to subsidized stumpage fees for softwood lumber, so presumably can they be to agriculture that is indirectly subsidized by water subsidies. As water prices for agriculture begin to rise, particularly in arid regions, countries that continue to support farmers by providing irrigation water virtually free, such as the USA (in California) and Australia, will, in effect, be unfairly subsidizing food production and may be challenged under the WTO.

High-technology industry and water use

High technology is the world's fastest growing industry and the foundation of the new, globalizing economy. In the interest of attracting investment and jobs in a globalizing economy, municipalities may offer high-tech companies incentives that have detrimental long-term impacts on water conservation and the environment.

Commonly perceived as being a 'clean' industry, according to Yaron (2000), the high-tech industry is, in fact, 'one of the most water-dependent and water-damaging sectors in the world'. Each 300 millimetre (mm) silicon wafer (computer) chip produced requires 8622 litres of de-ionized freshwater. Thus, the Intel plant in Rio Rancho, New Mexico, requires more than 2.24 million cubic metres of water annually. In Santa Clara, California, the electronics industry used about 24 per cent of the city's water between 1994 and 1995 (SVTC, 1999). In some of the states in the US South-West, there are no sites left for chip manufacturing because the aquifers cannot take the increased load of 4 million to 8 million litres of water required per day (SVTC, 2001).

Furthermore, computer electronics requires the assembly of parts containing more than 1000 materials, many of which are highly toxic, such as lead and cadmium, lead oxide, barium, mercury, acids and chlorinated and brominated substances (SVTC, 2001). Silicon Valley has more Environmental Protection Agency (EPA) toxic superfund sites than any other area in the USA (SVTC, 1999). Despite this impact on water and the environment, cities are willing to give high-tech companies – some of the most profitable in the world – discounts on their water rates in order to attract jobs and investment. For instance, in Albuquerque, New Mexico, Intel Corporation pays four times less than the city's residents for its water. As well, while residents had to decrease their water use by 30 per cent, Intel was allowed to increase its use by the same amount. The city of Austin, Texas, granted reduced water rates to industrial users for less than two-thirds of the residential tariff (Barlow, 1999). Phoenix, Arizona, gave Sumitomo Sitix, a Japanese wafer manufacturer, US$5.5 million for off-site sewer and water systems (Yaron, 2000).

While it is understandable that municipalities wish to attract high-tech companies in order to diversify their economies, low water rates and lax or unenforced water pollution standards are not in the public interest, particularly in a jurisdiction suffering from water shortages. Moreover, they are unnecessary, given, as discussed above, that there is no 'race to the bottom'. High-tech firms willing to pay the high labour costs of locating in the USA compared to developing countries are unlikely to relocate because of higher water prices and the requirement to treat wastewater adequately. Even if the cost of compliance for a high-tech firm is higher than the average of 2 per cent, such costs are still likely to be small compared to other costs. It is worth examining industrial water rates in both developed and developing countries, and ensuring that tariff structures are transparent. In jurisdictions where industrial water rates are too low, once the public becomes aware of this, public pressure will likely drive them up.

CONCLUSIONS AND RECOMMENDATIONS

We are at a critical threshold in the juncture of water management and development. Increasing population, pollution and urbanization all threaten the per-capita availability and the quality of freshwater. Such a juncture requires new ways of thinking about, and managing, water resources. Economic globalization offers some opportunities for making the necessary changes, but also poses risks. However, globalization is strongly rejected by some social and environmental activists who yearn for a nostalgic return to an idealized past – Weber's 'eternal yesterday'. Yet, past approaches are inadequate for meeting future challenges. Some would argue that the approaches of the past did not even meet the requirements in the past, if one looks at the persistent inequities in access to water and sanitation. The strongest criticisms of the market approach – that, for instance, raising prices and privatizing water service has a detrimental impact on the poor and public health – are not supported by available evidence. For the small volumes necessary to meet basic water requirements, less than 50 LPCD, the full-cost price of about US 5 cents per day per capita is affordable by almost everyone. Governments can mandate lifeline tariffs or other targeted, transparent subsidies for the extreme poor who cannot afford to pay this price. Furthermore, with source-water contamination on the rise, public health threats will continue to mount. Regardless of whether a water service is public or private, it is essential that governments develop enhanced drinking water and wastewater treatment standards, and follow up with prudent regulation and monitoring.

On the other hand, the excessive confidence that ultra neo-liberals have for Weber's vision of the 'eternal tomorrow' – based on progress, the efficiency of the market and economic globalization – is also flawed. It is true that globalization is creating wealth, but that wealth is unequally distributed. Some concerns raised by activists about privatizing water service have little basis and seem primarily based on the motivation to protect union jobs. If staff levels are excessive, as they are in many developing countries, this may not be in the interest of society. However, concerns relating to industry concentration, transparency, lack of conservation incentives and corruption are legitimate, and detract from the benefits that privatization offers for improving water service for the poor. The two largest private water firms control 70 per cent of the international market. If water corporations continue to grow in size, governments and regulators will find it challenging to control these giants, given their impact on the economy and employment. Governments may have to be more aggressive in their use of antitrust legislation, to block mergers and acquisitions, if they feel that the current or future industry concentration gives too much market power to a small number of firms, or to order the break up of firms that are already exhibiting anti-competitive behaviour. Ensuring transparency will address some of the other concerns. Governments and regulators must insist on transparency because corruption is far more difficult to practice in a transparent environment. More studies are essential to capture lessons learned from privatization experiences to date, the impact on the poor and the best way of offering lifeline tariffs or targeted subsidies to the extremely poor. A key question that privatization opponents must address is whether the status quo is better than the situation would be under a public–private partnership. The above-noted criticisms, including lack of transparency, the presence of corruption and, especially, high leakage levels, are also relevant for public utilities that are no longer accountable to the public.

Provided that concerns relating to corruption and lack of transparency are addressed, in many cases, private operators are able to improve water services in developing countries. The most important role for the government in these partnerships is to strongly regulate and to develop contracts that provide incentives for the private operator to conserve water, decrease leaks and serve the poor. However, the public–private approach is not necessarily the best in every context. While examples of successful reform of public utilities to make them more efficient and accountable are rare, they do exist. Such reforms, however, are more likely through public–public partnerships with other strong public utilities. The World Water Vision suggests that not only can public and privatized operations co-exist, but also that once regulation and accountability are established for private companies, their performance should be compared to public companies. Ultimately, the greatest benefit of the public–private partnerships may be that they force public companies to become regulated, accountable and efficient (Cosgrove and Rijsberman, 2000). Overall, equity is likely to be enhanced if utilities run on a commercial, self-financing basis, although, again, this does not preclude lifeline rates or targeted, transparent subsidies for the poor. Whether the utility is publicly or privately operated is less important.

Growing international trade associated with economic globalization poses potential threats to sustainable water management. Because of the increasing value of water in the industrial sector, particularly to high-tech industries, and the innovative means to transport water, pressure is mounting for bulk water exports that are already occurring on a small scale. Ultimately, the economic incentive for such exports will depend on further reductions in the cost of desalination, which has fallen rapidly during the last ten years. In the meantime, if exports become more common, environmental risks exist because trade agreements such as the NAFTA and the WTO restrict the use of the precautionary principle. This could have a significant impact if bulk water exports begin and can only be stopped after environmental damage has already occurred.

Economic globalization is also forcing water reallocation from agriculture to industries and tourism. Whether farmers willingly sell their water rights or are simply 'cut off', policies to mitigate the social impacts must be devised. Increasing the productivity of rain-fed systems and reusing treated wastewater in agriculture are essential to protect food production, especially in arid areas. Furthermore, as water prices for agriculture begin to rise, particularly in arid regions, countries that continue to support farmers by paying high subsidies for water will, in effect, be unfairly subsidizing food production and may be challenged under the WTO.

Finally, the foundation of the new, globalizing 'information' or 'digital' economy is high-tech industry. Some elements of high-tech, such as computer wafer manufacturing, are highly water intensive. The high-tech industry is not nearly as environmentally friendly as it is perceived to be because it uses many toxic chemicals in its production processes. Despite this, some municipalities, for example in the south-western USA, offer subsidized water prices to firms such as Intel, among the richest in the world. Some of these same municipalities have lax environmental regulations and monitoring records. Not only are such incentives unsustainable, particularly in arid areas such as Arizona and Texas, but they are also unnecessary because even with higher water prices and better on-site pollution control, environmental costs would still likely be small in proportion to the total costs of such firms. As a result, they would not move for these reasons alone. It is worth examining industrial water rates and cost structures in both developed and developing countries in order to derive policies that ensure sustainable and equitable water management without compromising economic livelihood. Furthermore, the development of such policies and tariff structures is best done in an open, multi-stakeholder environment to ensure that where industrial water rates are too low, public pressure drives them up.

NOTES

1   Blue water is renewable surface water runoff and groundwater recharge. It is the main source for human use and is the traditional focus of water resource management.

2   Canada's 2001 'Government Statement on Foreign Policy' states that it wishes to project 'Canadian' values and culture abroad, including respect for human rights, the rule of law and the environment (Government of Canada, 2001); see www.dfait-maeci.gc.ca/dfait/mandate-e.asp.

3   It is difficult to find exact figures because of all the variables involved. This statement is made on the range of tariffs included in Yepes and Diandras (1996) and the author's experience in other countries.

4   Based on the following estimation/average, water prices in developing countries are typically one fifth to one seventh the full cost of providing water (Bronso, 1998). Using an estimate of US$1 per m^3, and the more conservative figure of one fifth, the cost of this provision is US$0.2 per m^3. The poor typically pay 10 to 20 times this cost, or US$2 per m^3 to US$4 per m^3. Barlow notes a cost of US$3 per m^3 for Lima, Peru (Barlow, 1999).

5   A lifeline tariff is the rate charged for minimum human basic water requirements (for drinking, cooking and basic sanitation). In some countries, the cost of the lifeline water volume (estimates for which vary between 25 LPCD to 50 LPCD) is free.

6   South African Water White Policy Paper (1997) Section 5.2.1, 'Basic Needs'

7   A news release from the Ontario provincial government states the official conclusion of the probable causes of contamination:

> *With respect to the water supply wells, it is our opinion that it is probable that E. coli 0157:H7 from cattle manure entered Well #5 and then the distribution system. The method of transport to the well was by means of either, or both, the aquifer or surface runoff from a 12 May 2000 rainfall event. While it appears that activities with respect to manure handling were consistent with normal agricultural practices, the presence of the manure, probably containing E. coli 0157:H7, and the excessive rainfall events of 9 May to 12 [May] 2000, combined with a very low chlorine residual in the water distribution system, resulted in the outbreak observed in May 2000.*

See www.alertontario.org.

8   Vivendi, Suez Lyonnaise, Bouygues (SAUR), Enron (Azurix), RWE, Thames Water (1999), United Utilities, Severn Trent, Anglian (1999), Kelda Group (1999).

9   Such an approach was taken in the International Development Research Centre's (IDRC) Snow and Ice Hydrology Project, which helped the Water and Power Development Authority (WAPDA) Utility in Pakistan to develop an operational flow forecasting system for the Upper Indus River Basin. BC Hydro, the Crown Utility in British Columbia, acted as the implementing agency for the project through its consulting arm, BC Hydro International, and took all responsibility for training. One of the key comments of the WAPDA staff who were trained on the project related to the benefit of being exposed and working day to day with BC Hydro staff in Vancouver.

10   Professor Mark Busch, Queen's School of Business, Kingston, Canada, pers com, September 2001
11   This viewpoint is the likely US position. 'In 1993, then US Trade Representative Mickey Kantor said in a letter to a US environmental group, "when water is traded as a good, all provisions of the agreement governing trade in goods apply"' (Barlow, 1999).
12   For example, Sunbelt Water Inc of Santa Barbara, California, is suing the Canadian government because the company lost a contract to export water to California when the province of British Columbia banned the export of bulk water in 1991.
13   For example, according to the NAFTA, Canada must supply the USA with a quantity of energy greater than or equal to the average quantity supplied over the previous three years (CBC, 2001).
14   Under GATT Article XX, General Exceptions, to which Article 2101 of NAFTA refers, member countries can bypass normal trade rules to protect the environment, including measures 'necessary to protect human, animal or plant life or health...as well as in relation to the conservation of exhaustible natural resources if such measures are made effective in conjunction with restrictions on domestic production or consumption'. See www.wto.org.
15   Green water is the rainfall that is stored in the soil and evaporates from it.
16   One of IDRC's major research areas is entitled 'Cities Feeding People'. It focuses on helping the poor maintain food and water security by practising confined-space production techniques and safely reusing wastewater to grow cheap, nutritious food in and around cities. For more information, contact Naser Faruqui at nfaruqui@idrc.ca.

References

Barlow, M (1999) 'Blue gold: The global water crisis and the commodification of the world's water supply', Special Report, International Forum on Globalization
Barlow, M (2000) 'Commodification of water: The wrong perspective', *Water Science and Technology*, vol 43, no 4, pp70–84
Beyer, P (2000) 'Religions in global society: Transnational resource and globalized category', Paper presented at the conference Reinventing Society in a Changing Global Economy, University of Toronto, www.utoronto.ca/ethnicstudies/conferences.html
Bhalla, A S (1998) 'Introduction' in Bhalla A S (ed) *Globalization, Growth and Marginalization*, IDRC, Ottawa, Canada
Bhattia, R, Cesti, R and Winpenny, J (1995) *Water Conservation and Reallocation: Best Practice Cases in Improving Economic Efficiency and Environmental Quality*, World Bank – Overseas Development Institute, Joint Study, Washington, DC
Biswas, A K (2001), 'Missing and neglected links in water management', *Water Science and Technology*, vol 43, no4, pp45–50
Blokland, M, Braadbaart and Schwartz, K (eds) (1999) *Private Business, Public Owners; Government Shareholdings in Water Companies*, VROM, The Hague
Bosch C et al (2000) 'Water, sanitation and poverty' in *Poverty Reduction Strategy Sourcebook*, World Bank, draft
Britannica.com (2001) 'Luddite', Encyclopædia Britannica, www.britannica.com/eb/article?eu=50450

Bronso, A (1998) 'Pricing urban water as a scarce resource: Lessons from cities around the world' in *Proceedings of the CWRA Annual Conference*, Victoria, British Columbia, Canada

Brutciski, M and Banicevic, A (1999) 'Water, the WTO and NAFTA: Conservation, exports and the international trading system', Canadian Bar Association National Symposium on Water Law, 9–10 April, Toronto

Burchill, S and Linklater, A (1996) *Theories of International Relations*, St Martin's Press, New York

Canada, Department of Foreign Affairs and International Trade (DFAIT) (2001) Canada–United States Bureau, www.can-am.gc.ca/content/bw_trade-e.asp

Canada (1998) 'Government of Canada Statement on MMT', www.ethyl.com/products/pa/mmt/gov_ca_stmt.html

Canadian Broadcasting Corporation (CBC) (2001) 'Power play', CBC-TV, *The National*, transcripts, tv.cbc.ca/national/trans/T010515.html

Canadian International Development Agency (1995) 'Aid and trade: Critical for successful development', www.acdi-cida.gc.ca/xpress/dex/dex9504.htm

Catley-Carlson M et al (2000), *World Water Vision*, CD-ROM

Colander, D C (2001) *Microeconomics*, 4th edition, McGraw-Hill Irwin, Toronto

Cosgrove, W J and Rijsberman, F R (2000) *World Water Vision: Making Water Everyone's Business*, World Water Council, Earthscan, London

Drinkwater, K and Frank, K (1994) 'Effects of river regulation and diversion on marine fish and invertebrates', *Journal of Aquatic Conservation of Marine and Freshwater Ecosystems*, vol 4, no 2, pp135–151

Euronature (2001) 'EUROPE between hi-tech and nature', www.euronature.f2s.com/nature/water.html

Faruqui, N, Biswas, A K and Bino, M J (2001) *Water Management in Islam*, UNU Press and IDRC, Ottawa, Canada

Financial Times (1997) 'Aquarius: Water bags seize financial niche', *Financial Times Global Water Report 30*, 11 September 1997, p15

Fraser, N (December 2001/January 2002) 'Mario Monti, Commissioner for Competition: A monthly guide to the bureaucrats pulling the strings in Brussels', *Business Life*, p20

Gerth, H H and Wright Mills, C (1958) *From Max Weber: Essays in Sociology*, Galaxy Book, New York, p78

Glassman, J K (1999) 'A European recipe for increasing your returns: Just add water', *International Herald Tribune*, Neuilly-sur-Seine, France, 8 April 1999, p18

Globe and Mail (2001) 'The myths about globalization', 13 April 2001, p2

Globe and Mail (2001) 'The myths about globalization', 14 April 2001, p3

Government of Canada (2001) 'Government Statement on Foreign Policy', www.dfait-maeci.gc.ca/department/mandate-en.asp

Hall, D (2000) 'Water partnerships: Public–public partnerships and "twinning" in water and sanitation', Public Service International Research Unit, University of Greenwich, www.world-psi.org

Heckey, R E et al (1984) 'Environmental impact prediction and assessment: The Southern Indian Lake experience', *Journal of Fisheries and Aquatic Sciences*, vol 41, pp720–731

Heckey, R E et al (1991) 'Increased methyl mercury in fish in newly formed water reservoirs' in Suzuki, T et al (eds) *Advances in Mercury Toxicology*, Plenum, New York

Inglehart, R (2001) 'Technological change, cultural change and democracy: Who's afraid of Ronald McDonald?' Paper presented at the conference Reinventing Society in a Changing Global Economy, University of Toronto, Toronto, www.utoronto.ca/ethnicstudies/conferences.html

Komives, K and Brook Cowen, P J (1999) 'Expanding water and sanitation services to low-income households: The case of the La Paz-El Alto concession', World Bank Group, Washington DC

Kruger, A B and Grossman, G (1994) 'Economic growth and the environment', National Bureau of Economic Research Working Paper

Lobina, E and Hall, D (2001) 'Potential for public sector water operations in developing countries', Public Service International Research Unit, London

Lundqvist, J and Gleick, P (1997) 'Comprehensive assessment of the freshwater resources of the world: Sustaining our waters into the 21st century', Stockholm Environment Institute, Stockholm, Sweden

Mallat, C (1995) 'The quest for water use principles' in Allah, M A and Mallat, C (eds) *Water in the Middle East*, IB Tauris Publishers, New York

National Research Defense Council (NRDC) (1998) 'Pure drink or pure hype', Chapter 2, www.nrdc.org

Ottawa Citizen (2001) 'Fuelling the energy debate', 19 May

Postel, S (1995) 'Nile, Ganges, Colorado and Central Asian rivers cut off from the sea', Worldwatch – press release, May/June

Public Service International (PSI) (2000) 'Paying for privatization', PSI Briefing – World Water Forum, The Hague, 17–22 March 2000, www.world-psi.org

Rajaee, F (2000) *Globalization on Trial: The Human Condition and the Information Civilization*, IRDC, Ottawa, Canada

Rockström, J (2000) 'Green water security for the food makers of tomorrow: Windows of opportunity in drought-prone savannahs', *Water Science and Technology*, vol 43, no 4, pp71–78

Rose-Ackerman, S (1996) 'The political economy of corruption: Causes and consequences', World Bank Public Policy for the Private Sector, Note No 74, The World Bank, Washington, DC

Ruiz, C (1999) 'The thirst for water and justice', InterPress (IPS), 16 September, www.ips.org

Schneiderman, D (1999) 'MMT promises: How Ethyl Corporation beat the federal ban', *The Post*, a publication of the Parkland Institute, vol 3, no 1, www.ualberta.ca/~parkland/Post/Vol3_No1/Schneiderman-ethyl.html

Serageldin, I (2000) 'From vision to action after the Second World Water Forum', *Water Science and Technology*, vol 43, no 4, pp31–34

Shiva, V (1999) 'Monsanto moves to control water resources and fish farming in India and the third world', www.purefood.org/Monsanto/waterfish.cfm

Shulk, J (2000), 'Water fallout: Bolivians battle globalization', *These Times Magazine*, Third World Traveler, www.thirdworldtraveler.com/New_Global_Economy/Water_Fallout.html

Silicon Valley Toxics Coalition (SVTC) (1999) 'Sacred waters: Life-blood of mother earth', San José, California, www.svtc.org

Silicon Valley Toxics Coalition (SVTC) (2001) 'Water use and other material and wastes associated with semiconductor production', www.svtc.org/hitech_prod/larachart.htm

Silva, G, Tynan, N and Yilmaz, Y (1997) 'Private participation in the water and sewerage sector: Recent trends', *Private Sector*, pp1–2

Smith, G and Naim, M (2000) *Altered States: Globalization, Sovereignty, and Governance,* IRDC, Ottawa, Canada

Streeten, P (1998) 'Globalization: Threat or salvation?' in Bhalla, A S (ed) *Globalization, Growth and Marginalization,* IDRC, Ottawa, Canada

Tan, S (2001) China's Three Gorges Dam project, www.prairie.sierraclub.ca/gorges.html

Trade Aid (1998) 'Fair trade through trade aid: The philosophy of trade aid', www.canterbury.cyberplace.co.nz/community/tradeaid.html

Turton, P (1998) 'Leakage level update', UK Environmental Agency, www.environment-agency.gov.uk/modules/MOD31.255.html

Vogel, D (1999) 'Environmental regulation and economic integration', Hass School of Business, University of California, Prepared for a Workshop on Regulatory Competition and Economic Integration: Comparative Perspectives, Yale Centre for Environmental Law and Policy

Water and Sanitation Program (South Asia Region) (2001) 'Villagers treat water as an economic good', Olavanna, Kerala, India, Field note, Department for International Development

Webb, P and Iskandarani, M (1998) *Water Insecurity and the Poor: Issues and Research Needs,* Centre for Development Research, University of Bonn, Bonn, p34

World Bank (2000) Statistics on the World Bank's dam portfolio, www.worldbank.org/html/extdr/pb/dams/factsheet.htm

World Water Commission (2000) *A Water Secure World: Visions for Water, Life and the Environment,* World Water Vision and World Water Council, p70

World Water Vision (2000) *Making Water Everybody's Business,* CD-ROM

Yaron, G (2000) 'The final frontier: A working paper on the big 10 global water corporations and the privatization and corporatization of the world's last public resource', Polaris Institute and the Council of Canadians

Yepes, G and Diandras, A (1996) *Waste Waters and Utilities: Indicators,* 2nd edition, International Bank for Reconstruction and Development and The World Bank, Washington, DC

Chapter 5

Managing rain for the future

Johan Rockström

INTRODUCTION

There is a growing concern over the future of the world's water resources. A series of world water assessments, starting with the classic work of L'vovich (1979) and the fundamental work by Falkenmark (Falkenmark and Lindh, 1976) onwards to the latest freshwater assessments (Raskin, 1997; Shiklomanov, 1997, 2000; UN, 1997; Cosgrove and Rijsberman, 2000), have convincingly shown that humankind is, through increased pressure on finite water resources, heading towards a water resources scarcity.

The pressure is fourfold. First, human pressure on finite freshwater resources increases arithmetically as a result of basic human water requirements – amounting to some 1500 cubic metres (m^3) per capita per year for a person eating a decent diet. Second, human water withdrawals increase exponentially with development. The last century has seen a sixfold increase in runoff water withdrawals while world population has 'only' tripled. This is a result of increased water use with increased socio-economic development (industrial production increased 12-fold and gross world product with a factor 14 over the same period). Third, humans destroy water. Freshwater resources are polluted from industrial waste. Groundwater in industrialized countries is not potable due to nitrogen leaching from over-intensive agriculture. Slow and invisible deterioration of water quality at local and basin scale is reducing the volume of water that is accessible for humans. Fourth, humankind is affecting the source of water – namely, the intricate weather systems governing the hydrological cycle of the Earth. This is not only done through human-induced climate change (IPCC, 2001), but also through land degradation affecting local moisture feedback mechanisms (Savenije, 1995).

The present state of affairs is, in many respects, appalling. It is appalling because the water-related problems are, to a large extent, caused by human mismanagement rather than natural environmental shocks. Water-related diseases affect 3.3 billion people per year leading to 5.3 million deaths annually, which is closely related to the outrageous situation of 3 billion people lacking adequate sanitation and 1 billion people without a secured drinking water supply (Walter et al, 1999).

According to conventional water resources assessments, it is estimated that population growth alone is pushing 55 per cent of the world population towards water stress or severe water scarcity over the next generation, mainly due to the water needs of 4.6 billion people in Africa and Asia (Falkenmark, 1997).

Recently, the outlook for the 21st century has been made even more gloomy. According to Conway (1997), there is a large hidden food gap. After projected production increases and import estimates, there is still a predicted 400 million tonnes' deficit of food grain in 2025. This large deficit, corresponding to one-quarter of present global annual grain production, is mainly located in sub-Saharan Africa and South-East Asia.

Basically, all population growth (95 per cent) in the world occurs in developing countries, of which the vast majority is located in tropical climates. The poorest countries generally host a large proportion of their rapidly growing populations in water scarcity-prone savannah agro-ecosystems. In sub-Saharan Africa and South Asia, where the poverty and food challenge is huge over the next generation, some 40 to 45 per cent of the landscape is arid to dry sub-humid, the largest figures on Earth. Economies in these regions depend strongly on the rural sector. In sub-Saharan Africa, generally greater than 60 per cent of the populations make their living from rain-fed smallholder farming, generating between 30 to 40 per cent of country gross domestic product (GDP). As a result, a major challenge within the context of poverty reduction is rural development, with strong emphasis needed on managing water.

This chapter looks into the future, with a focus on challenges and opportunities in what probably is the most urgent water resources challenge – namely, how to feed tomorrow's rural poor and still achieve a sustainable environmental management. To do this, the chapter presents evidence that raises questions regarding the validity of the conventional view that humankind is rapidly heading towards an imminent water resources crisis – the simplistic view of projecting population growth against withdrawals of perennial and accessible runoff water is simply flawed.

With this done, the arena is opened for fresh, forward-minded thinking about what approaches may be embarked on in the field of integrated water resources management. The chapter focuses on rural water management, and presents a set of holistic approaches that, if properly anchored with local communities and within government policies, may contribute to attaining improved water productivity, increased socio-economic development, and improved food self-reliance while conserving the environment. Such win–win paths to development are often accused of being naive; but as will be shown in this chapter, there are plenty of examples where win–win strategies for environmental management are occurring. A major challenge is to create the enabling environment to sustain promising initiatives.

WATER AND FOOD SECURITY: SORTING OUT THE FACTS

Conventional freshwater assessments

Conventional water resources assessments project severe physical water scarcity problems affecting 30 per cent of the world population over the next generation. Such conclusions are based on a supply–demand analysis, comparing what is generally called 'freshwater availability' with 'freshwater withdrawals'. Availability of freshwater (at country, regional or global level) is taken as the assessed and accessible flow of stable and perennial surface and sub-surface runoff in lakes, rivers and groundwater. This water is defined as 'blue' water flow (Falkenmark, 1995) and is distinguished from 'green' water flow, which is the remaining proportion of the terrestrial hydrological cycle – namely, the return flow of vapour to the atmosphere as evapotranspiration. It has been estimated that we can realistically access some 12,500 Giga cubic metres (Gm^3) per year of blue water flow, out of a cumulative average of 38,000Gm^3 per year of runoff flow (Postel et al, 1996).[1] This corresponds to 11 per cent of the annual precipitation over land surfaces (approximately 110,000Gm^3 per year). Vapour flow over terrestrial areas accounts for 64 per cent of the annual precipitation over land areas.

Global 'freshwater withdrawals' are normally estimated at some 4000Gm^3 per year (Shiklomanov, 2000). These human withdrawals are used to cover water needs in industry (accounting for 23 per cent of the withdrawals), household and municipal use (accounting for 8 per cent) and agricultural use (accounting for 69 per cent). It is when such data on blue water availability (at country, regional or global scale) is compared with direct water withdrawals at present, and in the future, that severe regional water scarcity projections evolve. The forecast for 2025 is a global withdrawal of 5200Gm^3 per year (according to Shiklomanov, 2000). The increased withdrawal is a direct result of population growth and socio-economic development. Both are drivers behind increased water withdrawals. The reason for this can be stated quite simply – everything we do requires water in one way or another, and the more we do (and aspire to do), when economic development permits it, the more water per capita we demand. As freshwater resources are finite (under constant threat of human-induced deterioration), we seem to be heading toward an unavoidable crisis. For every newborn child, pressure on water will increase. Since we already are withdrawing one third of the estimated 'water ceiling' (12,500Gm^3 per year), how will the situation be with 2 billion new babies over the next 30 years, especially in dry regions with the most rapid population growth? Regional and local implications of human pressure on scarce water resources can already be seen in the overextraction of river base flow for irrigation and industrial use (for example, the Colorado River), the rapidly falling groundwater levels due to overextraction (for example, semi-arid parts of India), and the large-scale ecological collapse due to hydroengineering (for example, the Aral Sea).

All these cases of serious, often catastrophic, implications of overextraction of blue water are very worrying; but the question is: are they the first signs of a creeping global crisis or, rather, isolated hot spots in areas where mismanagement, scarcity and human pressures coincide? In an attempt to answer this question, it is relevant to step behind the assumptions used in water resources projections. Human pressure on freshwater resources has been expressed in several different ways, with the basic common feature that human demand for water is the key driver behind increased freshwater withdrawals. This pressure is generally expressed at country, regional or basin level, in the form of stress indices (such as the ratio between water withdrawal or water demand and water availability). For projections into the future, withdrawals or demand are based on estimates of projected human freshwater demand (in turn, based on estimates of human freshwater requirements). These vary between assessments and range in the order of $1200–1700m^3$ per capita per year. Water stress indices are generally based on this annual per-capita flow, where a country with a freshwater availability (read blue water access) lower than $1700m^3$ per capita per year is considered to be under stress (based on Falkenmark's water stress index; Falkenmark, 1986). This estimated annual per-capita need could be divided into pure 'blue' water uses, equal to direct use of liquid blue water flow, for drinking and household purposes, municipal use and industrial use. The global per-capita average need to cover direct blue uses amounts to some $190m^3$ per capita per year, which corresponds to a global withdrawal of $1100Gm^3$ per year (Shiklomanov, 2000). The remaining 90 per cent of per-capita water requirement is for food. This is explained by the fact that food production is the world's largest economic water-consuming sector, with approximately $1300–1600m^3$ per capita per year required to produce an adequate diet.[2]

Whether or not humankind is heading towards a global water crisis depends on whether there is enough freshwater to sustain food production (if, according to the conventional view, we focus only on direct human needs for water in industry, municipalities and agriculture). More broadly, if we also include indirect use of freshwater to sustain ecosystems, the water crisis challenge also requires that we address the need for an institutional and ethical environment at hand to deal with water trade-offs to sustain different water-using sectors.

But let us concentrate on the conventional assessments for the moment, based on direct water uses. The first critical conclusion is that drinking water supply, sanitation and industrial water requirement are issues of global water resources scarcity, even though in certain arid locations societies experience scarcity of blue water for direct blue water uses. Low percentage of populations connected to water supply systems, and often poor household water quality, are rarely issues of water scarcity but an issue of poor water management. Even a world population of 10 billion people will never claim more than $2000Gm^3$ per year, which is less than 20 per cent of realistically accessible runoff water, and only roughly 2 per cent of global precipitation over land areas. If we add the promising developments in desalination technologies, where the price for desalination is moving well below US$1 per m^3 of water (see Chapter 6), then the human 'blue' water demands seem even more 'under control'.

This means that for conventional water resources assessments, the dominant driver pushing humankind towards the ceiling of freshwater availability is water for food. However, the question is whether it is analytically correct to carry out water resources predictions by comparing freshwater availability in terms of country-level access of blue water flow, with human water requirement in terms of a general per-capita index of which 90 per cent is water for food.

Such a bias towards blue water flow (where the blue water branch in the hydrological cycle is considered equal with the freshwater resource) would be justifiable if the world's largest water users – namely, farmers – tapped their productive water to produce food from perennial and monitored blue water sources.

In order to shed some light on the issue, an analysis was carried out on the predominant source of water: either rainfall returning directly as green water flow in rain-fed agriculture or runoff blue flow in irrigated agriculture that, at present, is used to feed the world's population. Figure 5.1 shows a first attempt at developing a world map indicating the predominant source of water used to produce cereal foods. The data used to develop the map is based on grain production only. Data on blue water withdrawals in irrigation are taken from the International Water Management Institute (IWMI, 2000), as well as from data on areas under rain-fed agriculture and estimated grain yields in irrigated and rain-fed farming systems. The green water withdrawals were calculated assuming global water-use efficiency in rain-fed grain production of $3000m^3$ per tonne of grain (evapotranspiration flow).

As seen in Figure 5.1, the world is largely green, with 70 per cent of the countries depending primarily on green water flow (return flow of vapour in rain-fed agriculture) to sustain food grain production. This is still a strongly conservative estimate because the highly green water-dependent livestock sector is not included in the calculation. As will be seen below, there is strong evidence to suggest that the green water used to sustain permanent grazing for livestock is larger than the green water used in grain production, which would increase direct green water dependence.

The conclusion is that conventional freshwater assessments compare apples with pears. In other words, water scarcity is assessed by comparing the blue water availability with a general human water requirement index (the $1700m^3$ per capita per year) that, in most countries of the world, is covered by direct return flow of vapour in rain-fed agriculture, rather than blue water withdrawals. Not surprisingly, the countries that, in conventional assessments, are projected to face severe physical water scarcity in 2025 correspond largely with those countries marked blue in Figure 5.1. This indicates that when apples are compared with apples (blue water demand – as the countries' per-capita water demand is directly linked to irrigation – with blue water availability), the assessments deliver results indicating large blue water resource dependence.

Need for blue–green integration

The above points to the fact that we actually do not know how much water, or even what form of water, is needed to sustain present global food

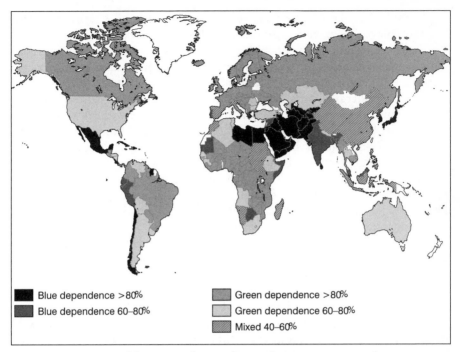

Figure 5.1 *World map analysing the predominant source of water – green or blue – to produce food*

production, or will be needed to sustain production in the future. It is true that humans may need between 1500 and 1700m³ per capita per year to cover water needs. However, in most temperate North European countries and tropical developing countries, only roughly 190m³ per capita are actually 'blue'. The water resource that sustains food production originates from rain where it falls and returns as vapour, and is never accounted for in water resource assessments. No country in the world has a projected per-capita blue water availability below 200m³ per capita per year (which is the volume threshold under which direct 'blue' water uses could be threatened).

The analysis appears to support three statements. First, there is little or no evidence to support the projections of a global creeping physical water crisis. It would seem more likely, in the words of year 2000 Stockholm Water Prize Laureate Professor Kader Asmal, that 'the water crisis is a symptom of inequity and poverty' (*Stockholm Water Front*, 2000). The disastrous examples of widespread water scarcity affecting 1 billion world inhabitants are primarily a result of mismanagement rather than physical scarcity per se. Second, the analysis suggests that more attention has to be given to green water dynamics, as a majority of the per-capita water requirements is fulfilled from direct return flow of green water in rain-fed agriculture. Here, another form of water scarcity is in focus – namely, recurrent droughts and dry spells caused by unreliable tropical rainfall. Third, it remains essential to conclude that physical blue water scarcity is a current reality and future risk for the dry semi-arid and arid regions of North Africa, the Middle East and parts of South and East Asia, where irrigation plays a dominant role in securing local livelihoods.

Based on the above, it is possible to carry out a broadened water resources assessment in an attempt to incorporate a more holistic approach to water resource management. In the conventional water resources assessments, agriculture generally falls out as the largest water-consuming sector, withdrawing roughly 70 per cent of 'annual freshwater withdrawals'. Table 5.1 shows a broader analysis, including both green and blue water flows to sustain water-dependent biomass-growing systems at a global scale. The assumption made is that human water withdrawals include both direct withdrawals (for food, domestic and industrial use) and indirect withdrawals to sustain ecosystem functions such as biodiversity, but also grasslands for grazing. The water flow to sustain these systems is taken as actual evapotranspiration flow, or green water flow.

In Table 5.1, 'blue food' denotes irrigated agriculture, and the water withdrawals originate from Shiklomanov's (2000) estimates of consumptive withdrawals (evapotranspiration flow). Green food denotes rain-fed farming systems, and the data originates from Rockström et al (1999). Grasslands, permanent grazing areas, and forests and woodlands are three categories where the annual water withdrawals (here considered only as direct return flow of green water as evapotranspiration to sustain the systems) have been estimated by correlating data from Rockström et al (1999) and the Food and Agriculture Organization of the United Nations (FAO) Statistical Databases (FAOSTAT).[3]

The column in Table 5.1 that can be most easily compared with conventional water resources assessments is the 'percentage of direct human withdrawals'. Here, only direct human withdrawals for food, industry and society are considered. The annual cumulative withdrawal amounts to $31,600Gm^3$ per year compared to conventional estimates of $4000–5000Gm^3$ per year. Irrigated agriculture accounts for 'only' 8 per cent of annual withdrawals, compared to 70 per cent as estimated in most studies (Gleick, 1993; Shiklomanov, 2000). Green food in rain-fed agriculture accounts for roughly twice the blue food (14 per cent of annual water withdrawals) and it appears that animal husbandry is by far the largest water-withdrawing sector. Sustaining the world's permanent grazing areas with a return flow of green water contributes the largest component of indirect human water withdrawals (here it could be argued that this flow should be considered a direct human water withdrawal because grazing directly sustains economic meat production). The large water dependence associated with raising livestock should, if anything, be a strong argument for more vegetarian diets.

However, the accusation that animal husbandry is an inefficient use of water is dubious because the opportunity cost of the rainfall used to sustain permanent grazing land may, in most cases, be zero. In other words, the land is used for permanent grazing simply because it cannot sustain other land uses, and therefore grazing is the most effective use of that water, which would otherwise evaporate back into the atmosphere anyway. As a percentage of total withdrawals, food production accounts for only 9 per cent (3 per cent for blue

Table 5.1 *Assessment of water withdrawals (systems depending on direct use of blue water flow) and water uses (systems depending on direct and indirect use of green water flow) to sustain direct and indirect human water dependence*

System	Annual estimated water withdrawals/uses (Gm³ per year)	Percentage of precipitation	Percentage of total withdrawals/ uses[v]	Percentage of direct human withdrawals/uses[vi]
Blue food	1800[i]	2	3	6
Green food	5000[ii]	5	7	17
Grasslands	12100[ii, iii]	11	18	
Permanent grazing	20400[ii, iii]	19	30	72
Forests and woodlands	19700[ii]	18	29	
Wetlands	1600[ii]	1	2	
Arid lands	5700[ii]	5	8	
Other systems	1100[i]	1	1	
Dom+Ind	1300[i]	1	2	5
		63[iv]	100	100

Notes: i Shiklomanov (2000). ii Rockström et al (1999). iii Estimated from a combination of Rockström et al (1999) and data from FAOSTAT (http://apps.fao.org/). iv The unaccounted 35 per cent is presently unused blue water flow. v Includes green water flow to support the generation of ecosystem services in forests, grasslands, grazing land, wetlands and agriculture. vi Includes only direct human water withdrawals for food, meat, industry, households and municipal water use.

foods and 6 per cent for green foods). This is largely explained by the dominant green water withdrawing systems – forests, grasslands and, perhaps surprisingly, green water flow from arid lands. Grain foods account for only 6 per cent of total precipitation over land areas. This is a strong indicator of the opportunity to sustain humankind in balance with nature by wisely using the remaining 94 per cent of freshwater. But there are 'no free lunches'. The largest remaining biophysical water challenge, then, is whether there is enough freshwater to sustain global food production while concurrently sustaining ecosystem services in the major biomes of the world.

Yield trends and food security

Developing countries are facing the world's largest food security challenge. Almost all of the projected population growth to an estimated 8.1 billion in 2030 and 8.9 billion in 2050 will occur in developing countries (United Nations medium projections). Furthermore, practically all challenges related to malnutrition and notoriously low food yields are concentrated in tropical developing countries. Similarly, the major global challenges of dealing with water scarcity in relation to food, nature and people are also concentrated in these regions. In other words, the regions of the world facing the largest food deficits are also facing the largest water deficits (Rockström and Falkenmark,

2000). There is, therefore, little doubt that the challenge of managing water resources for agriculture is largest in the drought-prone savannah areas, which host roughly 40 per cent of the world's population and cover an equal proportion of the land mass on Earth (Middleton and Thomas, 1992).

Nowhere else are the populations growing so quickly (at a rate of 2 to 3 per cent per annum), the nutritional and economic challenges so large (the majority of people earn less than US$1 per day) and the yields so low (oscillating around 1 tonne per hectare for food grains) than in sub-Saharan Africa.

Despite a deceleration of population growth, the required food-production increases to feed tomorrow's population are formidable. The FAO estimates that world grain totals have to increase by almost another 1 billion tonnes by 2030, up from the present 1.8 billion tonnes, corresponding to an annual increase of 1.5 per cent per year (FAO, 2000). In developing countries, the growth has to reach roughly 2 per cent per year, and in sub-Saharan Africa the rate must reach 2.5 per cent per year over the next 30 years (reaching Green Revolution levels).

It is important to remember that the bulk of world food is still produced by smallholder farmers, constituting more than 60 per cent of the population in many developing countries. These small-scale entrepreneurs, cultivating small plots of land (less than 5ha) are the largest individual water-consuming actors on Earth. The reason for this is the linear relationship between biomass growth and 'green' water use, with a range of 1500 to 3000m^3 of green water required to produce 1 tonne of cereal grain yield (or 150 to 300mm per tonne per hectare).

Evidence suggests that there is little new land to set aside for agriculture (McCalla, 1994), especially if we take into consideration ecosystem services produced from other ecosystems (forests, grasslands and wetlands). This means that increased food production will have to originate from growth in soil and water productivity – by producing more crops per drop and more crops per unit of farmland.

Yield levels for smallholder farming systems in drought-prone environments are low and oscillating, as in the case of sub-Saharan Africa at 1 tonne of grain per hectare. Many farmers experience even lower yields because of land degradation and soil nutrient mining (Rockström, 2000). Some regions of the world, for example the Sahel region, have even experienced a decline in yield levels of staple food crops over the last decade (Matlon, 1990).

MAKING MORE FOOD WITH THE SAME RAINFALL

Focus on vapour development

On a global and regional scale, the analysis thus far has shown that with a broader approach to water resources management, there are good opportunities to squeeze more development out of the hydrological cycle, without directly threatening human water requirements (at least not for domestic, industrial and municipal use). This requires focus on vapour development by increasing the amount of biomass per unit of green water flow. A starting point in assessing how far crop yields can be increased is by analysing the on-farm rainfall partitioning. As seen in Figure 5.2, only 15 to 30 per cent of the rainfall is actually used in productive food making, while 70 to 85 per cent of the rainfall in water-scarce farming systems is 'lost' from the crop field. These figures are synthesized observations from several semi-arid research stations in sub-Saharan Africa. The losses are generally even higher in degraded farmers' fields, with less than 10 per cent of the rain taking the productive green water path as crop transpiration (Rockström, 1997).

The on-farm hydrological cycle in Figure 5.2 is also a good indicator of the degree of mismanagement and land degradation in agro-ecosystems. The reason is the linear relationship between biomass production and green water flow, meaning that more biomass requires more green water flow. Furthermore, a healthy and well-managed agricultural system returns a large proportion of rainfall back to the atmosphere as green water. A degraded farming system returns a lower fraction. Therefore, one would be tempted to conclude that Figure 5.2 paints a depressing picture. It is depressing in the sense that it is a very strong indicator of the environmental and socio-economic problems facing many poor developing countries; but it also signals fantastic

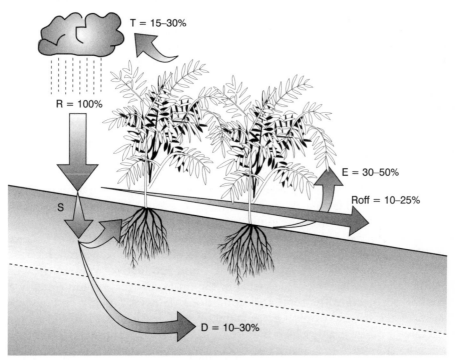

Key: R = seasonal rainfall, E = soil evaporation and interception, S = soil moisture, T = plant transpiration, Roff = surface runoff, D = deep percolation.

Figure 5.2 *General overview of rainfall partitioning in farmers' fields for semi-arid savannah agro-ecosystems in sub-Saharan Africa*

Table 5.2 *Water-related biophysical deficiencies affecting on-farm yield levels*

Deficiency	Cause	Manifestation
Hydroclimatic	Inadequate seasonal rainfall Extreme spatial and temporal variability	Yield-impacting droughts and dry spells
Soil	Poor soil texture Poor soil structure Shallow rooting depth Steep slopes Soil chemical properties	Low soil infiltrability Low water holding capacity (WHC)
Plant	Soil nutrient availability Crop species Pest and diseases Land management	Poor crop water uptake capacity

opportunities for improving the livelihood of the rural poor and the environmental condition of savannah landscapes. If up to 90 per cent of the water balance is lost to food production in the form of evaporation, runoff and drainage, this means that there are huge volumes of water out there in the landscape to tap for productive use. Verifying this requires an assessment of why yields are low, and how much they can be increased.

Rockström and Falkenmark (2000) show that low crop yields are attributed to a set of management-related water deficiencies (see Table 5.2).

The deficiencies are manifested in the inability to cope with dry spells – short periods of water stress during crop growth, poor performance of the crop water balance (high runoff, large evaporation and drainage losses), and poor soil fertility and crop management resulting in low crop water uptake capacity.

Rockström and Falkenmark (2000) also show that there are no hydrological limitations to a doubling or even quadrupling of crop yields in rain-fed semi-arid farming systems, from 0.5 to 1 tonnes per hectare at present to 2 tonnes per hectare. Not only does this seem possible, but they show it could be achieved with relatively small implications on the local water balance (a 15 to 25 per cent increase in soil infiltration, and a 15 to 20 per cent increase in the proportion of productive to non-productive vapour flow).[4] Hydroclimatically achievable yields in the on-farm situation are roughly 5 tonnes per hectare for semi-arid conditions. However, many commercial farmers in semi-arid tropical areas maintain yield levels of 8 to 10 tonnes per hectare of maize grain, which is close to the physiological potential of many varieties (Rockström, 2001).

'Marginal land' and 'dry lands': Time to shift the terminology

The above indicates that even on the farm level there is an urgent need to refocus our managerial minds. There are two dominating professional perceptions related to rain-fed farming in semi-arid areas. One perception we are dealing with is that of water-scarce dry land, where water is the primary limiting factor for crop growth. The second perception is that semi-arid lands are marginal, and can only contribute in a very limited fashion to food security and socio-economic development. Both notions are flawed.

To begin with, there is more precipitation in most dry lands than in most temperate wetlands. For example, in Stockholm, the very wet capital of Sweden, the annual rainfall amounts to only 550 millimetres (mm), with roughly 300 to 400mm falling during the short 120-day growing season. The conditions for agriculture should be considered marginal, to say the least, compared with the 700mm of seasonal rainfall under fantastic solar radiation conditions present in most semi-arid tropical landscapes. Many semi-arid regions have bimodal rainfall, giving two rainy seasons and the potential for two harvests per year, which is impossible in most 'non-marginal' temperate zones. Indeed, one cannot pass the month of June in Sweden without reading about the outcry from farmers over early-season dry spells hitting spring crops during germination. Subsidies and monetary compensation generally suffocate these signs of hydrological marginality in the North.

In the South, people go hungry as soon as the rainfall is not distributed or partitioned according to the wishes of the crop grown. Water scarcity, even over short periods, leads to social and physical disaster. There is nothing to cushion the effects of a poorly performing water balance. Inevitably, the semi-arid savannah turns harsh, threatening the poor. Of course, it is always necessary to acknowledge that temperate and tropical climates are never comparable in terms of precipitation alone. Atmospheric demand for water and variability of rainfall is generally a factor 2 to 3 times higher in tropical hydroclimates, resulting in a much higher risk of droughts and dry spells, and a lower proportion of effective water available for crop growth. However, the point here is that large volumes of water fall from the sky in tropical dry lands. Therefore, it is more constructive to focus on management options to minimize evaporation losses and mitigate dry spells and droughts, rather than succumb to the general perception of marginality, which automatically leads to the erroneous attitude of limited development potential.

So, one may wonder, have semi-arid savannahs always been perceived as marginal dry lands? There is evidence to the contrary. Only a century ago the most successful 'Sarki-Noma' farmers made fortunes from millet cultivation in semi-arid parkland savannah areas of the Sahel (Sidikou, 1974). How could that be? As shown by several scientists, farming systems have evolved rapidly over the last century as a result of demographic pressure from systems based on shifting cultivation (in the Sahelian case in productive and dense *Acacia fedherbia* parklands) to continuous production systems in exposed bare-soil landscapes. The shifting cultivation systems were based on long fallows (often 25 years) that enabled farmers to bridge a number of the water deficiencies discussed above.

The whole rationale of using fallows is to enrich the topsoil by lifting soil nutrients from deep soil layers. This requires deep-rooted trees. The fallows also assist in maintaining soil structure by keeping a mulch layer that reduces soil evaporation. This sustainable farming system linked with large land holdings, spread over large geographic areas to reduce the impact risks of high spatial variability of rainfall, was sufficient to keep yields and total production at levels that enabled the export of crops. Farmers made money, bought military protection, established dry-season sheltering contracts for manure replenishment with the warrior Touareg nomads, and conserved the environment. Furthermore, the rural societies were equipped with a broad set of social safety valves to cope with the unavoidable cycles of meteorological drought periods (first documented in the Old Testament, symbolized by the seven good rainfall years followed by seven drought years). Farmers saved during good years for the bad years. Old farmers in West Africa generally state that they do not remember having eaten the harvest of a certain year during that same year. The latest harvest was always stored under previous 'security' harvests, which meant that the meals were cooked using old grain (from previous years). Livestock pressure was low, which meant that these four-legged bank accounts (which is what livestock constitutes for the agro-pastoralists of semi-arid savannah farming systems in most parts of Africa) stood a good chance of survival and could support the society under periods of drought.

Today, all of that is gone. The farming systems are in a social and biophysical crisis, resulting in human tragedy each time rainfall drops below a critical threshold. The crisis is both social and biophysical in the sense that the safety systems have collapsed (there is barely enough food to take a rural family through to the next harvest *even* during good rainfall years). The degradation of soil fertility and soil structure means that large proportions of rainfall are lost, and even if water is available in the root zone no strong roots are there to absorb it. Actually, several scientists have shown that even in the semi-arid tropics of sub-Saharan Africa, soil nutrients often constitute the major limiting factor for crop growth, not water (Penning de Vries et al, 1991; Klaij and Vachaud, 1992; Fox, 2001). According to Sanchez et al (1997), agricultural development in Africa can only take place if initiated by an enormous soil fertility injection. This is not surprising, given the depressing figures on negative nutrient balances for African farming systems, with an annually estimated net loss of nitrogen less than 50 kilograms (kg) per hectare for many regions (Braun et al, 1997).

The crisis is related to the abandoning of one farming system based on reasonably sustainable soil property conservation (especially in terms of soil nutrients) in favour of another system that never has experienced the introduction of an alternative mode of soil nutrient and soil structural management. Compare this to the very similar agricultural development in Europe, where the soil nutrient crisis caused by abandoning the shifting cultivation system was initially solved by the enclosure revolution (enabling manure application on grain fields from stables), and later by the fossil fuel revolution leading up to the last agricultural revolution.

Therefore, little historical or present evidence exists to support the notion of semi-arid savannahs being agriculturally inferior, with little or no development potential. On the contrary, there is historical support to suggest that rain-fed agriculture in semi-arid tropics has a very bright future.

The challenge: Changing the development paradigm

The above statements would normally result in two groups of academics roaring their disapproval. Firstly, the arid hydrologists and rural anthropologists would claim that there is very strong evidence to show that water is causing serious and recurrent crop failure and that there is also a strong possibility that the deterioration of farm productivity is related to a decline in rainfall. This can be shown not only from hydrological observations, but also from surveys among rural communities where water is generally the primary concern of most rural households. It is hard to counter these arguments; but do they really support the general marginality paradigm? No. Water in semi-arid tropics is scarce due to the character of tropical rainfall, and not because of the absolute scarcity of water. Rainfall is highly erratic, with huge intensive storms falling in a very unreliable pattern over time and space. Coefficients of variation vary in the range of 20 to 40 per cent, even higher with lower annual rainfall. The atmospheric thirst is huge, generally exceeding rainfall depths even during rainy seasons (potential evapo-transpiration ranging from 5 to 10mm per day). High rainfall intensity and large rainfall depths over short periods of time lead to high surface runoff and significant drainage (even in dry lands). The problem, then, is not necessarily a lack of water, but that when water is there, it is in abundance and often at the wrong time. And, if it is left to form open water surface, it evaporates quickly.

Therefore, the challenge is not necessarily an absolute lack of water, but rather how to deal with large spatial and temporal variability, and how to reduce water losses. In comparison, the region of Cherrapunji in India, referred to as the world's wettest 'desert', receives an annual rainfall over 10 metres (m), and still suffers from severe water scarcity problems that are related to large variability of rainfall and huge water losses due to land degradation (Agarwal, 2000).

High rainfall variability leads to meteorological droughts (occurring one or two times every decade) (Stewart, 1988) and to dry spells. Meteorological droughts are generally the focus of the professionals who claim that water scarcity is to be blamed for poor agricultural productivity. Reliable historical climatic records show that meteorological droughts have occurred over history with serious social impacts (Nicholson, 1978). They form a natural part of the semi-arid context, and there is nothing we can do about it. Other research indicates that meteorological dry spells are a major concern for farm management in semi-arid tropics. Rainfall and water balance analyses indicate a high risk of occurrence of dry spells exceeding ten days for semi-arid locations in Eastern and Southern Africa (Barron, 2001). For example, during the stress-sensitive flowering stage of maize there is a 60 to 80 per cent risk of dry spells exceeding ten days. This is serious but manageable. Dry spells may not only explain a large proportion of the yield losses in semi-arid tropics, but they may also form the backbone of risk management among farmers. If the risk for yield-reducing dry spells is too high, a farmer will not invest capital in that business venture. The risk of losing invested capital contributes to the decision of not investing in fertilizers, crop varieties and pest management. This leads to opportunities lost during well-distributed rains. But, on the other hand, it also results in little loss during dry spell years (which may occur in four out of five crop seasons). These farmers have no insurance, no societal back-up if the enterprise goes bankrupt, and the only option available for dealing with indebtedness caused by climatic variability is often to migrate to urban shanty towns and start new lives.

The second outrage originates from the rural development community. Farmers have 5000 years of trial and error upon which to build their experience and management. They know their landscape, and there is little that can be brought in externally to improve things. To put it bluntly, how can one claim that there is no water problem in marginal dry lands? The dominating school of thought praises bottom-up approaches that rely on participatory methodologies. The goal is not to introduce new technologies, but rather to empower local communities to develop their own know-how. Local communities have the answers to all the problems inherently rooted within their own society. The problem is that the so-called enabling environment allowing these capabilities to bloom is not there. The solution is to facilitate a process that stimulates the enabling environment. A broad set of participatory methodologies – such as participatory rural appraisal (PRA), rapid rural appraisal (RRA) and co-management – have been developed in order to assist in this endeavour of giving help for self-help. This bottom-up wave is probably a result of the appalling development failures encountered during the 1960s and 1970s, when technology transfer from the industrialized and temperate North to the developing and tropical South, dominated. Large-scale, high-tech concrete projects were parachuted into the jungle, with complete lack of local ownership, capacity building and maintenance. This top-down approach was a catastrophe and led only to rust and decay.

The problem today is that the development pendulum has swung too far from one extreme (the top-down Northern-bias approach) to another (the farmers-first approach). The latter approach is humble, culturally sensitive, gives good tools to distil gender differences and is theoretically (and rhetorically) very seductive. The effect, however, is that engineers have suddenly become one of the scapegoats of underdevelopment. It must be acknowledged that neither approach is adequate, and that the pure bottom-up paradigm is causing many problems. The reality of bottom-up approaches to development that rely on indigenous knowledge alone is that they tend to get stuck in the assessment of problems and needs. Such approaches fail to address challenges and opportunities, much less actual solutions (even if the approaches were not intended to stop at problem assessment). They are well suited for rural communities that are socially and economically stable and not in a transitional phase. Unfortunately, the dramatic increase in demographic pressure on finite soil and water resources has resulted in rural crises, where indigenous land-use practices are no longer able to generate livelihood security. A symptom of this crisis is the extremely low yield climax in many semi-arid farming systems in sub-Saharan Africa, where yield levels oscillate in the range of 0.5 to 1.0 tonnes per hectare.

The great advantage with bottom-up approaches is that local ownership of development is enabled (which is absolutely crucial to sustainable development), and the full complexity of causes and effects behind is unearthed. A genuine, potentially egalitarian exchange of knowledge and ideas is achieved between the service-providing agent and the recipient of development. However, once the problems and local capacities are identified, innovative solutions to solve the problems are not considered. Instead, the process goes into an introverted spiral of self-development that may have significant results, but not in the order of magnitude required to lift poor societies permanently out of misery. The core of the problem is that indigenously based development paradigms, even though potentially promising, will never by themselves solve the enormous task of lifting poor communities out of the poverty trap. And this is strongly the case in the field of agricultural development.

First, the challenge is so outrageously large – over the next year even a 'Green Revolution pace' in yield increase will not be enough to feed the newly born and lift undernutrition status in sub-Saharan Africa (yields have to more than double over the next 20 years). Second, the argument that farmers not only know it all, but have also tested all, is not valid anymore (one may strongly question if it ever was). It was the case some 50 to 75 years ago when the farming systems were still operating in their original mode (shifting cultivation with a sustainable balance between virgin land, cropland and grazing land).

Today, this is not the case. Farmers are facing an agrarian crisis, and it has been overwhelmingly proven that such crises over the history of humankind have more often than not been solved through painful revolutions with very strong external influence (import of ideas and technologies) (Boserup, 1992). However, even if we acknowledge that rural societies in poor water scarcity-stricken countries are in a transitional crisis phase, many workers would argue that the rationale of introducing innovative and perhaps alien technologies will still never work (the crisis argument is simply not a valid rationale for technology transfer). Nothing is more wrong. History is full of examples of how completely alien technologies, (top down) parachuted into traditional rural societies, have been absorbed and today form the very basis for their mode of survival and economic endeavour. The historically recent introduction of sweet potatoes from South America to Papua New Guinea (Diamond, 1997), potato, wheat and barley in Northern Europe, and the horse in North America are a few examples. The reason for rapid and complete absorption of such alien technologies, according to Diamond (1997), is the simple fact that the innovations dramatically surpassed indigenous technologies in performance. We should not make the mistake of underestimating the open-mindedness and curiosity for the unknown among poor rural societies. A poor African farmer meeting a development worker to discuss his/her problems in a full PRA is expecting a solution to problems, new or old, internal or external – it does not matter. The challenge is to anchor ownership and secure capacity to master the technology, not to avoid novelty.

In sum, water is there but at the wrong time, and the farmer competes for the resource in a thirsty atmosphere. The rural crisis is so deep in most parts of semi-arid developing countries that we can talk of an agrarian crisis. Indigenous approaches, despite all their merits in assessing causal complexities and the ability to anchor ownership, will not do the job. Innovations, genius and novelty are needed. New technologies are required. The social engineer has to fully enter the development scene.

Tilting the water resource management approach

Linking the biophysical analysis on water availability for development with the conceptual analysis on development paradigms detailed above opens up an exciting avenue for future development opportunities. What came out in the biophysical analysis was that there is a need for a tilting in water resources management from river to raindrop, from 'blue only' to the consideration of 'green–blue blending'. This will widen the management options and assist in the prioritization of management and policy strategies. If a broadened green–blue hydrological integration is applied, it may also be useful to adopt a more holistic approach to farming-systems development. Normally, we distinguish between rain-fed and irrigated farming systems, which have created their own 'water-tight' governing structures. For example, water is divided among different ministries, where, generally, rain-fed agriculture falls within the mandate of a ministry dealing with agriculture, while irrigation schemes are the domain of a ministry dealing with water resources. This divide, where green and blue waters are governed by different line ministries, often with little bridging between sectors, requires some thorough rethinking.

First, many of the most promising opportunities to improve water productivity in rain-fed agriculture involve some form of protective or supplemental irrigation to mitigate dry spells – for example, using surface or sub-surface runoff flow in water harvesting systems. Thus, already in rain-fed or green water development, blue water management from both surface and sub-surface water resources are becoming more prominent (often used by farmers for centuries, applying traditional indigenous technologies). Similarly, rainfall generally supplements crop water requirements in conventional irrigation schemes. The fact is that large parts of worldwide food production originate from hydrologically blended production systems, integrating green and blue water flows at the farm level.

The policy and management implications should not be underestimated. First of all, an integrated hydrological approach to rain-fed farming systems, even in semi-arid areas, will show that there are larger management options accessible to the farmer than is generally perceived as being the case, as is shown in the yield gap analysis in Figure 5.2 and Table 5.1. The policy changes entail moving from a situation where so-called dry lands are seen as marginal because of soil moisture deficits to a situation where surface and sub-surface runoff flow generated from intensive rain storms are seen as a potential source of water for food production.

Second, the bulk of development efforts has been allocated to conventional irrigation schemes. The majority of rural people still live beyond the reach of irrigation conveyance channels. A shift towards seeing the blue opportunities in rain-fed agriculture is a shift towards building local capacity to develop small-scale technologies and methodologies for improved water security (such as drip irrigation, river diversion systems, small dams, sand- and sub-surface dams, and improved shallow wells).

WIN–WIN SOLUTIONS BASED ON INTEGRATED RAIN MANAGEMENT

One of the major challenges in the water-for-food nexus in semi-arid tropical regions over the next 25 to 50 years is to achieve a sustained doubling of on-farm soil and water productivity. This will be done to improve livelihoods, to improve the crop-per-drop ratio and, in doing so, to secure the generation of essential ecosystem services. The following brings out some promising and, from the local farming context, novel technologies and practices to improve water productivity in agriculture.

Conservation farming systems

A major cause of human-induced land degradation in smallholder farms is the intensive soil preparation by hoe or plough, which together with the removal or burning of crop residues leaves the soil exposed to climatic hazards such as rain, wind and sun (Benites et al, 1998). Conventional tillage using ox- or tractor-drawn ploughs has, over the years, been perceived as the indicator of agricultural modernization in tropical developing countries. It is, however, becoming more apparent that ploughing techniques developed in temperate regions with gentle rains and low wind and water erosion problems can have seriously adverse effects on the long-term productivity of erosion-prone tropical soils.

Moreover, conventional tillage practices require high labour and energy inputs and are generally associated with poor timing of farming operations. These two latter factors strongly affect poorer, small-scale farmers who generally depend on ox-traction for ploughing operations. Many smallholder farmers, especially female-headed households, do not have their own pair of oxen due to resource limitations and/or lack of grazing areas.

Conservation tillage is generally defined as any tillage sequence with the objective of minimizing soil and water loss, and having an operational threshold, leaving more than 30 per cent mulch or crop residue on the surface throughout the year (SSSA, 1987). Translated onto farm operations, this means no soil inversion, by abandoning the plough in favour of alternative tillage practices with a minimum of soil disturbance. From a rural development perspective, this means that for the small-scale farmers in tropical regions conservation tillage is not a 'new' production system, but rather a novel development of the original farming practices based on shifting cultivation and long fallows.

Conservation tillage (CT) systems, ranging from zero-tillage to minimum- or reduced-tillage systems, have been widely adopted in several parts of the world. In the USA, 30 per cent of the agriculture is presently under conservation tillage, and in Brazil zero-tillage systems have been adopted on a large scale because of trials initiated during the early 1970s (Derpsch, 1998; Derpsch and Moriya, 1998). Examples of successful CT systems – where crop yields, reduced soil erosion and water conservation have been significantly increased – can be found in several sub-Saharan countries, such as Ghana, Nigeria, Zimbabwe, Tanzania, South Africa and Zambia (Elwell, 1993; Oldreive, 1993; Vogel et al, 1994), and in Asia, such as Pakistan and Nepal (Hobbs et al, 2000). However, the adoption of conservation tillage systems is mainly confined to commercial farms with little adoption among smallholder farmers.

In sub-Saharan Africa, several conservation-farming initiatives have been initiated over the last couple years, all aiming at increased promotion and adoption of CT systems among smallholder farmers. The African Conservation Tillage (ACT) network was launched in early 2000 in an effort to improve the exchange of experiences and to support capacity building and research on CT systems for smallholder farmers.

From a water productivity perspective, CT systems have four attractive attributes:

1　The focus on water and soil productivity, while simultaneously reducing soil erosion.
2　The focus on farmers as entrepreneurs and not only as subsistence maintainers.
3　Their attractiveness in supporting efforts to increase water-use efficiencies in drought-prone areas.
4　Their ability to be scaled up as the systems generally fit on all arable land (compared to storage-water harvesting systems that only fit in zones where biophysical and economic catchment parameters are conducive).

Experiences on CT systems in Eastern Africa during the recent drought from March to July 2000 illustrate the opportunity to improve land and water productivity even under water-scarce conditions. Ethiopia has experienced crop water deficits in large parts of the country. However, through improved timeliness of farm operations, conservation of soil water and reduced weed competition, the non-governmental organization (NGO) Sasakawa Global 2000 reported successful crop yields on maize and tea crops (in areas where farmers have suffered complete crop failure). This was caused by abandoning the conventional intensive Maresha ard-plough system in favour of zero-tillage systems (using hybrid seed, fertilizers and herbicides) (Quinones, 2000, pers comm).

Similarly, in Kenya, where an estimated 4 million people suffer from severe food deficits due to crop failures, farmer-managed zero-tillage trials facilitated by Monsanto have yielded 3 to 4 tonnes of grain per hectare in areas experiencing complete crop failure (average yield levels are less than 2 tonnes per hectare) (Lawrence-Brown, 1999, pers comm).

In north-western Tanzania, within villages located in semi-arid areas around the Arusha district, farmers participating in demonstrations using animal-drawn rippers and sub-soilers to assure maximum infiltration of rainfall and to enable pre-season dry planting were able to harvest a crop during the water-scarce long rains of 2000. Meanwhile, neighbouring farmers using mouldboard ploughs and disc ploughs suffered from complete crop failure (Mwalley, 1999, pers comm).

However, soil compaction resulting in impermeable plough pans due to continuous conventional ploughing leads to crop water stress even during years of adequate rainfall distribution. In many conventionally ploughed farming systems, neither soil water nor crop roots can penetrate deeper than 12 to 15 centimetres (cm) into the soil. This results in high surface runoff as the topsoil rapidly gets saturated, and in crop water stress a couple of days after rainfall events because there is only a very limited volume of available soil moisture.

Figure 5.3 shows results from three years of on-farm conservation trials in the Arusha area of north-western Tanzania. The conservation tillage systems tested in partnership with farmers originate from research in West Africa and in Zambia (IMAG, 1999). These include animal-drawn rippers and sub-soilers. These implements fit on the conventional plough beam but were otherwise completely alien to the farmers in the three villages where the participatory research was initiated. Farmers were initially exposed to conservation-farming technologies around the world and then, among themselves in a dialogue with the scientists, designed their own innovative conservation tillage system from the smorgasbord of technologies exposed to them. They decided on implements, timing of operations and cropping patterns, and how to deal with weeding, mulching and cover crops. The conservation tillage systems, which above all conserve water, are shown in the two columns to the left in Figure 5.3. The combination of soil fertility (fertilizer application in this case because all treatment received manure) and conservation tillage gave by far the highest yields – on average 4 tonnes of grain per hectare, a factor three times higher than the conventional practice of ploughing without fertilizer. Interestingly, only the synergy between water (conservation tillage) and soil fertility (fertilizer application) gives a yield take-off. Soil fertility management alone gives slightly higher average yield than water conservation alone in this semi-arid environment. This supports the earlier statement that water is not necessarily the primary limiting factor in these dry lands.

Normally, promoting conservation-farming practices is worthwhile even if yields are not necessarily enhanced as a result of the beneficial impact on soil conservation and reduction in labour requirements. Here, in the context of semi-arid smallholder farming, where the soils are seriously affected by

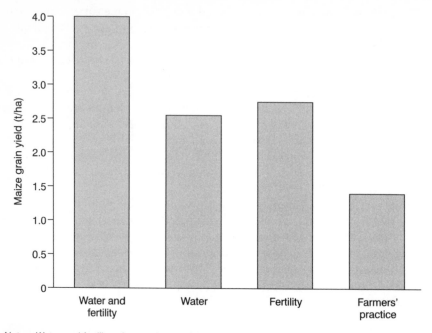

Notes: Water and fertility refers to the combination of conservation tillage for water harvesting and application of fertilizer; Water refers to conservation tillage alone; *Fertility* refers to fertilizer application alone; *Farmers' practice* refers to the current farmers' practice of conventional ploughing with no fertilizer application.

Figure 5.3 *Maize yields from on-farm trials in Arusha and Arumeru districts, Tanzania, 1999–2000*

structural degradation, assuring full rainfall infiltration combined with a small soil fertility input, corresponding only to the recommended levels for smallholder farmers, results in very significant yield increases. This is encouraging not only because of the increase, but also because a beauty of conservation farming is that it 'fits' basically all cropland. Compare this with small irrigation dams that, irrespective of success, will never support more than a very small fraction of the cropland in need of water supply.

Runoff management for supplemental irrigation

As previously mentioned, sheet, rill and gully runoff are generally not perceived as water resources until they reach permanent/semi-permanent rivers and streams. However, there are large opportunities in mitigating dry spells and even droughts by harvesting surface runoff upstream in catchments for supplemental irrigation of crop during periods of water stress.

On-going research in the Sahel (Burkina Faso) and Eastern Africa (Kenya) has shown that 50 to 100mm of supplemental irrigation during critical periods of crop water stress can increase crop yields of maize and sorghum two or three times (Fox and Rockström, 2000; Barron et al, 1999). The rainwater

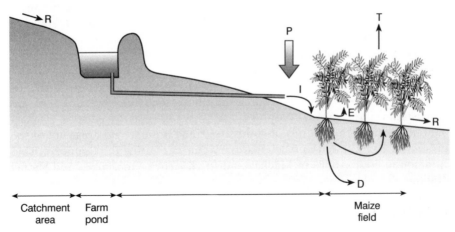

Key: R = runoff, P = precipitation, I = irrigation, E = soil evaporation, T = plant transpiration, D = deep percolation

Source: Barron et al (1999)

Figure 5.4 *Longitudinal transect of water harvesting system for supplemental irrigation of Maize in Mwala Division, Machakos district, Kenya*

harvesting system used is very simple, involving limited investments (mainly labour) and requiring small catchment areas of less than 10ha. Figure 5.4 shows the principle outline of the system, where sheet and rill surface runoff is harvested in a small farm pond (~ 300m^3 storage capacity), and where the water is fed by gravity onto the cultivated area. The catchment area consists of communal land covering degraded grazing areas, dirt roads, degraded fallows and homesteads. Gravity-fed application of the water is a key feature of the system, as farmers would rarely consider lifting the large volumes of water required to sustain a crop (Jurdell and Svensson, 1998).

The research in Kenya and Burkina Faso also indicates the possibility of bridging very serious dry spells that, due to complete crop failure, are defined as droughts. The long rains in Kenya and the 2000 rainy season in Burkina are good examples of this. In the Kenyan case, a large rainfall event at the onset (80mm) was followed by a devastating and prolonged dry spell during flowering and grain filling. Total crop failure hit most farmers. On the research site, the onset rainfall was harvested in the farm pond enabling the bridging of the stress period and generating a very high grain yield of approximately 2 tonnes of grain per hectare (compared to an average yield level of 1 tonne per hectare for the region). Similarly in Burkina, yields exceeding 1 tonne per hectare were maintained using supplemental irrigation during the 2000 rains, which hit flowering with a serious dry spell, resulting in total crop failure for many farmers in the region.

The crops per drop implications of supplemental irrigation in rain-fed farming systems experiencing temporally unreliable rainfall are very large. In the Mwala example, where long rains were experienced in 2000, on average

6.2kg of grain was produced per mm of rainfall, or 3.0kg of grain per mm of total water supplied (rain + supplemental irrigation). These are average to very good water-use efficiency values. The maize, depending only on rainfall, had, on average, a crop per drop ratio of 0.33kg per mm per hectare, indicating large unproductive losses in the water balance.

In cases where the catchment and command area are owned by different actors, then a new form of trading may have to be developed where the downstream farmer trades cropland against water (gravity fed from a micro dam upstream). These kinds of soil-water trade in semi-arid areas are in the process of being tested in participatory water harvesting development using common interest groups in Machakos district, Kenya (Rockström and Shone, 2000).

Drip irrigation

Modern drip irrigation methods date back to experiments in Israel during the 1960s, and have since spread to arid and semi-arid areas all over the world among large-scale commercial farms. The benefits are significant, with large reductions on overall water requirements in crop production (by at least 50 per cent), and reduced labour and energy needs combined with the possibility of precision application of fertilizers. The drawback has been the high investment costs, and only recently have cheap low-pressure systems for small-scale farmers reached the market. Small bucket-kit systems (water supplied with 20-litre buckets) with drip-lines for 15m^2 vegetable cultivation strips are being successfully promoted by Chapin Living Waters Foundation in several countries in sub-Saharan Africa. In Kenya, gross margins of US$50 to US$130 per bucket kit per season have been reported by female farmers participating in promotion of bucket kits (Ngigi et al, 2000). This is a significant amount of money generated with little labour input from a small piece of land (15m^2) by using water in a very efficient manner, through large reductions in evaporation and percolation losses, and a continuous supply of available soil water.

Systems approach to innovative adoption

Conservation farming, supplemental irrigation and drip systems all involve significant changes in both production systems and in the way we look at smallholder farming in developing countries. Successful conservation farming involves not only the change of tillage implement, but also more focused farm management regarding timing of operations, precision farming, cropping patterns, post-harvest management and weeding. Zero-tillage systems, where inputs such as herbicides are used to management weeds, require a development from subsistence-oriented farming to business-oriented farming. Fertilizers, knapsack sprayers for herbicides and improved seed require a surplus production to generate a cash income. Often, micro-credit schemes must be established to kick-start the process of moving farming systems that are stuck in a soil-degraded yield climax of less than 1 tonne per hectare. This is because of decades of soil-nutrient mining, erosion, compaction and exhaustion of organic matter through a positive cycle of progressive investment in soil and water management. Markets have to be accessible, and market information available.

Water harvesting systems for supplemental irrigation, drip systems and productive water points involve large time and capital investments for small-scale farmers who require profit returns. The risk of crop failure in semi-arid farming systems (due to frequent droughts and dry spells) is often explained as one core reason why farmers (on a rationale basis) are reluctant to investment in improved seed, pest management and fertilization (organic and inorganic). Securing a water source during dry spells can be the incentive needed for investments on improved soil and water management, which in turn can result in progressively increasing yields and profits. The conclusion is that farming-systems improvements among smallholder farmers in water-scarce regions can be achieved if a broad, holistic approach is adopted, where technologies and methodologies are integrated with entrepreneurship, markets and credit schemes at a watershed or river-basin scale.

Planning rain at the catchment scale

Isolated efforts of technology adoption, however successful, are a risky approach in the development of innovative systems for upgrading rain management in rural landscapes. Every increase in green water flow in one farming system upstream will affect water availability downstream. Hydrological implications downstream, both for surface and sub-surface blue water flow, need to be assessed and negotiated in all attempts at improving food production. There are no systematic studies carried out in semi-arid tropical catchments that assess the impact on water availability downstream of system innovations upstream. This is urgently needed as the implications may not only affect humans, but also the generation of ecosystem services upon which humans depend. For example, on a global scale, Rockström et al (1999) estimated the total human dependence on green water flow at 88 per cent of available green water, only to sustain ecosystem services from major biomes of the world. This indicates that most of the precipitation that returns to the atmosphere as vapour flow is actually already producing ecological goods and services for us, in the form of food, timber, wetland fauna, grasslands and grazing land.

This indirect human dependence on water for ecosystem goods and services in terrestrial ecosystems is not taken into account in conventional water assessments. These comprise assessments that trickle down the scales and are not properly integrated in catchment planning. There is a growing focus on these upstream–downstream links between green and blue water flows. South Africa has taken a global lead in recognizing forestry as a water user (Ministry of Water Affairs and Forestry, 1998). This is based on the experience that large upstream forest plantations may result in reduced blue water flow downstream. In Australia, large-scale tree planting has been suggested as a measure to reduce a worrying trend of increased soil salinity problems, caused by extensive tree clearing that results in rising saline groundwater tables. There is evidence suggesting that such large-scale tree planting may actually result in decreased blue water flow in downstream rivers (Vertessy and Bessard, 1999) given the high evapotranspiration of trees.

Fox's (2001) estimates of the hydrological implications of upgrading water harvesting systems for supplemental irrigation in a semi-arid river basin in northern Burkina Faso show that less than 1 per cent of the rainfall would be able to support dry-spell mitigation on 15 to 20 per cent of the basin farmland. This very minor impact on the hydrological cycle is supported by research in southern Zimbabwe, where groundwater extraction for small-scale gardening presented a similarly low impact on water resources (Lovell et al, 1996). Furthermore, field observations in semi-arid Sahel imply that the fate of a large proportion of the generated surface runoff is actually direct evaporation from inundated lowlands, rather than direct human or indirect productive use in ecosystems (Rockström, 1997). Findings that indirectly support this are by Evanari et al (1971), who concluded that more productive use of runoff could be made from small-scale systems upstream than large-scale dams downstream, as a result of the losses involved when water flows through a landscape.

This indicates that there still remains a lot of work to be done on how to achieve sustainable development at catchment or river-basin level, especially with regard to trade-offs between green and blue water flows – between liquid blue water flows and vapour green water flows.

CONCLUSIONS

The majority of population growth over the next generation will occur in developing countries. It is here that the major food security challenges are centred, as are the water resources challenges because food is the largest water-consuming activity. If we can solve the water challenges facing poor communities in the scarcest water regions, than we stand a good chance of doing so in less water-scarce regions.

This chapter suggests that, even for these extreme environments, there are large development opportunities. They only surface by adopting a shift to a more holistic hydrological thinking, combined with a more optimistic view of semi-arid environments and an open mind towards novel technologies and innovations.

Shift in hydrological thinking

The starting point is to break free from conventional 'blue' water bias in water resources policy and management in favour of a holistic approach that takes rainfall (precipitation) as the starting point for integrated catchment management. This step is required to open the managerial arena for proper prioritization of all the options available to improve soil and water productivity in water-scarce agrarian landscapes. This broadened 'water' approach needs to be shouldered by a broadened sectorial approach, where the water implications for all water-dependent service-providing processes in the landscape are taken into consideration. This is crucial, as it has been shown that a large proportion of accessible green water flow is already used to produce ecosystem services from the major biomes on Earth. Humankind will, despite a holistic rain-based approach, be confronted with a set of difficult trade-offs over the next couple of generations, especially between green water flow for food production in rain-fed agriculture and green/blue water flows to sustain ecosystems downstream. Furthermore, a wider green–blue emphasis requires more attention to the risks involved in rainwater depending on land-use activities. This is especially important because evidence shows that risk management in tropical smallholder agriculture is, to a large extent, driven by the risk of rain-induced crop water stress. Therefore, rainwater management may be an important entry point in the effort to upgrade rain-fed agriculture.

The responsibility of science

Administratively, nature is split up in a number of managerial islands, where management is carried out in a piecemeal fashion with little cause–effect considerations in time or space. Agriculture, environment, water resources, health and infrastructure generally fall under different ministries with little or no linkages, either in law or in policy and regulations. Obviously, in the real world, all of these sectors meld together at the river-basin, and even at the watershed, scale, and a farmer is, in his/her daily work, forced to take decisions that affect several sectors. A severe integration gap is in the water/food/environment nexus, where there is an urgent need to break management barriers and to develop common policies and regulations. A good example where progress had been made is in South Africa where the new water act protects water requirements for domestic, agricultural and environmental uses.

The problem is that we cannot expect such pragmatic reforms to occur as long as policy-makers are not served with solid scientific evidence that integrated environmental management is the most beneficial way to proceed. It is not enough that rhetoric claims that integration is beautiful. Hard data that shows societal and economic benefits as a product of integration is needed.

In water-scarce regions, rainfall partitioning can function as a good entry point for integrated environmental management, as every land-use decision impacts water and, at the same time, depends on it. A land-use decision to shift from conventional ploughing to minimum-tillage farming will, in the long term, increase infiltration and return flow of productive transpiration on cropland. Simultaneously, more biomass will be produced per unit of land and water, and animal traction requirements will be reduced. This, in turn, may reduce grazing pressure and minimize the need for slash-and-burning of fallow, or marginal, land for new cultivation – often this is the only avenue resource-poor land users can take to feed growing families when yields are stuck at stubbornly low levels. With more fodder available on the farm, zero-grazing units for dairy production may become viable. This will generate a stable source of income from selling milk. In turn, this may enable households to shift from inefficient stoves to improved stoves or even solar-power or small-scale biogas units, which reduce deforestation in upstream areas of the river basin. Such shifts, if occurring at a community level, will have impacts on the hydrological cycle, erosion patterns and social livelihoods.

Stakeholders in the driving seat

Without a doubt, any development effort, whether based on external and alien technologies or indigenous technologies, will have to evolve ensuring a broad stakeholder involvement and ownership. This is the top-down–bottom-up blend discussed earlier. The small-scale farmer is an entrepreneur who calculates investment ventures based not only on cash flow but on the risks involved. Risks in semi-arid tropics are directly proportional to rainfall variability (not to rainfall amounts). Innovative technologies for coping with temporal rainfall variability can shift farmers from the present attitude of risk aversion to an attitude of productivity maximization. It can only be achieved by anchoring the innovations deep in the mental soil of the farmer.

Technical and biophysical integration: Finding synergy

A sub-catchment or watershed within a river basin is probably the most appropriate level of local management. It is small enough to ensure local decision-making but is still large enough to host natural resource parameters that can enable spatial synergies. Watershed planning where biophysical conditions (for example, slope, soils, rainfall and vegetation) are linked to technological options can generate synergies resulting in improved benefits for the environment. For example, it is very difficult to successfully promote conservation farming in farming communities in Eastern Africa where animal husbandry is an important part of the farming systems, and post-harvest grazing on cropland is common practice due to the communal land tenure system. The crucial mulching for reduction of evaporation, improvement of soil infiltration capacity and soil-water holding capacity becomes virtually impossible to achieve. Therefore, promotion of improved cropping systems must be addressed on a community or watershed scale where competition for crop residues can be addressed and possibly even sustainably solved.

The art of blending indigenous and innovative technologies

The conceptual challenge for rural development in the 21st century is to break out of the business-as-usual closet that, at best, generates 1.5 per cent per year increases in staple food yields. Instead, we must open our minds to more dynamic and innovative efforts that can give the development injection so badly required. For example, as shown by Sanchez et al (1997), soil fertility depletion in smallholder farming in sub-Saharan Africa is so bad that, regarding phosphorus, even the most effective business-as-usual approaches (subsidies to increase farm use of fertilizer, etc) will simply not work. All the phosphorus will be tied up in the soil and is not available for crops. The deficit is simply too large! They suggest a one-off government-supported phosphorus-injection scheme of unprecedented scale to 'fill up the fix costs' of phosphorus storage in the soil. Only then can 'normal' development efforts have an effect. The same may apply to water management in semi-arid tropics. The conventional plough-based farming systems have created so much land degradation, resulting in plough-pans, that the soil simply is no longer the rain 'sponge' it once was. We need to do something more drastic than preach isolated efforts of composting, more efficient manure management, dry planting and intercropping. Instead, we must think in terms of new farming systems – abandon the plough completely, once and for all. Introduce sub-surface farm tanks for supplemental irrigation, and so on. However, this eccentric approach cannot sustain itself. It must be combined with indigenous capacities, know-how and interests.

The ethical dimensions: After all, who owns the rain?

In the past, the tendency has been to focus on the allocation of river flows between various upstream–downstream human actors through formal water rights. This form of water management based on claims and disputes over water volumes needs to be broadened as water competition sharpens, and the role of vapour flow and water to sustain ecosystem values are fully understood. It has been argued that such a broadened conceptual framework at the river-basin scale requires the development of the ethical dimension of hydrology, in an equitable sharing of water resources between humans and nature, by adopting a mutual hydro-solidarity (Lundqvist and Falkenmark, 2000).

An emphasis on rain management upstream will stress the need to address legal and ethical dimensions of water allocation for different users in a river basin. At present, the legislation can only deal with 'blue' water flow in perennial rivers, lakes and accessible groundwater. But as this chapter has shown, most people's livelihoods depend upon water that is currently outside of the legal framework – namely, direct return flow of green water from either rainfall or local storm flows of blue water. Rain is generally considered to be god given, and in most rural societies in sub-Saharan African it would be inconceivable to introduce private ownership to rain. This is fine as long as farming systems only depend on rain that falls on a certain section of farmland. Once supplemental irrigation becomes an adopted tool for farmers dealing with dry spells, the local surface runoff produced from communal land upstream ceases to be 'everyone's' storm flow and becomes 'someone's' water source. Even more, it becomes a private source that can generate money. The ownership of local storm flows and rainfall at the field and watershed level will have to be addressed as an integral component of any serious effort to upgrade rain-fed agriculture in semi-arid tropics.

NOTES

1   1 Gm^3 = 1,000,000,000 m^3, equivalent to 1 km^3.

2   An estimated 1m^3 of green water (evapotranspiration) is required to produce 1000 kilocalories (kcal) of vegetarian foods (grain, legumes, tubers, etc) and 5m^3 of green water to produce 1000 kcal of meat (the difference is primarily accounted for by the conversion rate from grain feed to meat). To produce a balanced diet of 2700kcal per capita per day where 2200kcal derives from vegetarian food and 500kcal from meat, some 4.7m^3 per capita per day are required, or approximately 1700m^3 per capita per year (Klohn, 1998, pers comm).

3   This was necessary as the data on permanent grazing land from the FAO (34 million km^2) was larger than the estimated grassland area (29.5 million km^2) in Rockström et al (1999). Similarly, the forests and woodland area in the FAOSTAT Database on Agriculture at the global level is estimated at 55.5 million km^2 compared to 27.4 million km^2 in Rockström et al (1999). This can be explained by the combined effect that only a proportion of the grassland is used for grazing, and there is a large proportion of permanent grazing within the forest and woodland category in Rockström et al (1999). Therefore, in this chapter, the difference in area between the data from FAOSTAT and Rockström et al (1999) on the forest and woodland category (55.5 million km^2 – 27.4 million km^2 = 28.1 million km^2) constitutes permanent grazing, and the remainder used to attain the FAOSTAT estimated area for permanent grazing (34 million km^2 – 28.1 million km^2 = 5.9 million km^2) is the permanent grazing within the grassland category in Rockström et al (1999). This explains why the annual water withdrawals for the grasslands (12,100Gm^3 per year), forests and woodlands (19,700Gm^3 per year) are lower than the estimated withdrawals in Rockström et al (1999): 15,100Gm^3 per year for grasslands and 40,000Gm^3 per year for forests and woodlands.

4   The ratio between crop transpiration (T) to total evapotranspiration (ET), showing the proportion of productive green water to total green water (evaporation + transpiration flow).

REFERENCES

Agarwal, A (2000) 'Drought? Try capturing the rain', Briefing paper for members of parliament and state legislatures, Centre for Science and Environment, New Delhi, India

Barron, J (2001) *On Farm Water Management for Dry Spell Mitigation in Semi-Arid Sub-Sahara Africa*, Licentiate in Philosophy thesis, Department of System Ecology, Stockholm University, Stockholm,

Barron, J, Rockström, J and Gichuki, F (1999) 'Rain water management for dry spell mitigation in semi-arid Kenya', *East African Agricultural and Forestry Journal*, vol 65, no 1, pp57–69

Benites, J, Chuma, E, Fowler, R, Kienzle, J, Molapong, K, Manu, J, Nyagumbo, I, Steiner, K and van Veenhuizen, R (eds) (1998) *Conservation Tillage for Sustainable Agriculture*, Proceedings from an International Workshop, Harare, 22–27 June, Part 1 (Workshop Report), Deutsche Gesellschaft, GTZ, Eschborn, Germany

Boserup, E (1992) *The Conditions for Agricultural Growth: The Economics of Agrarian Change under Economic Pressure*, Earthscan, London

Braun, A R et al (eds) (1997) 'Maintenance and improvement of soil productivity in the highlands of Ethiopia, Kenya, Madagascar, and Uganda', AHI Technical Report Series, No 6, ICRAF, Nairobi

Conway, G (1997) *The Doubly Green Revolution*, Cornell University Press, Ithaca, NY

Cosgrove, W J and Rijsberman, F R (2000) *World Water Vision: Making Water Everybody's Business*, Earthscan, London

Derpsch, R (1998) 'Historical review of no-tillage cultivation of crops' in Benites, J et al (eds) *Conservation Tillage for Sustainable Agriculture*, Proceedings from an International Workshop, Harare, 22–27 June, Part II, Deutsche Gesellschaft, GTZ, Eschborn, Germany, pp205–218

Derpsch, R and Moriya, K (1998) 'Implications of no-tillage versus soil preparation on sustainability of agricultural production', *GeoEcology*, vol 31, pp1179–1186

Diamond, J (1997) *Guns, Germs and Steel: The Fate of Human Societies*, WW Norton & Company, USA

Elwell, H A (1993) 'Development and adoption of conservation tillage practices in Zimbabwe', *FAO Soils Bulletin*, vol 69, pp29–164

Evanari, M, Shanan, L and Tadmor, N H (1971) *The Negev: The Challenge of a Desert*, Harvard University Press, Cambridge

Falkenmark, M (1997) 'Meeting water requirements of an expanding world population', Philosophical Transactions of the Royal Society London, Series B, vol 352, no 1356, pp929–936

Falkenmark, M (1995) 'Land and water interactions: A synopsis', *Land and Water Integration and River Basin Management. FAO Land and Water Bulletin*, no 1, pp15–16

Falkenmark, M (1986) 'Fresh water: Time for a modified approach', *Ambio*, vol 15, pp192–200

Falkenmark, M and Lindh, G (1976) *Water for a Starving World*, Westview Press, Boulder, CO, p201

Food and Agriculture Organization (FAO) (2000) *Agriculture: Toward 2015/30*, Interim Report, July, www.fao.org/WAICENT/FAOINFO/ECONOMICS/ESD/gstudies.htm

Fox, P (2001) *Supplemental Irrigation and Soil Fertility Management for Yield Gap Reduction: On-Farm Experimentation in Semi-Arid Burkina Faso*, Licentiate in Philosophy thesis, Department of System Ecology, Stockholm University, Stockholm

Fox, P and Rockström, J (2000) 'Water harvesting for supplemental irrigation of cereal crops to overcome intra-seasonal dry-spells in the Sahel' *Physics and Chemistry of the Earth, Part B Hydrology, Oceans and Atmosphere*, vol 25, no 3, pp289–296

Gleick, P (ed) (1993) *Water in Crisis – A Guide to the World's Fresh Water Resources*, Oxford University Press, Oxford

Hobbs, P R et al (2000) 'New reduced and zero tillage options for increasing the productivity and sustainability of rice-wheat systems in Indo-Gangetic plains of South Asia', Paper presented at the ISTRO 2000 Conference, 1–6 July 2000, Fort Worth, Texas

Inter-Governmental Panel on Climate Change (IPCC) (2001) *Climate Change 2001: Impacts, Adaptation and Vulnerability*, Working Group II Report, IPCC, WMO, Switzerland

International Water Management Institute (IWMI) (2000) *Water Supply and Demand in 2025*, IWMI, Colombo, Sri Lanka

Jurdell, F and Svensson, M (1998) 'Making blue water green: The viability of small-scale earth dams for supplementary irrigation of cereals in semi-arid Africa (Kenya)', *Minor Field Studies*, No 42, International Office, Swedish University of Agricultural Sciences, Uppsala

Klaij, M C and Vachaud, G (1992) 'Seasonal water balance of a sandy soil in Niger cropped with pearl millet', *Agricultural Water Management*, vol 21, pp313–330

Klohn, Wulf (1998) Personal communication, FAO, Rome

Lawrence-Brown, D (1999) Personal communication, Monsanto Central Africa Inc, Agricultural Sector, Nairobi

Lovell, C et al (1996) *Small Scale Irrigation Using Collector Wells Pilot Project – Zimbabwe*, Final Report, October 1992–January 1996, Institute of Hydrology, Wallingford, UK

Lundqvist, J and Falkenmark, M (2000) 'Towards hydrosolidarity: Focus on upstream-downstream conflicts and interests', editorial in *Water International*, vol 25, no 2, pp168–171

L'vovich, M I (1979) *World Water Resources and their Future*, Litho Crafters, Chelsea, MI (translated by American Geophysical Union; translation edited by R L Nace)

Matlon, P J (1990) 'Improving productivity in sorghum and pearl millet in semi-arid Africa', *Food Research Institute Studies*, vol 22, no 1, pp1–43

McCalla, A F (1994) *Agriculture and Food Needs to 2025: Why We Should Be Concerned*, Consultative Group on International Agricultural Research (CGIAR), Washington, DC

Middleton, N and Thomas, D (eds) (1992) *World Atlas of Desertification*, 2nd edition, UNEP, London

Ministry of Water Affairs and Forestry (1998) *National Water Bill*, as amended by the Portfolio Committee on Agriculture, Water Affairs and Forestry (National Assembly), no [B 34B – 98], Republic of South Africa

Mwalley, J (1999) Personal communication, SCAPA Programme, Ministry of Agriculture, Arusha, Tanzania

Ngigi, S N et al (2000) *Technical Evaluation of Low-Head Drip Irrigation Technologies in Kenya*, Research report, Nairobi University and the International Water Management Institute (IWMI), Nairobi

Nicholson, S E (1978) 'Climatic variations in the Sahel and other African regions during the past five centuries', *Journal of Arid Environments*, vol 1, pp3–24

Oldreive, B (1993) *Conservation Farming for Communal, Small-Scale Resettlement and Co-operative Farmers of Zimbabwe*, Farm management handbook, Mazongororo Paper Converters Ltd, Zimbabwe

Penning de Vries, F W T and Djitèye, M A (eds) (1991) *La Productivité des Pâturages Sahéliens: Une Étude des Sols, des Végétations et de l'Exploitation de Cette Ressource Naturelle*, PUDOC, Wageningen, p522

Postel, S L, Daily, G C and Ehlich, P R (1996) 'Human appropriation of renewable fresh water', *Science*, vol 271, pp785–788

Quinones, Marco (2000) Personal communication, Sasakawa Global 2000, Addis Ababa, Ethiopia

Raskin, P (1997) *Comprehensive Assessment of the Freshwater Resources of the World. Water Futures: Assessment of Long-range Patterns and Problems*, Stockholm Environmental Institute, Stockholm, p75

Rockström, J (2001) 'Green water security for the food makers of tomorrow: Windows of opportunity in drought-prone savannahs', *Water Science and Technology*, vol 43, no 4, pp71–78

Rockström, J (2000) *Green Water Security for the Food Makers of Tomorrow: Windows of Opportunity in Drought Prone Savannahs*, Proceedings from the 10th Stockholm Water Symposium, 14–17 August, keynote address (forthcoming), Stockholm International Water Institute (SIWI), Stockholm

Rockström, J (1997) *On-Farm Agrohydrological Analysis of the Sahelian Yield Crisis: Rainfall Partitioning, Soil Nutrients and Water Use Efficiency of Pearl Millet*, PhD thesis in Natural Resources Management, Department of Systems Ecology, Stockholm University, Stockholm

Rockström, J and Falkenmark, M (2000) 'Semi-arid crop production from a hydrological perspective. Gap between potential and actual yields', *Critical Reviews in Plant Science*, vol 19, no 4, pp319–346

Rockström, J et al (1999) 'Linkages among water vapour flows, food production, and terrestrial ecosystem services', *Conservation Ecology*, vol 3, no2, pp1–28

Rockström, J and Shone, G (2000) 'Project document for upscaling of rainwater harvesting learning sites in Machakos and Makueni districts, Kenya', Workplan for Year 2001, Regional Land Management Unit (RELMA), Nairobi

Sanchez, P A et al (1997) 'Soil fertility replenishment in Africa: An investment in natural resource capital', *Replenishing Soil Fertility in Africa*, SSSA Special Publication No 51, pp1–46

Savenije, H (2000) 'Water scarcity indicators: The deception of the numbers', *Physics and Chemistry of the Earth (B)*, vol 25, no 3, pp199–204

Savenije, H (1995) 'New definitions for moisture recycling and the relation with land-use changes in the Sahel', *Journal of Hydrology*, vol 167, pp57–78

Shiklomanov, I A (2000) 'Appraisal and assessment of world water resources', *Water International*, vol 25, no 1, pp11–32

Shiklomanov, I A (1997) 'Assessment of water resources and water availability of the world', Background report to the Comprehensive Assessment of the Freshwater Resources of the World, Stockholm Environment Institute/World Meteorological Organization, Geneva

Sidikou, A H (1974) 'Sédéndarité et mobilité entre Niger et Zgaret', *Études Nigériennes*, no 34, Niamey, Niger

Soil Science Society of America (SSSA) (1987) *Glossary of Soil Science Terms*, SSSA, Madison, WI

Stewart, J I (1988) *Response Farming in Rain-fed Agriculture*, The Wharf Foundation Press, Davis, California

Stockholm Water Front (2000) No 2, Stockholm International Water Institute (SIWI), Stockholm

United Nations (UN) (1997) *Comprehensive Assessment of the Freshwater Resources of the World*, World Meteorological Organization (WMO), Geneva

Vertessy, R A and Bessard Y (1999) 'Conversion of grasslands to plantations: anticipating the negative hydrological effects' in Eldridge, D and Freudenberger D (eds) *Proceedings of VI International Rangeland Congress*, 19–23 July 1999, Townsville, pp679–683

Vogel, H, Nyagumbo, I and Olsen, K (1994) 'Effects of tied ridging and mulch ripping on water conservation in maize production on sandveld soils', *Der Tropenlandwirt*, Journal of Agriculture in the tropics and subtropics, vol 3–4, pp33–44

Walter, R et al (1999) United Nations Environment Programme, United Nations University, www.unep.org/unep/per/ipa/pressrel/r03-1799.001

Chapter 6

Recycling and reuse of 'derivative water' under conditions of scarcity and competition

CHRISTOPHER A SCOTT

INTRODUCTION

Around the world, but particularly in regions facing water scarcity, there is rapidly growing dependence on non-conventional 'derivative' water sources. The restricted access of the poor and marginalized groups to primary freshwater resources (runoff and naturally occurring groundwater, or 'blue water') has often required innovative use on their part of other water sources, including water reuse and recycling, as well as water harvesting to convert runoff to groundwater. At the same time, there has been increasing scientific research and investment attention paid to the recovery and recycling of degraded water, specifically through desalination or direct use of brackish water and groundwater recharge (for example, soil-aquifer treatment). Many of these practices are increasingly being mainstreamed. In fact, future integrated water resources management will increasingly have to depend on the successful sustainable replacement, at least partially, of more conventional water sources with derivative supplies.

The approach of our 'peer' generation to water management has largely been supply driven, based on major capital investment and centralized, bureaucratic management institutions that grapple with environmental and social issues (particularly resettlement and indigenous people's rights) associated with water resources development. Nevertheless, there is recent welcome recognition of demand-side options. A significant attraction of derivative water is that its very use helps to overcome the demand–supply debacle. As options that impose high access costs (social, institutional, financial and environmental), derivative sources internalize the need for conservation. This chapter aims to open the debate on the use of non-conventional water sources by addressing how relevant they are compared to primary water sources, as well as a range of questions related to access. Cross-sectoral linkages have confounded conventional management approaches and water multipliers despite the fact that water used for human purposes follows cycles, as in its natural state. While water recycling and reuse may not currently appeal to increasingly consumer-oriented societies, they will become central to water management for a variety of reasons related to the need to internalize the changes and costs associated with particular water uses, and to growing scarcity and competition for water worldwide. This is particularly the case in arid and semi-arid regions with moderate-to-high water demand.

BRIDGING THE SCARCITY DIVIDE: RECYCLING SECONDARY OR 'DERIVATIVE' WATER

Throughout the world over the past century, the withdrawal of primary water from surface or groundwater sources, used once and disposed of – with, or more frequently without, treatment – increased at rates outpacing growth in human population, economic output and the ability to handle 'waste' water and waste loads. At the same time, rapid growth in water use effectively committed a large share of developed water resources to existing or short-term future uses. As well, numerous countries face 'economic water scarcity', where investment and infrastructure are inadequate to utilize water that may physically be available. In other cases, nations have negotiated access to water originating outside of their national boundaries and have fixed future supplies (see Chapter 9). As a result, many regions and nations are faced with little or no prospects for growth in water supply with the assumption that social and economic development will be constrained. In numerous instances, the supply-side paradigm of a single use of primary water has reached or significantly exceeded its limits. The strategy from within the prevailing paradigm is to devise innovative ways to augment supply.

A significantly more useful approach, however, is to drop the strict definitions of 'supply' and 'available water resources', on the one hand, in counterbalance or imbalance with 'demand' and 'water use', on the other. There are ranges of practices that do not fit neatly on one side or the other of this artifice, but bridge the divide. Because these practices are not based on primary water – fresh surface or groundwater withdrawals – let us refer to them as secondary sources or *derivative* water. Included here are brackish water use through desalination or direct use, water harvesting for groundwater recharge (surface water impoundment remains a primary use) and reuse of urban sewage effluent and agricultural drainage. Increasing use of, and demand for, derivative water is required to meet the undeniable needs of societies and ecosystems for water. Appropriate derivative-use practices will eventually help to shape a new definition of 'water security' given that multiple uses are linked, that costs and benefits are shared, and that access to derivative sources is not yet as restrictive as for primary sources.

Within the broader conception of derivative sources are several that, while they hold considerable promise, remain essentially supply-side approaches – specifically, desalination of brackish water and water harvesting, which will be examined briefly here. There are limits to growth for the widespread adoption of multiple productive uses of water from both of these 'sources', although for different reasons. Desalination entails high energy costs and brine management challenges, while watershed-scale water harvesting (as opposed to in-situ plot- or field-scale moisture conservation) in arid and semi-arid conditions may simply translocate finite water supplies – 'robbing Peter to pay Paul'. There is still little hard evidence to test this translocation hypothesis. Even assuming that it does occur, it is a beneficial practice under the following conditions:

- if runoff would otherwise flow to saline water bodies;
- if runoff would otherwise flow to downstream water bodies and evaporate;
- if upstream use is better distributed among poor smallholders, compared with downstream use by users with other economic or water options.

The practice with the greatest scope for future growth in water resource and economic terms is water reuse, which will be the focus of subsequent discussion and analysis in this chapter.

Salt water, pure water: The prospects for desalination

The dictum 'the salt of the Earth' refers to a person, generally, who is reliable, constant, to be counted on. The same could be said of dissolved salts in water; they are inevitable, unavoidable. Yet, the past generation has seen impressive gains made in desalination technology, particularly with respect to unit costs, which are as low as US$0.50 to US$0.80 per cubic metre (m^3) for sea water and US$0.20 to US$0.35 per m^3 for brackish water, and falling (Semiat, 2000). Even under operational conditions with the need to include finance, maintenance and related costs, the unit costs have dropped considerably. The current cost that the private sector is willing to put in a desalination plant and assume all risks over a 30-year period (including actual energy costs) is in the range of US$0.70 to US$0.75 per m^3. This may drop to around US$0.50 per m^3 in the next 10 to 15 years (Asit Biswas, pers comm).[1] Issues associated with financing, particularly of urban water infrastructure, are discussed in Chapter 11.

Even lower unit costs of US$0.33 per m^3 are possible under commercial production conditions with 40,000 milligrams (mg) per litre total dissolved solids in and 240mg per litre out – using Rapid Spray Distillation© (RSD©, AquaSonics International, http://waterbank.com/Aquasonics%20WaterTech%20Article.htm).[2] While such assertions must still be verified, this technology is reported here as an example of the continuing rapid development in desalination technology with further prospects for lowering costs.

Desalination remains very attractive, for example, when compared with the costs of developing (and treating) new primary sources of water. In fact, as surface water development gets increasingly expensive, in part as a result of increased recognition of the social and environmental costs of large infrastructure, on-demand desalination will become increasingly mainstreamed. Where captive or inexpensive energy sources are readily available, desalination may already be a preferred technology for water supply. For this reason, desalination has been adopted widely in water-scarce, energy-rich countries in the Middle East. The Gulf Cooperation Council (GCC) states had a combined installed desalination capacity of 2.14 billion m^3 per year in 1997, with actual output of 1.7 billion m^3 (Al-Rashed and Sherif, 2000) that represents a large share of the world's desalination production. Still, this is largely reserved for drinking and industrial purposes, with costs rendering desalination water too expensive for agricultural, landscaping or environmental purposes. It is interesting to note that even in the unique water-scarce and energy-abundant conditions in GCC countries, the annual volume of desalination is scarcely comparable to the volume of treated effluent, and is less than annual groundwater extraction by a factor of ten.[3]

A number of factors raise significant questions about the mainstreaming of desalination for general water-supply augmentation purposes. Cost has been addressed earlier; this is generally cited as the primary obstacle to more widespread adoption of desalination. Additionally, two important environmental problems are associated with desalination technology, specifically carbon dioxide (CO_2) release from the enormous generation of energy it requires, and the production of concentrated brine that poses a host of management problems of its own. At the small and, to a lesser extent, medium scales, these issues can be externalized. However, when considering options for massive implementation that would be required in order for desalination to make a significant dent in water scarcity, environmental impacts must be internalized.

Harvesting new water or appropriating a resource already claimed?

Water harvesting represents a critical though often overlooked water use strategy practiced in a wide range of geographical, climatic, social and economic contexts (Oweis et al, 1999; Agarwal and Narain, 1997; Scott, 1994).[4] This is distinct from, but overlaps with, in-situ rainwater management as described by Rockström in Chapter 5. Given their dispersed nature, relatively small size and suitability under resource-poor conditions (which are not likely to attract significant external support or imposed management), water harvesting systems are often locally managed as common property resources, with major implications for poverty eradication and equitable resource access.

The fact that catchment and downstream water use (irrigation, livestock, domestic water) are collectively managed, however, does not a priori ensure equity (Kerr et al, 2000; Ahluwalia, 1998; Meinzen-Dick and Zwarteveen, 1998). Clearly, a combination of factors shapes the equity of water harvesting resource management – factors that are both specific to the resource and users group (water scarcity, social stratification and organization) and generic to the larger context in which these are embedded (water competition, government intervention and economic forces). Upper-catchment resource use is linked to the timing, supply and quality of water harvested; however, as common property rights may be insecure (often ill defined spatially and variable by season), the opportunities for collective action to address resource degradation may be limited. Shen, in Chapter 8, provides a more in-depth treatment of water rights.

In the context of water-scarce river basins, where demand for water exceeds supply, and 'closed basins', where there is no outflow of water that is not already committed to downstream uses, there may be upstream–downstream trade-offs associated with water harvesting extraction at the watershed scale as defined in this chapter. Other basins with apparently abundant water resources often face dry-season scarcity, such as the Ganges-Brahmaputra-Meghna (see Chapter 10). 'Dry' water harvesting results when water is simply translocated within the watershed. It is stored upstream instead of flowing to downstream reservoirs, as opposed to 'wet' water harvesting, which generates 'new' water.

More distributed water use resulting from dispersed upstream sources certainly has implications for equity (the poor often farm marginal hillside land), productivity (supplemental upland irrigation usually generates more 'crop per drop' than incremental full lowland irrigation) and water resource (gravity is conserved by storing water at higher elevation). It may not, however, create 'new' water, which is why this form of water harvesting is defined as 'derivative water' in this chapter. There is still a research gap in identifying which practices (with clearly defined soil, climatic and scale conditions) represent 'wet' or 'dry' water harvesting.

The recharge of shallow groundwater is a major positive outcome of water harvesting, although this is often an unintended benefit. Shallow groundwater is accessible to anyone with the means to extract it, and invariably benefits domestic and household water consumers who rely on hand pumps or other means to extract shallow groundwater. Kemper, in Chapter 7, indicates the complexities of the major challenge represented by groundwater management. However, given that most water harvesting systems rely on relatively small surface storage ponds with shallow depths that are rapidly 'sealed' through sediment accumulation, evaporative losses may be high in comparison with groundwater recharge through induced infiltration (Scott and Flores-López, submitted).

As demand for water increases downstream, political and economic pressure may be brought to bear in an attempt to limit upstream water harvesting, even though its impact in reducing peak flood flows is significantly lower than its ability to reduce low flows that would otherwise reach downstream diversions or storages. As a result, further research is required to ascertain whether water harvesting, indeed, captures 'new' water, a process that must be assessed from a basin-wide perspective with specific emphasis on inter-sectorial competition among agricultural, urban, industrial and environmental uses. Because water harvesting systems are invariably small and dispersed, it is unlikely that they are subject to basin-level water allocation agreements. However, as rising demand in the face of constant supply drives river basins increasingly towards 'closure', there will, no doubt, be more attention paid to water use and management in water harvesting systems.

How reassuring is the assured rapid growth of water reuse?

The third important set of derivative water use practices is water reuse. Of course, recycling within specific water-use sectors has been commonplace. For instance, 'excess' or 'wasted' irrigation water is frequently recaptured as runoff or drainage for further irrigation use, or it percolates to groundwater for subsequent extraction. Similarly, industry has attempted to recycle water primarily to save lost chemical or other process reagents for which water acts as a solvent and for reasons of enforcement of point-source pollution. However, considerable volumes of water are transferred inter-sectorally as 'wastewater'.[5]

The principal transfers occur from urban users who generate sewage to agricultural users for whom this represents a resource. As urban populations and the rates of both water supply, as well as sewerage coverage, around the world grow, the volumes of urban effluent generated are increasing dramatically. The 1998 estimated volume had surpassed 450 cubic kilometres (km^3) (Population Information Program, 1998); however, the timing and location of effluent discharges cause a fraction of this to actually be available for reuse. At modest assumptions of growth in population and coverage, the volumes available for reuse can be expected to rise.

Much of the current effluent production occurs in countries with economies capable of financing sewage collection and, therefore, adequate treatment. However, much of the growth will undoubtedly take place in developing countries with limited financial resources to permit adequate treatment, if any whatsoever.[6] These are many of the same regions facing water scarcity with the pressing twin needs for drinking water to satisfy rapid (mostly urban) population growth and for irrigation to meet food security goals. In water-scarce conditions (currently experienced in much of the Middle East and Southern Africa, and projected to grow in parts of South, Central and East Asia and sub-Saharan Africa), the drinking water–irrigation water–wastewater triad is likely to generate increasing trade-offs. The often illusory search for 'win–win' solutions will perforce shift to 'win–hold' or even 'hold–lose' strategies, unless appropriate safeguards are implemented to counter the clear human health and environmental risks associated with the practice. As a result, the practice of water reuse is assured to increase dramatically.

There are clear risks, principally to human health and environmental quality, associated with the practice of using untreated effluent. As will be discussed in this chapter, some water managers take a cautionary view under the assumption that restrictions and bans on irrigation with untreated effluent can effectively reign in the practice. Experience would suggest otherwise, as farmers in countries such as Mexico, Pakistan and Jordan (see case descriptions later in this chapter), as well as Palestine, Senegal, Ghana, Vietnam, and Brazil (Medeiros-Leitão, 2001, pers comm) are essentially lining up to irrigate with semi-treated or untreated effluent. A realistic approach is called for – one in which the risks of the practice can be effectively minimized while the benefits to society of reduced demand for primary sources of water coupled with agricultural production can be realized.

Effluent irrigation: Resource and nutrient multiplier or health and environmental threat?

Irrigation with urban effluent is widespread and has been documented in over 50 countries (Scott et al, 2000). In many cases, it is an undeniably important source of livelihood and supports the rural or peri-urban economy (Faruqui, 2000). Rough estimates suggest that at least 20 million hectares (ha) worldwide are irrigated using partially diluted or undiluted effluent. The growing nature of the practice is a result of the direct benefits accrued to farmers, who have insecure access to primary water sources as alternatives. There are a number of clear societal benefits, too. In general, effluent irrigation:

- reuses water, as has been the primary thrust of the discussion on derivative water in this chapter;
- represents a highly reliable supply of water, available throughout the year and in proximity to urban markets;
- conserves nutrients by putting them to beneficial use, which reduces the use and costs of agricultural fertilizer inputs;
- adds organic matter that may improve soil structure and tilth;
- reduces direct pollution of surface receiving water, which would further degrade water quality and render it unsuitable for a range of subsequent uses;[7]
- represents a low-cost option for land application of urban waste that, through conventional treatment and sludge management, might otherwise be land applied.

Nevertheless, there are considerable risks associated with intensive and prolonged irrigation using untreated or partially treated urban effluents:

- health risks for the irrigators and communities through prolonged exposure (see case descriptions later in this chapter);
- health risks for the consumers of produce irrigated with effluent, particularly vegetables and greens, grown in or on the ground, a practice that significantly increases their direct contact with irrigation water;[8]

- contamination of surface and groundwater, often the drinking water source for the same communities who irrigate with effluent;
- build-up of chemical pollutants in the soil (salinity, heavy metals, etc);
- creation of habitats for disease vectors, particularly mosquitoes, by creating year-round pools of standing water.

As urban populations and rates of water supply and sewerage coverage increase worldwide, so will the supply of urban effluent. It is inconceivable in the context of growing water scarcity and competition that effluent irrigation will not follow suit, despite efforts to ban or restrict its use. The value of the water and nutrients is simply too high for farmers to forego the opportunity, despite the risks that farmers themselves acknowledge. In many instances, urban effluent itself is a highly competed for resource among vying individuals or collective groups of aspiring irrigators. This raises serious social, economic and legal issues of access, equity and allocation rights (Buechler and Scott, 2000).

Prevailing wisdom would suggest that, given effluent's connotation as 'dirty' or 'impure', cultural and religious barriers might prevent its reuse, particularly in traditions where notions of ritual purity are highly articulated – Islam and Hinduism. Fundamental to this issue, however, is the presence and level of sewage treatment. Adherents of both faiths (in the Middle East, Pakistan and India) use untreated effluent, although religious authorities do not condone the practice. On the other hand, the Council of Leading Islamic Scholars in Saudi Arabia issued a *fatwa* in 1978 that treated effluent may be used for ritual ablution and for drinking, provided that treatment is adequate to eliminate any health risk (Faruqui et al, 2001). For agricultural reuse, there is no contradiction, then, between Orthodox Islam, or the cultural practices of many Muslims, and the World Health Organization (WHO) guidelines on wastewater use (WHO, 1989; Naser Faruqui, pers comm).

There are a number of difficult policy implications of this overlooked resource. Which official agency has jurisdiction over urban effluent – the municipal authority responsible for releasing it; the irrigation agency that oversees most other irrigation water use; the sanitary/public health authorities? This and other ticklish questions raised previously can no longer be avoided, as has been the tendency among many water managers with regard to the practice itself. They will not go away by simply ignoring them; instead, the issues need to be put on the table and discussed openly to devise creative solutions and alternatives. The costs and risks are simply too high to do otherwise, while the benefits to farmers and society are too tangible.

MANAGEMENT AND POLICY OPTIONS FOR EFFLUENT IRRIGATION

It should be clarified at the outset that irrigation with untreated effluent is not a substitute for treatment. Instead, a range of management approaches and policy alternatives need further investigation and discussion based on the realization that the conventional model of treatment under centralized sewage collection presents huge investment challenges in most developing countries. Some options have already found articulation in countries with longer backgrounds in effluent irrigation, while others are proposed here and need to be seriously considered. The recommendation to ban irrigation using untreated effluent should be rejected as unrealistic and untenable (because of the very direct benefits outlined previously). It is not the most optimal way to reduce risks even if strict enforcement were possible, given that the degradation of the receiving waters would greatly increase risks for downstream uses – human and ecological. Land application of urban waste, whether through treatment and sludge spreading or through effluent irrigation, remains a critical alternative to widespread water pollution.

There are four principal options for effluent management, described below, while the fifth is really a source mitigation approach that would reduce both effluent volumes and their constituent concentrations through practices such as dry sanitation.[9] While this fifth alternative may be the ultimate solution, it is not feasible for widespread adoption in the foreseeable future. Therefore, it is prudent to advocate an evolutionary approach under the realization that water will continue to be used for its solvent properties and that water-based hygiene practice is intrinsic to human nature.

The four principal options for effluent management, from least to greatest feasibility (in my opinion), are:

1   Strict prohibition and enforcement – 'just say NO!'[10]
2   The status quo – 'turn a blind eye'.
3   Beneficial use without treatment, seeking to minimize risks.
4   Appropriate treatment followed by regulated reuse with flexible standards linked to specific reuse.

'Just say NO!'

A common reaction on the part of many water managers convinced of the need to treat all effluent to secondary level or better, but when confronted with the prospect of untreated effluent irrigation, is to recommend banning the practice entirely. As discussed earlier, this appears unworkable and generates grave problems of its own. This approach is rejected as untenable and will not be dealt with here.

'Turn a blind eye'

The most common reaction, which is not really an option per se but a deeply pervasive view on the practice of effluent irrigation, is abject indifference. Many water managers, decision-makers and the general public simply do not care – or it comes as a shock – that untreated effluent is being applied to crops at the very margins of, and sometimes within, city limits. Again, this practice is old and pervasive and it should come as no surprise that it will continue to grow. Ignoring or wishing it away is neither realistic nor responsible. It may be, however, in my view, a somewhat more helpful starting position than the strict ban and enforcement approach, which simply transfers risks and generates wider pollution-management problems. The challenge with indifferent or uncomfortable managers or decision-makers is getting them to take the issue seriously. Effluent reuse clearly is serious business for the reasons outlined and must be dealt with openly.

Beneficial use without treatment

This alternative offers wide latitude but must not be confused with indifference. A set of supporting activities are necessary on the part of the water management agency, with the onus placed preferably on the municipal sewage authority or utility company, but with support from irrigation, public health and environmental agencies. These include water quality monitoring with full public disclosure, as well as identification and separation with the requirement for reduction or treatment of harmful point-source discharges (particularly industries discharging heavy metals, toxic pollutants, carcinogenic substances, or other contaminants linked to specific health and environmental risks). Beneficial use of effluent for irrigation requires some oversight through phytosanitary controls, public health monitoring and environmental quality protection.

Appropriate treatment with regulated reuse

The precautionary approach – followed, for example, in California – of treating effluent to tertiary levels does not appear feasible for financial reasons or necessary on epidemiological grounds. Nevertheless, secondary treatment is necessary, particularly where industrial effluents are involved; but domestic/residential sewage may only need to be treated to the primary level for agricultural reuse. As a result, the prescribed treatment and standards for effluent water quality should be linked to the specific reuse. For example, the Mexican regulations (Government of Mexico, 1996) stipulate maximum allowable limits for basic contaminants by use class and by receiving water bodies that serve as the source for that subsequent use. This approach is based on sound principles, but could easily become constrained by a confusing array of receiving waters and subsequent use classes, making for loopholes and impossible enforcement. At a minimum, agricultural reuse of effluent discharged to irrigation canals or natural water bodies requires effective standards.

Israel has adopted principles (Government of Israel, undated), if not official standards, that link effluent quality (principally biochemical oxygen demand and suspended solids) with the subsequent specific use, and require that barriers be used to limit exposure to health risks. Barriers (two to three required, some obligatory, depending on effluent quality and crop) include sand filtration, disinfection, setback distances, plastic ground cover, sub-surface irrigation, etc. Specific crops that require no barriers after primary effluent treatment include cotton, fodder, crops dried at least 60 days in the sun after the last irrigation (cereals), woody crops and grass with no public contact during cultivation. Other crop types, including citrus, nuts, deciduous and tropical fruits, require two barriers for high-quality (disinfected) effluents, and two to three barriers for oxidation pond effluents.

CASE DESCRIPTIONS OF PLANNED AND UNPLANNED REUSE

Agricultural reuse requires supervision and monitoring. A workable planned approach, even beneficial use without treatment, is preferable to unplanned effluent irrigation ('turn a blind eye'). Planned use involves:

*   primary treatment or better;
*   blending with freshwater;
*   crop restrictions – for example, crops not for human consumption (fodder, trees, etc) or crops that are not consumed raw (grains, etc);
*   green belt or landscaping applications;
*   use-specific water-quality standards (as distinct from absolute standards).

In contrast, unplanned reuse remains the norm in most developing countries, with a range of practices characterized by:

*   domestic sewage and industrial effluent 'disposal' in drains or natural waterways;
*   no treatment;
*   unregulated, unrestricted irrigation of all types of crops;
*   little or no monitoring or management of health or environmental risks.

The implications of various planned, semi-planned or unplanned agricultural reuse schemes will shed some light on the trade-offs involved.

Mexico: Planned and unplanned reuse

Of the 7.3km^3 of effluent generated annually in Mexico, 5.5km^3 are sewered, while only 0.53km^3 are adequately treated; the remaining 6.8km^3 are discharged into the environment without treatment (CNA, 1997). An estimated 91 per cent of this volume is generated inland in arid to sub-humid conditions with potential demand for irrigation water, suggesting that some 200,000 to 250,000ha are under effluent irrigation in Mexico. The practice has grown around a number of Mexican cities and towns. Cirelli (1998) reports on the social and political dynamics of effluent irrigation outside of San Luís Potosí, where effluent users have secured rights through a series of presidential decrees.

Mexico City is the largest urban population in the world living in a closed hydrologic basin, with no natural outflow to the sea. It also discharges effluent to the largest single agricultural reuse system in the world. Of the raw sewage

Table 6.1 *Effluent flow and its uses, Mexico City*

Source/fate	Flow (m³ per second)	Comments
Wastewater generated in Mexico City	45	194 litres per day per capita. At 70% return rate, water supply is 260 litres per day per capita.
Primary treatment for irrigating parks/green areas within Mexico City	10	Could irrigate up to 10,000ha of land, but may be used to maintain wetlands and 'floating gardens'.
Primary and secondary treatment for Texcoco Lake reclamation	1.0 ~ 1.5	Reclamation of sodic soils, reforestation and Nabor Carillo Lake.
Tertiary treatment for animals and/or groundwater injection, Texcoco Lake	0.05	Sedimentation, flocculation, filtration (sand, activated carbon) and chlorination.
Untreated wastewater	34	Discharged to Tula Irrigation District (Hidalgo State) through a network of tunnels, one > 60km.

from Mexico City, 1.5km³ are estimated to be reused for irrigation every year (approximately 45m³ per second), far and away the largest single user in the world (Khouri et al, 1994). Tunnels – both historical and modern – are used to reduce flood risks and to carry effluent out of the basin, where it is used for semi-restricted irrigation of 100,000ha in Tula and Alfajayucan irrigation districts, principally of fodder (alfalfa) and grain (maize and wheat). Not coincidentally, this remains the largest irrigation district in the country whose management has yet to be fully transferred from public (Comisión Nacional del Agua – CNA) control to the users. The high land (and water) values in Tula precipitated armed confrontation between rival communities in 1999.

Table 6.1 lists the breakdown of the approximately 45m³ per second of effluent flow generated in Mexico City.

Other cities in Mexico have unplanned agricultural reuse of urban effluent. Scott et al (2000) assessed the costs and benefits of unplanned effluent irrigation outside the city of Guanajuato. Multiple recycling loops were observed in a short 20km stretch of the Guanajuato River before drainage flows entered the Purísima Reservoir, the first 'official' or primary source of water on the river that supplies water to an established irrigation district. The city plans to treat and sell its effluent to a potential buyer who plans to build a golf course. This raises a number of difficult questions on the water rights of farmers who have been using the water for generations. Table 6.2 presents annual nitrogen (N) and phosphorus (P) loads applied in effluent irrigation, at measured irrigation volumes, and effluent total N and P concentrations, before and after the proposed treatment plant. The bottom lines of the table compare per-hectare applications with alfalfa's N and P requirements. Effluent treatment would leave a considerable phosphorus deficit for alfalfa.

Table 6.2 *Nutrient implications of treatment, Guanajuato, Mexico*

	Untreated		Treated		Percentage change	
Canal	N (kg)	P (kg)	N (kg)	P (kg)		
San José de Cervera	45,483	7553	3556	711		
Santa Catarina	63,865	10,308	11,397	1698		
	N (kg/ha)	P (kg/ha)	N (kg/ha)	P (kg/ha)	N (%)	P (%)
San José de Cervera	455	76	36	7	-92.2	-90.6
Santa Catarina	1597	258	285	42	-82.2	-83.5
Alfalfa requirements	88	115	88	115		

The total annual value of effluent irrigation was estimated to be approximately US$135 per hectare per year, while the agronomically usable nutrient value represented US$0.02 per m³ of effluent. Table 6.3 presents an assessment of nutrient replacement costs for farmers switching from free effluent irrigation to commercial fertilizers, including application costs. It should be noted that Guanajuato may not be representative of many other cities for its lack of heavy manufacturing or processing industries.

Table 6.3 *Fertilizer replacement costs, Guanajuato, Mexico*

N source	Percentage N	Cost (M$/50 kg)[i]	Cost (US$/kg N)
Urea	46.0	87.50	0.40
Ammonium nitrate	33.5	82.50	0.52
Ammonium sulphate	20.5	36.50	0.37
Average			0.43

P Source	Percentage P	Cost (M$/50 kg)	Cost (US$/kg P)
Super triple	46.0	112.50	0.51
Simple sulphate	18.0	47.50	0.56
Di-ammonium phosphate (DAP)	46.0	137.50	0.63
Mono-ammonium phosphate (MAP)	52.0	140.00	0.57
Average			0.57
Application cost, combined N+P (US$/ha)			31.58

Note: i The exchange rate of the Mexican peso (M$) was M$9.50 per US dollar in 1999 at the time of the study.

Pakistan: Semi-planned reuse

Researchers of the International Water Management Institute are studying effluent irrigation in Haroonabad, Pakistan (van der Hoek et al, 2002). Because of its value to farmers, effluent is auctioned in bulk to the highest bidder, who subsequently retails it to farmers. Farmers have been organizing to bid for effluent themselves, thus cutting out the intermediary. Unrestricted cropping permits vegetable cultivation, which leads to significant health risks for producers and consumers alike. Additionally, irrigation canals or shallow groundwater, which is essentially canal water, serve as the source of domestic and drinking water for numerous rural communities in Pakistan, as in other countries. As a result, effluent irrigation increases the risk levels of gastroenteric disease outbreaks, although a major determinant of diarrhoea disease was found to be water handling and storage practices within the household.

Jordan: Planned and semi-planned reuse

Like neighbouring Israel and Palestine, future water resource demands in Jordan must increasingly be met through effluent reuse. The city of Amman's sewage is treated at the Khirbit As Samra wastewater treatment plant and discharged to Wadi Zarqa, where it is retained in the King Talal Reservoir.[11] There is some lift irrigation from the *wadi* above the reservoir; but the bulk of the water is released downstream to the Jordan Valley, where reuse is essentially semi-planned. Two principal constraints make this a difficult prospect: salinity and agricultural marketing.

Treated effluent in Jordan is significantly higher in total dissolved solids (TDS) and biochemical oxygen demand (BOD), as well as other contaminants, than in water-abundant countries. This is because of low per-capita water supply rates, which themselves have increasing TDS at an average 580 parts per million (ppm) in 1998, with more or less constant waste loads (Nazzal et al, 2000; Al-Kharabsheh, 1999; Government of Jordan, 1998). For example, Khirbit As Samra effluent has approximately 1200ppm TDS, while Wadi Dulail TDS is as high as 5000ppm. These levels limit the range of crops that can be irrigated. Alfalfa is a common choice, given that it is tolerant of high TDS and because humans do not consume it. However, alfalfa is also deep rooted and water consumptive. Tree crops may be suitable for irrigation with treated effluent, as the fruit does not come in contact with the water. However, apricots, peaches and other stone fruit do not tolerate high chloride levels.

CONCLUSIONS: NEXT GENERATION ISSUES FOR DERIVATIVE WATER USE

This chapter has provided an overview of the use of derivative or secondary sources of water. These are not really 'unconventional'. In fact, many have been, and are being, used conventionally around the world, particularly rainwater harvesting and effluent reuse. Together with desalination, however, they represent important examples of water resources that might otherwise not be used productively. As a result, they are important in addressing water scarcity. The review of water harvesting and desalination suggests that the scope for significant growth may be limited; to the contrary, urban effluent generation is growing rapidly and will continue to do so into the future.

- Under what conditions can the benefits of effluent irrigation be accepted without undue damage to the environment and public health?
- How can unplanned use be converted to safe, low-cost planned use?
- Effluent reuse standards must be tailored to the specific use.
- There is a need for sensitivity mapping of soils and groundwater in order to determine where the practice is appropriate and where it is not.

It has been shown that derivative water use will grow rapidly in the years to come; however, this is not without risks and trade-offs of its own. Desalination holds considerable promise as unit costs decrease dramatically. Nevertheless, environmental costs associated with brine and CO_2 production from this energy-intensive practice will have to be internalized. Techniques for 'wet' water harvesting that capture water that would otherwise be lost to evaporation must be identified, contextualized and tested. The potential to increase productivity and equity appear to be great, particularly if downstream hydrologic impacts are minimized. Finally, reuse of inadequately treated or untreated effluent must be addressed using innovative technical and institutional approaches. Crop restrictions represent one practical step toward converting unplanned reuse to beneficial use; this has been applied successfully in a number of countries. While derivative use of water represents one future solution to water scarcity and security, adequate management will be critical. This chapter has reviewed a number of the relevant issues that must be considered.

NOTES

1   Commercial bids by the TotalFinaElf group for a desalination plant in Kuwait are said to be at US$0.67 per m^3.
2   To achieve these costs, the process relies on waste heat from power stations, landfills, wastewater treatment plants, refineries, cement kilns, etc. RSD can use off-peak power for production or flared natural gas (William Turner, pers comm). In general, the use of waste energy has reduced the share of energy cost in relation to total desalination cost, as in the example of the Tampa Bay, Florida, proposal.
3   Groundwater extraction is estimated to exceed recharge in the GCC countries by a factor of approximately six. While groundwater exploitation is a separate issue, it is illustrative to note that despite the GCC states' unique advantages in pursuing desalination, it is deemed expensive or restrictive enough to continue overabstracting groundwater.
4   *Water harvesting* here refers to the capture, diversion, storage and subsequent use of surface runoff generated in watersheds. Although increasing attention is being

paid to in-situ soil moisture management at the plot scale, which has tremendous biomass and crop productivity potential without significant downstream hydrologic impacts (see Chapter 5), for definitional purposes this is not 'derivative water'. The *watershed* as a unit is considered to include both the upstream catchment and downstream use of water. Groundwater recharge is a major, though often unintended, outcome. Large areas in India (referred to as 'tanks' or 'minor irrigation systems') and in Mexico (*'bordos'*), for example, fall in this category. Water productivity is often extremely high where the systems are subject to intensive management and labour inputs.

5   A note on the nomenclature used here: the term 'wastewater' carries the connotation of low-value, inferior quality and something to simply be disposed of, which in fact reflects an urban perspective. To correct for this bias, the term *water reuse* is preferred when referring to the practice and effluent when referring to the resource. Of course, effluent can be treated or untreated, as will be elaborated.

6   Paradoxically, the cost of secondary-level treatment of sewage is often as low as, or lower than, the cost of developing additional freshwater supplies. For example, developing new supplies in Jordan and Saudi Arabia costs US\$1.15 per m^3 and US\$2.63 per m^3, respectively (World Bank, 2000), compared to sewage treatment in the range of US\$0.50 per m^3.

7   Shiklomanov (2000) addresses the urgent need to avoid water degradation, though does not prescribe or advocate irrigation using untreated effluent.

8   Several of the benefits to farmers of effluent irrigation – proximity to urban markets and reliable supply through time – cause them to choose vegetables that command higher prices at market than other produce. This also greatly increases the risk of disease, such as typhoid and paratyphoid A and B in Dakar, Senegal, in 1987, and cholera and typhoid in Santiago, Chile, in 1992.

9   Sanitation and treatment alternatives to centralized wastewater collection, treatment and reuse range from dry sanitation (Jonsson, 1997; Córdova, 2000) to grey water separation – without faecal waste – to on-site natural treatment or remediation. Several of these options will continue to gain strength in the coming years. However, for municipal investment, multilateral and bilateral funding and construction industry imperatives, growth in water supply will continue to give de facto predominance to conventional centralized systems, certainly in the medium term. It is relevant to note that some practices such as urine separation and semi-dry systems used commercially at large scale in Scandinavia are, in fact, gaining considerable support in developing countries, for instance in East Africa.

10 No apologies to Nancy Reagan, who as First Lady of the USA advocated the 'just say NO!' approach for drugs in the US, with the deplorable results that are plainly evident today.

11 The plant is designed for secondary treatment; but due to hydraulic overloading, the resulting effluent is considered to be treated only to an advanced primary level.

REFERENCES

Agarwal A and Narain S (eds) (1997) *Dying Wisdom: Rise, Fall and Potential of India's Traditional Water Harvesting Systems*, Centre for Science and Environment, New Delhi

Ahluwalia M (1998) 'Representing communities: The case of a community-based watershed management project in Rajasthan, India', Paper presented at Crossing

Boundaries, the seventh annual conference of the International Association for the Study of Common Property, Vancouver, Canada, 10–14 June 1998

Al-Kharabsheh, A (1999) 'Ground-water quality deterioration in arid areas: A case study of the Zerqa river basin as influenced by Khirbet Es-Samra waste water (Jordan)', *Journal of Arid Environments*, vol 43, no 3, pp227–239

Al-Rashed, M F and Sherif, M M (2000) 'Water resources in the GCC countries: An overview', *Water Resources Management*, vol 14, no 1, pp59–75

Buechler, S J and Scott, C A (2000) 'Para nosotros, esta agua es vida: El riego en condiciones adversas: los usuarios de aguas residuales en Irapuato, México' in Scott, C A, Wester, P and Marañón-Pimentel, B (eds) *Asignación, Productividad y Manejo de Recursos Hídricos en Cuencas*, Serie Latinoamericana no 20, International Water Management Institute, Mexico

Cirelli, C (1998) 'El riego con aguas negras: Apuntes metodológicos', *XX Coloquio de Antropología e Historia Regionales*, Agua, Medio Ambiente y Desarrollo en México, pp29–42, Colegio de Michoacán, Zamora, Mexico

Comisión Nacional del Agua (CNA) (1997) *Congruencia del Marco Regulatorio en Materia de Descargas de Aguas Residuales*, duplicated, CNA, Mexico City

Córdova, A (2000) 'El saneamiento seco como estrategia para reducir la huella hídrica de las ciudades' in Scott, C A, Wester, P and Marañón-Pimentel, B (eds) *Asignación, Productividad y Manejo de Recursos Hídricos en Cuencas*, Serie Latinoamericana no 20, International Water Management Institute, Mexico

Cosgrove, W J and Rijsberman, F R (2000) *World Water Vision: Making Water Everybody's Business*, World Water Council, Earthscan, London

Faruqui, N I (2000) 'Wastewater Treatment and Reuse for Food and Water Security', International Development Research Centre, Ottawa, Canada

Faruqui, N I, Biswas, A K and Bino M J (eds) (2001) *Water Management in Islam*, United Nations University Press, Tokyo and International Development Research Centre, Ottawa, Canada

Gleick, P H (2000) 'The changing water paradigm: A look at twenty-first century water resources development', *Water International*, vol 25, no 1, pp127–138

Government of Israel (undated) *Principles for Giving Permits for Irrigation with Effluents (Treated Wastewater)*, unofficial English translation, Ministry of Health

Government of Jordan (1998) *Wastewater Management Policy*, Policy Paper No 4. June, Ministry of Water and Irrigation, Amman

Government of Mexico (1996) *Límites Máximos Permisibles de Contaminantes en las Descargas de Aguas Residuales en Aguas y Bienes Nacionales (NOM-001-ECOL-1996)*, Secretaría de Medio Ambiente, Recursos Naturales y Pesca, Mexico City

Jonsson, H (1997) 'Ecological alternatives in sanitation', Proceedings of SIDA Sanitation Workshop, Paper presented at Assessment of Sanitation Systems and Reuse of Urine, 6–9 August 1997, Balingsholm, Sweden

Kerr, J et al (2000) 'An evaluation of dryland watershed development projects in India', *Environment and Production Technology Division Discussion Paper No 68*, International Food Policy Research Institute, Washington, DC

Khouri, N, Kalbermatten, J M and Bartone, C R (1994) 'Reuse of wastewater in agriculture: A guide for planners', *UNDP-World Bank Water and Sanitation Report No 6*, World Bank, Washington, DC

Meinzen-Dick, R and Zwarteveen, M (1998) 'Gendered participation in water management: Issues and illustrations from water users' associations in South Asia' in Merrey, D J and Baviskar, S (eds) *Gender Analysis and Reform of Irrigation Management: Concepts, Cases and Gaps in Knowledge*, Proceedings of the

Workshop on Gender and Water, 15–19 September 1997, International Irrigation Management Institute, Colombo, Sri Lanka

Nazzal Y K et al (2000) *Wastewater Reuse Law and Standards in the Kingdom of Jordan*, Ministry of Water and Irrigation, Amman

Oweis, T, Hachum, A and Kijne, J (1999) *Water Harvesting and Supplemental Irrigation for Improved Water Use Efficiency in Dry Areas*, SWIM Report 7, International Water Management Institute, Colombo, Sri Lanka

Population Information Program (1998) *Solutions for a Water-Short World*, Population Report M(14), The Johns Hopkins School of Public Health, Baltimore

Scott, C A (1994) 'Facing environmental degradation in the Aravalli Hills, India', in Millington, A C and Pye, K (eds) *Environmental Change in Drylands: Biogeographical and Geomorphological Perspectives*, Wiley, Chichester, UK

Scott, C A and Flores-López, F J (submitted) 'Evaporation and infiltration from water bodies in the Lerma-Chapala basin, Mexico', *Journal of American Water Resources Association*

Scott, C A, Zarazúa, J A and Levine, G (2000) 'Urban-wastewater reuse for crop production in the water-short Guanajuato River Basin, Mexico', IWMI Research Report 41, International Water Management Institute, Colombo, Sri Lanka

Semiat, R (2000) 'Desalination: Present and future', *Water International*, vol 25, no 1, pp54–65

Shiklomanov, I A (2000) 'Appraisal and assessment of world water resources', *Water International*, vol 25, no 1, pp11–32

van der Hoek, W, ul Hassan, M, Ensink, J H J, Feenstra, S, Raschid-Sally, L, Munir, S, Aslam, R, Ali, N, Hussain, R and Matsuno, Y (2002) *Urban Wastewater: A Valuable Resource for Agriculture. A Case Study from Pakistan*, IWMI Research Report 63, International Water Management Institute, Colombo, Sri Lanka

World Bank (2000) *Wastewater Treatment and Reuse in the Middle East and North Africa Region (MENA)*, The Initiative for Collaboration to Control Natural Resource Degradation (Desertification) of Arid Lands in the Middle East, World Bank, Washington, DC

World Health Organization (WHO) (1989) *Health Guidelines for the Use of Wastewater in Agriculture and Aquaculture*, WHO, Geneva

Chapter 7

Rethinking groundwater management

KARIN E KEMPER[1]

INTRODUCTION

Until a few years ago, it would have been difficult to find a water-related issue less attractive than groundwater. First of all, groundwater, by definition, is under the ground and therefore out of sight. This means that it cannot be captured in fascinating colour photographs that could in turn be published in photo magazines. Second, for politicians, investing in groundwater savings or pollution control is less interesting than financing large constructions – pumps are not as visible as monumental irrigation schemes or reservoirs. And researchers (other than hydrogeologists) may be frustrated once they learn how difficult it is to find reliable data on flow, chemistry, recharge and discharge patterns.

Thus, since there did not seem to be any tangible problems with groundwater, it was largely left alone – in the socio-political, economic and regulatory sense – in most countries. In another sense, however, it was not left alone. Whenever surface water was not sufficiently available, becoming too polluted, or when it was otherwise profitable to drill wells, private and public investors would start exploiting their groundwater resources. This would eventually lead to significant dependence on groundwater. Worldwide, 70 per cent of groundwater is used for irrigation, 20 per cent for industry and 10 per cent for residential uses (Brown et al, 1999). The latter figure does not seem very impressive, but it actually translates into 1.5 to 2 billion people worldwide who are dependent on groundwater for their drinking supply, as shown in Table 7.1.

Slowly, the aggregated effect of groundwater use is now becoming evident. It is estimated, for example, that 10 per cent of the world's crops are irrigated with overdrafted groundwater, effectively taking out a loan on the future. The Worldwatch Institute in its *State of the World 2001* devotes an entire chapter to groundwater, illustrating that – in addition to groundwater quantity

Table 7.1 *Groundwater as a share of drinking water use,*
by region in the late 1990s

Region	Share of drinking water from groundwater (percentage)	People served (millions)
Asia-Pacific	32	1000 to 1200
Europe	75	200 to 500
Latin America	29	150
USA	51	153
Australia	15	3
World		1500 to 2000

Note: Data on Africa not available.
Source: Worldwatch Institute (2001)

problems in arid and semi-arid areas – pollution is increasingly an issue to be taken seriously worldwide. Globally, a situation has developed in which some countries are regionally suffering from overdraft of their aquifers, such as Mexico, Yemen, the USA, China, Jordan and India, while others are more known for groundwater quality problems, such as Argentina, The Netherlands, Germany and Bangladesh. A neglected aspect is that those countries traditionally more concerned with groundwater overexploitation are also subject to groundwater pollution. The issue just has not been as prominent due to the over-riding quantity problem.

Given the importance of groundwater, its increasing role in domestic, municipal, industrial and irrigation supply, and the socio-economic, environmental and health problems related to current trends, the aim of this chapter is to highlight the importance of providing groundwater users with adequate incentives to begin a more sustainable era of groundwater management. These incentives need to be bundled and include both economic incentives, as well as the power for the different groundwater users to make decisions about their resource.

This chapter is not an attempt to provide a sole solution to groundwater management, which would be impossible. It is important, however, to think about the underlying issues that prevent effective groundwater management and how to tackle them. Addressing groundwater issues from a technical perspective alone – as has been tried unsuccessfully in a number of cases – is clearly not sufficient. Consequently, the chapter discusses a shift in groundwater management approaches, stepping away from laissez-faire and towards active aquifer management.

The focus of this chapter is primarily on developing countries and on issues related to the need for groundwater management due to aquifer overexploitation and, to a certain extent, pollution. While not all areas in developing countries experience aquifer overexploitation, it is an increasing problem and, even in those regions where groundwater seems to be abundant, unmanaged groundwater abstraction can eventually lead to local problems (Moench, 2001). The emphasis of this chapter, then, is on management, even for those regions where some would prefer to take the traditional route of 'abstraction now, management later'.

DETRIMENTAL IMPACTS OF GROUNDWATER NON-MANAGEMENT

Groundwater development can be highly beneficial in the short to medium term. In the long term, however, there are many negative effects of uncontrolled groundwater abstraction and pollution. The following sections concentrate, firstly, on the physical characteristics of groundwater and then on three particularly important areas with regard to the following juxtaposition – namely, socio-economic development, equity and public health.

Physical characteristics of groundwater

Groundwater has played a vital role in the development process, both in urban and rural areas worldwide, because of its:

- quality, which is generally very good and offers substantial savings in treatment costs compared to surface water sources;
- security as a source of supply during extended dry periods compared to most surface water resources;
- suitability for independent public supply and private use, notably during the early stages of development;
- attractiveness in terms of capital investment because exploitation can progress in stages with rising water demand; and
- availability where needed, without being confined to streams and riverbeds (Foster et al, 1998).

Depending on the hydrogeological and climatic characteristics of a given region, groundwater can be susceptible to overexploitation (more water is withdrawn from the aquifer – a waterbearing geological formation – than is naturally recharged during a given time period) and/or to pollution. The vulnerability of the aquifer depends, inter alia, on its depth and the lithology and the general hydrogeological environment. There is extensive literature about groundwater characteristics from a hydrogeological perspective (Foster et al, 2002b).

Since groundwater is, by definition, under the ground, specific and often costly measures are required in order to study the characteristics of a given aquifer. Ideally, an aquifer would be managed so that it would not be polluted (because cleaning up groundwater is far more costly than cleaning up surface water and, in some deteriorated aquifers, remediation is practically impossible) and its yield would be perpetually sustained.

In the absence of management – often due to the perceived high cost of better studying the aquifer – groundwater abstraction can lead to both pollution and decline in aquifer water levels. Serious declines can reduce well yields, in turn provoking an expensive and inefficient cycle of well-deepening to regain productivity, or even premature loss of investment caused by the forced abandonment of wells. Other major threats are saline intrusion in cities and irrigation areas, land subsidence in susceptible environments – such as the effects in Mexico City where land subsidence has severely damaged the inner city – and disappearance of wetlands. Shah et al (2000) provide an extensive list of problems affecting groundwater-dependent areas worldwide.

Groundwater development can be highly beneficial in the short to medium term. In the long term, however, there are many negative effects of uncontrolled groundwater abstraction and pollution. The following sections concentrate on three particularly important areas with regard to the juxtaposition of short- and medium-term benefits versus possible long-term negative effects of groundwater abstraction and pollution.

Socio-economic development

Groundwater is important for development in both agriculture and industry. For instance, in Mexico, 2 million out of the country's 5 million irrigated hectares (ha) rely on groundwater supply (see Chapter 6). Worldwide, a large part of the Green Revolution has been based on groundwater use. The development impact becomes obvious. At the same time, however, if groundwater is overabstracted, well yields will fall over time. The immediate effect is increased cost (diesel, electricity) to pump the water, thus decreasing farmers' income margins. If the trend continues, their wells have to be deepened and more powerful pumps purchased, further increasing costs. Finally, the water level may have fallen so far that it is not economically viable to continue growing certain crops or to continue growing at all.

The socio-economic impact of such detrimental development on a regional economy can be dramatic, as is the case in the Mexican city of Guaymas where the groundwater level is too deep to permit viable agriculture. The region now focuses on tourism as a development tool.

As previously mentioned, overabstraction can also lead to saline intrusion, as is happening in the Mexican city of Hermosillo, parts of California, in Israel and Dakar, Senegal. Saline intrusion is reversable, if at all, only at exceedingly high cost. Its immediate effects are that a variety of crops cannot be grown any more due to their low salt resistance and that the potability of the water declines.

Finally, land subsidence due to overdraft, which compacts the soil, can have effects not only on buildings in urban areas, water mains and sewerage networks, but also on irrigation infrastructure, destroying canals and requiring costly rehabilitation works. In addition, and not unexpectedly, the decline in water availability can lead to social conflicts, both in the rural and in the rural–urban domain.

In conclusion, overabstraction may first lead to increased benefits of a regional economy (irrigated lands can be expanded, cheap and good quality water supply is available for domestic and industrial purposes); but the same incentives users have to engage in economic activities based on groundwater use can lead to negative effects in the long run – depending on the characteristics of the hydrogeological regime. These issues linking sustainability of groundwater management and socio-economic development also take us to the important issue of equity.

Equity

Especially in areas with relatively shallow aquifers, groundwater is a very equitable resource. For instance, the expansion of the treadle pump in India during recent years shows that low-income farmers can benefit from easy access to groundwater and increase their productivity and economic well-being (Shah et al, 2000). In large areas of Africa and South Asia, people dig their own shallow wells or are able to invest in relatively shallow boreholes.

However, when numerous people do the same in a given area, the many incremental uses will eventually lead to the negative effects of overabstraction mentioned above and a reverse effect can be observed. The first groundwater users to have to abandon their wells if groundwater levels sink too low can be expected to be the poor who do not have the financial resources to afford pumping water from increasing depths or to invest in new wells. They are also the first ones hit if their wells turn saline or when their urban well runs dry or becomes polluted. As a consequence, they may have to abandon farming, seeking their livelihood in the city or – if they are urban dwellers – purchasing more expensive water from private vendors (given that the public water supply system often does not reach the poor).

While development efforts and the literature have focused on the access to groundwater and the potential benefits of its use as an equity issue (Kahnert and Levine, 1993), the increasing numbers of overexploitation and pollution scenarios need to enter the global groundwater agenda. Unfortunately, until now, very few studies have been carried out in this regard and significant research about the equity dimension of sustainable groundwater management in developing scarcity and pollution situations is still required. Such research should provide clues on when to start investing in groundwater management.

With the prevailing attitude among many groundwater developers that groundwater is a freely exploitable resource, it is often more costly to put simple management measures in place once problems have already appeared. By then, vested interests have already developed among users (for instance, relating to amounts of water used and perceived as entitlements, or provision of access to privately developed wells for monitoring purposes) that may make it difficult to develop a clear picture of an aquifer's characteristics and to put in place such measures as monitoring and agreements for more efficient use of the groundwater. At the same time, groundwater management does entail costs to society and to the users, so that a balance needs to be found between the cost of management investments compared to the benefits of long-term sustainability of groundwater use.

Public health

Often, the overabstraction of groundwater is the focus of concern, especially in arid and semi-arid regions. However, groundwater pollution due to heavy metals and toxins has very detrimental health effects. The Worldwatch Institute (2001) warns of a ticking time bomb in this regard. Given that groundwater nowadays often substitutes for already polluted surface water, the groundwater pollution trend is certainly worrisome because users and policy-makers are basing their future on a 'safe' resource, which frequently is far more vulnerable to pollution impacts than surface water.

Another health hazard is posed by naturally occuring trace metals such as arsenic. The most well-known case in this regard is Bangladesh, where high arsenic levels are contaminating the groundwater. The reasons for this are not entirely resolved; but the fact is that large areas are affected and the years of investing in wells for local communities are now turning into a public health threat rather than a benefit as was envisaged (Government of Bangladesh et al, 2000). Other countries in the region, such as Cambodia, may be facing the same dilemma if they do not take action now.

Arsenic is not the only naturally occuring contaminant that has been neglected. For example, fluoride, soluble iron, manganese and selenium are also found in groundwater supply areas (Foster et al, 2002a). At present, no clear strategies exist on how to balance the costs and efforts of pre-investments in identifying potential long-term threats with the need to quickly and affordably supply water to growing populations.

Having shown the detrimental impacts of groundwater non-management, the need for adequate groundwater management becomes obvious. In the following sections, a shift in groundwater management approaches is discussed.

A SHIFT IN GROUNDWATER MANAGEMENT APPROACHES: TOWARDS PROVIDING INCENTIVES FOR MORE SUSTAINABLE USE

Groundwater has not really been managed in many developing countries and laissez-faire would be the most appropriate term to describe the situation. Increasingly, however, the negative effects of overabstraction and pollution are becoming evident, and such diverse countries as Thailand, Yemen, Mexico and China are looking for solutions.

What has been the approach to groundwater management until now?

As with other water resources, for a long time groundwater management was either neglected entirely and the focus was on furthering groundwater exploitation – often without the basic hydrological knowledge of a given region – or regarded from a technical point of view.

In the latter case, a first step would be to study the groundwater resource (typically carried out by the government and/or universities) and to model it. In cases of sinking groundwater levels, certain areas would then be delineated and declared off-limits for further abstraction. Examples are the 'dark blocks' in India and the '*vedas*' in Mexico. These approaches have not been successful in curbing groundwater overexploitation or pollution. Groundwater levels in these countries keep sinking; in several parts of Mexico, levels are sinking by 3 metres (m) per year (World Bank, 1999). Equally unsuccessful is the same recipe followed for groundwater quality management. Studies result in protection zones that are often not controlled due to absence of legislation and enforcement capacity.

A different approach to groundwater management is now developing, based on the recognition that – as with all common pool resources – users need to have incentives and effective management instruments and mechanisms to preserve the resource. For this, different and better institutional arrangements for groundwater management are needed.

Institutional economics and groundwater management

This chapter takes its perspective from the New Institutional Economics, which over the past decades has developed as a complement to mainstream neo-classical economic theory. Rationality, institutions, transaction costs and path dependence bound its key concepts. In this section, these concepts are described and applied to groundwater resources management issues.

In the face of local crises due to water scarcity, groundwater depletion and pollution, groundwater should be managed in a more efficient manner, both with regard to its inter- and intra-sectorial allocation and with regard to its use.[2] It needs to be recognized in this context that 'efficient' groundwater management is not a simple concept. Assuming, for instance, that a groundwater user pumps a certain volume per month, but experiences 'losses' due to transmission leakage, she may lose because she has spent energy with sub-optimal results. On the other hand, the water will return to the aquifer. In that sense, her loss is the aquifer's gain. Thus, making more efficient use of water by reducing leakage, as is often recommended, may actually increase the total use of groundwater and lead to more rapid aquifer depletion. More efficient use in the sense of this chapter, therefore, refers to an explicit reduction of total groundwater consumptive use (Foster et al, 2002b).

Bounded rationality

In neo-classical theory, individuals are assumed to be rational and constantly trying to maximize their individual utility by making choices according to their predetermined preferences. This view implicitly assumes that the individual has all of the information needed to make an optimal decision and will be able to process all available information. Institutional economists challenge this concept and assert that individuals try to be rational and maximize utility; but they are not completely able to do so because, in the real world, they never have complete information, and even if they did, they would not be intellectually capable of processing it all. For this reason, their rationality is limited (Simon, 1982). Nevertheless, the concept of bounded rationality does recognize the attempt to be rational in an economic sense. This is important because it means that individuals react to incentive structures in a predictable manner. For example, if a good is free – as, for instance, a public good such as groundwater – individuals are assumed to use more of it than if they had to pay for it. The implication is that an analysis of the incentive structures that individuals face can explain why they behave in a certain way, while the design of a management mechanism that permits the application of economic instruments to induce certain behaviour, such as the efficient use of a given resource, is possible.

Institutional arrangements

If we assume that individual actors are susceptible to incentives, we have to ask where these incentives originate. Institutional economists maintain that incentives are provided by institutional arrangements, such as legal regulations and laws; but they can also be informal, such as customs and codes of behaviour. Here we follow the North's distinction between institutions as the 'underlying rules of the game' and actors – the individuals, agencies and organizations. The latter interact with, and influence, the institutional framework, but they are not institutions. In everyday language, the expression 'institution' is applied to agencies and organizations. Therefore, the use of the word institution in relation to rules and regulations frequently causes confusion. Here, the term institutional arrangement is used for more clarity since it better indicates the structural nature of institutions. Together, institutional arrangements and actors compose the institutional framework.

Contracts and property rights

An institutional arrangement of major importance in the context of groundwater management relates to contracts and property rights. Economic activity takes place in the form of contracting. Contracts, formal or informal, are used to exchange goods, to obtain access to public goods and to retain the rights of acquired goods. The institutional framework can facilitate these actions – for instance, by providing clear rules on contract layout and by helping to enforce such rules.

The existence of a contract presupposes a property right in some form (see Chapter 8). The most well-known type of property right is the right of ownership. The right of ownership in an asset is composed of three elements: the right to use the asset (*usus*), the right to the returns from the asset (*usus fructus*) and the right to change the asset's form, substance and location (*abusus*). The last element is the most fundamental and far-reaching feature of the right of ownership since it encompasses the right to transfer the asset, or parts of the rights connected with the asset, to others (Furubotn and Richter,

1991). Due to this possibility, the owner of the asset has an infinite planning horizon and will be interested in the efficient allocation and use of the asset over time. Although the right of ownership is exclusive, it is not unrestricted. Society usually imposes rules constraining the actual power of decision over the asset.

In relation to groundwater, the above has important implications. Firstly, it makes clear that the introduction of property rights to water can take different forms. For example, the property right can be established in relation to the right of the use of the water. This is the case in several areas of the USA (Colorado, New Mexico) and Chile, where permanent ownership of the water right exists – owners of water rights can use the water, are entitled to appropriate its returns and can transfer the water right to others. However, the ownership of the water resource itself remains with the US government (Kemper and Simpson, 1999). Often, the ownership of groundwater rights is limited in a number of respects, the most important being that the water rights can be transferred only in a limited area, such as an irrigation district, a groundwater basin or within one state; but they cannot be sold or given away outside. The reason for this restriction is based on political decisions that the water source is destined for the benefit of this particular area and should remain there. This example demonstrates that property rights are embedded in rules, which can be designed, changed and adapted to different situations. It must be recognized, however, that the constraints imposed on ownership rights influence their value in the eyes of the owner, potential acquirers and other interested parties.

Property rights thus influence the use and allocation of an asset. Property rights, or the lack thereof, have been thoroughly discussed in the literature about natural resources, principally in relation to common property, open access resources and exclusive property rights.

In much of the economics and political science literature, the distinction between open access and common property resources has been blurred. This is dangerous when giving policy recommendations or analysing the allocation, and use of, a resource such as groundwater. Many analysts have adopted Hardin's point of view (1968) that common property resources are prone to overconsumption because everyone has the right to use and no one has an incentive to preserve. However, a distinction has to be made between common property and free access resources. A resource may be a common property resource; but that does not necessarily imply that everyone who wants to has free access to it. A free access resource can be used by anyone without any control mechanism or, as Bromley and Cernea (1989, p20) point out:

> *Open access results from the absence – or the breakdown – of a management and authority system whose very purpose was to introduce and enforce a set of norms of behaviour among participants with respect to the natural resource. When valuable natural resources are available to the first party to effect capture, it is either because those natural resources have never before been*

incorporated into a regulated social system, or because they have become open access resources through institutional failures that have undermined former collective or private property/ management regimes.

As Ostrom (1990) has shown for water, a number of societies have developed rules over the years to regulate the use of their water resources without attributing property rights to individuals. Ostrom argues that if a number of conditions are fulfilled, communities are able to manage a common property resource without individual privatization. Thus, the distinction between common property and free access resources is important. A groundwater resource that is treated as a common property resource need not be overexploited if the appropriate institutional arrangements exist to take care of its management.

Transaction costs

Over the past decades, the concept of transaction costs has become widely used in fields such as industrial organization and, increasingly, in the application of institutional analysis in natural resource studies. Transaction costs, following Ostrom, Schroeder and Wynne (1993), are the inevitable transaction costs in terms of time and effort of negotiating, monitoring and enforcing the terms of a contractual agreement, the strategic costs and the information search costs.

Each category consists of ex-ante and ex-post transaction costs. Concerning the first category, examples of ex-ante transaction costs are those related to obtaining relevant information, negotiating agreements, making side payments and communicating with relevant parties. Ex-post costs relate to the monitoring of the performance of contract participants, sanctioning and governance costs, and renegotiating. Williamson (1984) points out the importance of taking into account ex-post transactions that are frequently neglected in analyses, although they may constitute the bulk of the costs incurred in relation to institutional arrangements. With regard to groundwater, this cost category is critical. Since in most countries groundwater is not regulated and often not sufficiently studied, the first step towards any type of management is very costly. Aquifers need to be studied, models need to be developed to be able to assess management necessities and options, groundwater users need to be identified, inventories of wells and registers must be created, groundwater use concessions/permits/rights must awarded, etc. Thus, the transaction cost in terms of time and effort to put in place a system is significant and certainly one of the reasons why groundwater management in so many countries is insufficient, given the more readily visible needs that they may be facing. The same is true for ex-post transaction costs. Where once a system is in place, it needs to be maintained, thus implying recurring costs for monitoring, updating and enforcing.

The inevitable strategic costs are complemented by the second category, summarized under the heading 'strategic costs'. Strategic costs arise when, due to asymmetric distribution of power or a lack of information or transparency, one actor or actor group can resort to opportunistic behaviour to improve their own welfare at the expense of others. Strategic costs occur in the form of adverse selection, moral hazard, shirking, free riding and corruption.[3] In an environment where the potential for opportunistic behaviour is high, the strategic costs can add significantly to the basic transaction costs in the first category.

In the case of groundwater, strategic costs are of significance due to the fact that groundwater users generally depend on their own wells and that aquifers may range from a handful to tens of thousands of users. This increases the cost of effective monitoring, affording users the opportunity to incorrectly state the volume of water they have been using (for example, when water use rights are awarded based on historical use). In addition, it is easy to tamper with water meters and thus avoid penalties for exceeding concession volumes, thus rendering a management system less effective and providing other users with lower incentives to follow agreed rules.

The inevitable and strategic transaction costs are complemented by information search costs. Information search costs relate to time and effort spent to obtain requisite information for a contractual agreement, and to monitor and enforce it. For example, when the transparency of a system is so low that it is not clear who takes decisions and on which criteria, information search costs are very high. At the same time, the potential for moral hazard increases. Therefore, as Ostrom, Schroeder and Wynne (1993) point out, 'institutional arrangements that help to generate information or distribute it serve crucial roles in reducing all types of transaction costs'.

As will be argued in subsequent sections, the increase in transparency and availability of information to all users is crucial to reduce information search costs. Governments, universities and groundwater management authorities have an important role to play in this regard. In the absence of sufficient information, or if the transaction costs in terms of time and money for obtaining it are too high, groundwater users do not have incentives to use water efficiently. If they do not know how much water they have access to, they will behave rationally and withdraw all of the water they can get, since they do not know if others are not overpumping the resource, eventually causing scarcity for all.

Path dependence

Historical and current institutional structures condition our possibilities of bringing about change. The notion of path dependence is taken from the technological realm where the initial investment in one particular technology frequently leads to further development of that technology rather than to a radical switch to newer, more efficient solutions due to the transaction costs of developing and introducing an entirely new alternative.

If applied to groundwater management, one can argue that in an area where groundwater has been dealt with according to the laissez-faire approach, the change to active groundwater management will imply costs for current users. These costs may hurt their interests, increasing the transaction costs for groundwater managers to convince them of the necessity to introduce groundwater monitoring, licensing and/or pricing. The previous laissez-faire situation has set the standard for users, and they will be reluctant to incur these new costs. This links back to the equity question because different strata of users will perceive costs and benefits of an active management approach in different ways. Depending on their overall power, this will determine the chance of improving groundwater management in their aquifer, region or country.

Path dependence helps to explain why the same type of institutional changes can lead to substantially different outcomes if applied to different settings. The concept demonstrates the need to analyse the evolution and status of current institutional structures, both in order to explain them and to analyse the possibilities of change.

Institutional arrangements influencing water resources allocation and use

All actors (such as groundwater users, water management agencies and government entities) are susceptible to incentives provided by the institutional arrangements around them. Institutional arrangements and actors together constitute the institutional framework and how the different parts of an institutional framework interact. For instance, laws mandating more efficient groundwater use to avoid groundwater overexploitation will not be effective if they are not enforced. And they will not be enforced effectively if the different actors have no information about them or if, as in many countries, there is no interaction between the users and the water administration. Moreover, laws mandating the achievement of a certain water quality, although laudable, will have little effect if the water users have no incentives to improve their water treatment process – not even if the treatment technologies are available. Thus, the institutional framework needs to be treated as an integrated whole to achieve the proposed objectives.

Figure 7.1 shows the four variables for efficient groundwater resources allocation and use and relates them to the institutional framework. The arrows point in both directions to indicate the feedback within the system.

Here we distinguish three categories of institutional arrangements: formal and informal institutional arrangements in the water sector, and institutional arrangements originating in other sectors.

Examples of *formal institutional arrangements* in the water sector are the constitution, water laws, subsidiary legislation and administrative rules. The number and specific content of these institutional arrangements vary between and within countries. Often, legal provisions on water resources are scattered in different laws. For instance, some countries do not have a national water law, but they have a water chapter in the environmental law. Mexico, for example, has had a national water law since 1992. Brazil's national law was passed in 1997. Groundwater is generally, and logically, dealt with under national water laws (an exception is the state groundwater law of Arizona in

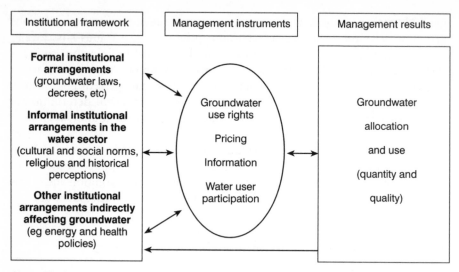

Notes: The institutional framework defines the management instruments to be used, which in turn has an impact on the management results; management results feed back into the system for reinforcement, adjustment and refinement.
Source: Adapted from Kemper (1996)

Figure 7.1 *Institutional arrangements influencing groundwater allocation and use*

the USA); but often it is not very explicit, thus leaving ample scope for uncertainties and diverging interpretations.

An additional caveat is that these formal institutional arrangements are not necessarily enforced. This is especially the case in developing countries. When a law or decree is not enforced, and if stakeholders are aware of this fact, then the law will not have any effect on their behaviour. They will know that the cost in social or financial terms of disregarding the law will be zero, so there will be no reason for them to adhere to the law, except if they see other gains. Consequently, the simple existence of a formal institutional arrangement cannot be taken as a conditioning factor for actors' decision-making. The enforcement and monitoring aspects have to be taken into account and, as we shall see later, are particularly complicated – involving high transaction costs – with regard to groundwater management.

Customs, generally accepted codes of behaviour and social norms are examples of *informal institutional arrangements*. Ostrom (1990) cites an example of an irrigation project in Spain where farmers had built up a social norm that water would not be stolen. Although there were no financial penalties involved, the social costs were perceived by farmers as so high that infractions on neighbours' water rights seldom occurred. Experiences in the states of Arizona and New Mexico in the USA also indicate that groundwater users self-report their annual water use and that state water administrators accord these self-reports significant credibility, effectively using the data provided as a basis for their groundwater management decisions.

This shows that informal arrangements can also develop in the absence of a functioning formal framework. Water users might perceive that they all lose by overexploitation of the resource and organize themselves to allocate and monitor water use. These arrangements may not be contractual, but everyone is aware of them. They thus function as working rules, complementing or replacing de jure rules. Another example is informal water markets that develop in the absence of a (functioning) formal framework. We can find such markets in places as different as India, Yemen and Brazil (Shah et al, 2000; Kemper et al, 1999). In addition, in Mexico there are indications that informal rental water markets exist alongside the more recent formal markets (World Bank, 1999).

Certain *institutional arrangements* have an impact on the water sector, although they are geared towards other sectors. Electricity pricing plays an important role in areas of groundwater use. If electricity is free, the cost of pumping the water is restricted to some capital costs, operation and maintenance of the pump, which renders water quite cheap. The types of electricity tariffs also influence the indirect price of the water. If they are flat, it does not matter to the water user how much water she pumps because the price she has to pay is already fixed and does not depend on the volume. The picture changes if the tariff is progressive. Then each additional unit of water has a price that would discourage wasteful water use.

A further arrangement that must be taken into account concerning agricultural use of water is the market access for crops. In the literature, there is a general call for the reallocation of water from low-value to high-value crops to increase allocative efficiency (Postel, 1992). In a zero transaction-cost world, this change could take place easily – farmers would adapt their production in accordance with price movements. In the real world, however, farmers not only often lack information about how much water different crops need, but also often lack access to the market for high-value crops. In many cases, especially in rural areas in developing countries, middlemen take on the marketing of products. This can be due to local farmers' lack of information and transport infrastructure. However, since they know that farmers are forced to sell very quickly, they can offer very low prices so that, in the end, the crop may not have a higher value for the farmer than a traditional food crop. The difference in value is only perceived in the urban market. In addition, the prices of high-value crops may fluctuate more unpredictably than for basic food crops. In all cases, farmers will not have an incentive to shift their production from low-value to high-value crops.

An analysis along these lines provides a picture of the current institutional framework and permits a judgement of the results that it produces in terms of groundwater allocation and use efficiency.

Institutional arrangements can provide incentives, but it is harder than it seems

Based on the previous sections, one would expect an aquifer that is subject to overdraft, conflicts and pollution, as well as inefficient allocation and use, to have an institutional framework with insufficiently defined groundwater use rights, weak enforcement and sanctioning mechanisms, perverse incentives from other sectors, as well as informal norms that encourage waste rather than efficient use of water.

Conversely, to achieve sustainable use and avoid pollution, an adequate institutional framework for groundwater management would have to encourage more efficient allocation and use, while taking into account regional socio-economic development, health and equity aspects.

Allocative efficiency is achieved if a resource is put to its highest-valued use. Many times, however, an abundance of water is, for example, used for low-value irrigation, while it could be used for high-value irrigation – thus generating higher returns per m^3 of water used – or a part of it could be made available for industry and domestic uses. This is where allocative and use efficiency interacts. In many countries, irrigation is the largest water user, and a comparatively modest share of the water could be transferred to other sectors if the irrigation sector became more efficient (Postel, 1992).

For instance, in New Mexico in the south-western USA, a de facto reallocation is taking place, with urban areas expanding into surrounding farmland and urban utilities purchasing groundwater rights. The transfer of groundwater out of agriculture into urban uses has been taking place in a win–win mode, with farmers being compensated.

For any transfers to happen, the appropriate institutional arrangements need to be in place. On the technical side, groundwater use must be monitored, and widely accepted transfer mechanisms need to occur. In Mexico, for example, where groundwater also is tradable, there seems to be a preference by farmers to lease the groundwater rather than sell it. A mechanism to do so does not exist, however, so trade does not take place or only takes place informally. This, in turn, renders monitoring of the environmental and socio-economic impacts difficult.

Rural–urban transfers also used to take place in Arizona (Schiffler, 1998). With the state's groundwater law of 1980, however, groundwater trading, as well as trading farmland to acquire groundwater rights, was essentially curbed. The state has now implemented a system that provides incentives for rights holders to save groundwater and accrue credits for future use – and possible sale – in a groundwater savings bank. This reflects a more regulatory management approach with incentives that are not based on private seller–buyer interactions, but rather on interactions between groundwater users and state managers.

To improve the use efficiency of groundwater, other mechanisms need to be in place, as well. For instance, irrigators need to be informed of water-saving technologies and need access to credit for implementing these, as well as access to markets to sell their products. In addition, groundwater needs to be adequately priced to provide the incentive for more efficient use. This also implies the analysis and reorientation of other subsidies that may distort the price of water – such as energy subsidies rendering groundwater mining profitable – at a high cost to society.

As previously mentioned, it needs to be recognized that more efficient use alone may not be the solution. Often, the fact that water is used 'inefficiently' – when there are many leaks in the system – actually replenishes the groundwater table. Once more efficient technology is introduced, net groundwater consumption may actually increase because a larger part of the water disappears from the basin through non-beneficial evapotranspiration.

Components of the institutional framework

In this section, the different instruments devised by the institutional framework – groundwater use rights, pricing, information and, above all, stakeholder participation – will be discussed.

Groundwater use rights

Groundwater use rights are often ambiguous and difficult to define. This is due to the previously mentioned difficulty of defining the magnitude and availability of the resource itself. Groundwater modelling is intricate and expensive, and if no good models are available that provide information about available yield over time, then the basis for giving any type of water rights, be it concessions or tradable rights, is very weak (see Chapter 8).

At the same time, there is a need for well-defined groundwater rights. Countries such as Israel, Jordan and Mexico have taken steps to implement groundwater rights systems. Well-defined groundwater usage rights entitle individual users or user groups to an abstraction allocation at a certain point in time or during a specified time period. Without a clear definition of who the users are and how much water they are entitled to, the users themselves have no incentive to use the water efficiently because they have no guarantee that if they save water today, the aquifer's yield will permit them to abstract what they need tomorrow. In addition, if water allocations are to be shifted to a different user, without defined groundwater usage rights, there is no information about how much can be reallocated, who would win and who would lose.

Thus, the existence of groundwater usage rights has an essential effect on enforcement, sanctioning systems, application of pricing mechanisms, water reallocation mechanisms, and the need for the generation of information and its management.

It is important to note that to achieve better groundwater management, groundwater usage rights need not be tradable. Obviously, tradability would introduce an increased efficiency aspect; but often the first, most important, step is to register the users and get a better estimate of the types and magnitude of abstraction. This information can then be compared to information about aquifer recharge and thus long-term water-use sustainability (Garduño et al, 2002; Kemper, 2001)

At the same time, it needs to be mentioned that the right to trade is very powerful because the rights holder will have a long-term perspective. He will not only consider what the water can produce for him (in tonnes of rice for example), but also the opportunity cost of the water (for example, the value added by using the water in car manufacturing). Thus, the highest value of water use is taken into account and provides an incentive for more efficient use and reallocation of surplus water to a higher-valued use. Reallocation by trading means getting compensated. This is different from administrative reallocation, where rights holders may not receive any compensation when water is reallocated to a different use (although recent water laws now tend to provide for compensation when water is reallocated through no fault of the rights holder).

Water use rights are embedded in rules that can be designed, changed and adapted to different situations. They are advocated here as a tool to provide a long-term horizon to water users. Tradable groundwater use rights per se will not resolve overexploitation of an aquifer unless a certain percentage of the aquifer volume is reserved to achieve certain stabilization. Theoretically, this could take place the same way as air pollution rights, where each year a certain amount of water is designated as tradable, effectively decreasing the consumptive use on a yearly basis. In practice, however, the opposite seems to occur. In a number of cases, the first step to assign water rights is based on initial self-assessment by groundwater users of their historical use. These self-assessments are often strongly exaggerated; but groundwater administrators do accept them as a starting point. The challenge, then, is to eventually reduce the overall volume of rights in order to arrive at the actual amount of groundwater withdrawn. Only in the next step will groundwater use actually be decreased. This gradual decrease can only take place if the institutional framework is sufficiently developed to permit follow-up actions (re-registering of wells and permits; use of licensed drillers, etc). Clearly, this is a long-term process that does not show immediate results.

Another important aspect in the allocation of groundwater rights is the distinction between open access and common property resources. Aquifers are a typical example of a common property resource. Frequently, they also are an open access resource – namely, when neither private nor collective groundwater use rights exist. The introduction of water rights would try to ameliorate this situation by offering an incentive towards a long-term perspective by individuals and an interest in controlling fellow users. But, as previously noted, high transactions costs can be expected in the introduction of groundwater use rights due to existing vested interests by current users. They can be especially high if an aquifer is already overexploited and decisions for curbing groundwater use have to be taken. For this reason, it is recommended to start groundwater management in situations that require less sacrifice, and not to wait until situations become critical.

In addition, the crux of groundwater is the size of the stakeholder community. Groundwater aquifers can be very small, with only tens or hundreds of users. Such is the case for some aquifers in Mexico, California and in Southern Africa. It is conceivable that users would be able to arrive at a joint management framework, even without individual property rights. As pointed out by Shah et al (2000), many aquifers, especially in Asia, have thousands of users. In that case, it is far more difficult to envision one integrated framework at the 'community level', and obviously transaction costs for both introducing and maintaining any groundwater framework increase significantly. As a result, sub-management structures are required.

In summary, groundwater use rights are essential to provide incentives for better groundwater management. But perhaps even more than with surface water, they need to be designed in a flexible and locally adapted manner to allow for local needs and circumstances. For this, the characteristics of the aquifer, individual or common property right cultures, different lengths of validity of the rights, and transferability must be taken into account.

Water pricing

When dealing with the need for more efficient groundwater use and allocation, a prime recommendation is, usually, the introduction of better pricing (see Chapters 4 and 11). The rationale is that groundwater users have an incentive to use water efficiently when it has a price. If it is free, they will use more than they would otherwise, unnecessarily reducing the availability of water for everyone and increasing scarcity of, and thus competition for, the resource. If 'the price is right', users will have incentives to use less water and introduce water-saving technologies, thus freeing water for other uses.

In groundwater, pricing issues are distinct from surface water, given that the extraction of the groundwater resources usually takes place on private land, with private equipment. For this reason, there are actually two options for pricing – namely, the resource itself or the other inputs needed to pump groundwater: the pump, the borehole and, most importantly, energy.

Energy pricing

The cost of energy is usually seen as the most important incentive to reduce overpumping. In Figure 7.2, the Mexican situation is depicted and we can see that there was a noticeable decrease of electric consumption during 1990, when an increase in the '09' energy tariff took place. One can infer from the results that the elasticity with regard to energy pricing is significant. Usually, however, this type of action is not easy to apply due to political reasons – as was the case in Mexico and reflected in the downturn in the price curve in Figure 7.2, and a corresponding increase in pumping from 1992 to 1993.

Even here, innovative ways need to be sought. While energy pricing is seen by many politicians as an effective means of subsidizing rural producers, the detrimental effect on groundwater aquifers needs to be taken into account. The well-intentioned 'pro-poor' policy may eventually turn into an 'anti-poor' policy when the aquifers become overexploited and only the rich can afford to continue pumping.[4] For this reason, other types of subsidies must be contemplated. An option could be lump-sum payments to small farmers that would permit them to either pay the full electricity bill or reduce their pumping, pay a lower bill and use the 'gain' for something else. In this way, the energy tariff would not distort the true price of groundwater, without hurting the poor.

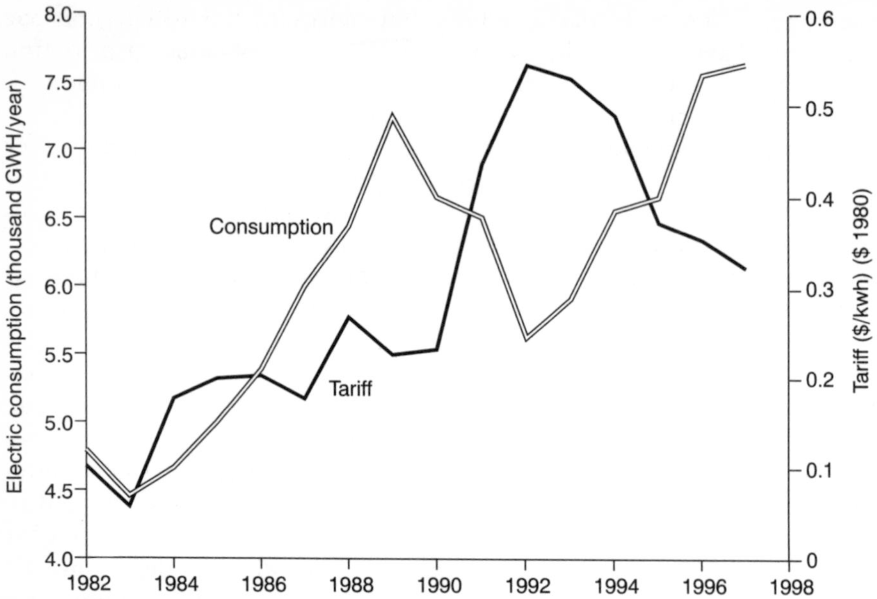

Note: Tariff deflacted by using the implicit price index of GDP.

Source: World Bank (1999)

Figure 7.2 *Variation of electric power consumption and the 09 tariff*

Pricing the resource

Another way to provide an incentive is to price the resource itself (users pay for the abstraction of the groundwater resource). For the most impact, this should be based on volumetric metering, thus giving an incentive to users to use less water. However, frequently metering equipment is not installed on wells or they are not effectively monitored by the groundwater management agency. Therefore, few countries practice groundwater pricing, or often only industrial and municipal users pay while agricultural uses are exempt. Given that agriculture is the largest user, pricing as an instrument to reduce overall water demand becomes relatively ineffective.

Due to the cost of monitoring individual wells – and also due to the possibilities of corruption in meter reading or tampering – there are now efforts to develop remote-sensing tools that can help calculate groundwater use based on the observed crop cover. The advantage of these tools is their visual power and the fact that water users themselves can learn to interpret them. This affords the possibility for aquifer self-management rather than reliance on well-by-well monitoring, thus increasing transparency in aquifer management and reducing strategic transaction costs. By using remote-sensing information, users can monitor each other's groundwater use, enabling peer pressure to enforce abstraction agreements and reducing possibilities of shirking.

Despite some caveats (for example, how to accurately model and calculate evapotranspiration), remote sensing can develop into an important and increasingly affordable tool for groundwater management. Attempts at its use are taking place in Idaho in the USA.

Information, awareness raising and participation

As has become clear from the above, a number of instruments exist to introduce more efficient groundwater use and allocation. These range from the clear definition of property rights to pricing the resource.

At the same time, all of these instruments have one fundamental prerequisite: enforcement. Groundwater is distinct from surface water in that many different users are involved in abstracting the resource, and monitoring their individual behaviour is very costly. Users, of course, are well aware of this and their incentive to comply with metering regulations and prohibitions against sale/lease of water or tariff payments is typically very low.

What, then, would provide an incentive to preserve the resource? Experiences in the USA and Mexico have shown that *information* is an essential one. Groundwater users who do not know what the conditions of their resource are will be less willing to sacrifice their current income than those who are aware that overexploitation is going to hurt them in the foreseeable future. For this, however, they need comprehensible and reliable information, which often is not available.

Blomquist (1992) provides a comprehensive analysis of the development of local management structures in eight Californian groundwater basins. Interestingly, each development started with the recognition that the groundwater resource was under increasing stress (as noticed by sinking water levels and sometimes saltwater intrusion), and with the collection of data about the aquifer, its recharge and potential safe yield. Once the data was obtained and confirmed on the ongoing overdraft, water users were able to forecast the potential consequences of non-action and began organizing for sustainable use and management of their aquifers.

These examples show that groundwater users must be recognized as true stakeholders entitled to information about the resource upon which they are so dependent. For many water agencies, this implies a significant shift from being centralized agencies that keep the information about water availability to themselves and take decisions without the participation of other stakeholders. Obviously, the trend towards definition and official allocation of groundwater use rights (such as in Brazil, Chile, Israel, Jordan and Mexico) contributes to a move towards transparency. Information is essential for decision-making among all levels of stakeholders in order to determine what planning horizon to consider, which savings measures to propose and accept, what investments to make, and what service to require from water agencies and government authorities. With a better-defined basis of groundwater use rights – and responsibilities – information becomes more valuable and more crucial to the different stakeholders.

Groundwater users, however, need more than one-way information: they also need a voice in decision-making. While, in principle, the aim of groundwater management is to make the resource last perpetually, there may actually be situations where an aquifer is already so overexploited that it is impossible to rescue it. If it consists of fossil water and there is no recharge, then stakeholders will have to come to a decision on how to deplete it in a strategic manner. This is, for instance, the case with the Ogallala Aquifer in the USA, which sinks roughly 1m per year.

In such cases, if stakeholders have no information, no decision-making power and no joint decision-making forum, then each one will try to capture as much for herself as she can, eventually leading to depletion, with all of the negative consequences described above. It is clear that monitoring social behaviour (not only groundwater tables) is essential to understand successes and failures in the implementation of groundwater stabilization strategies.

Countries such as the USA and Mexico are moving towards the management of aquifers by groundwater-user associations in an attempt to involve users in decision-making and to increase compliance with decisions that have been taken collectively. In both cases, a range of other demand management instruments discussed in this chapter accompanies these developments. In the USA, this shift has been taking place over the past five decades and is showing positive results (see Blomquist, 1992).

An important issue in this regard is the recurring assertion that since groundwater and surface water are hydrologically connected, aquifers cannot be managed in isolation. This argument is relatively weak given that, in many cases, surface waters are managed – if at all – without ever taking into account the connected groundwater resources. Nowadays, many aquifers are under such pressure that pragmatism would dictate tackling them directly without neglecting basic principles of integrated groundwater management as identified in the course of time (Kemper and Alvarado, 2001; Foster et al, 2002b). In those cases where the hydrological connection to surface water resources is significant, conjunctive use could, and should be, taken into account – as is the case in New Mexico (DuMars, undated) – but without stifling the process.

CONCLUSIONS

A new institutional framework for groundwater management is on the horizon. There is a clear shift from the laissez-faire approach, focusing on the exploitation of the resource without consideration for long-term sustainability, towards an approach centred on providing incentives to the different stakeholders for better and more equitable management of their resource.

Providing incentives is not enough. An enabling environment (the government's regulatory role, capacity building) and a fine-tuned combination of top-down and bottom-up approaches are also required. This new management tool package not only focuses on market-based instruments, such as water pricing and groundwater use rights, but is bundled in a larger package, including groundwater users themselves in decision-making structures. Groundwater management, compared with groundwater development, is still in its infancy and few working examples can be presented, especially in the developing world. It is clear, however, that increasing groundwater overexploitation and pollution worldwide are causing a shift in awareness about groundwater resources. From having been the 'invisible resource', groundwater is now becoming highly visible in those areas where groundwater overdraft and pollution are taking place and affecting different stakeholders. A democratization trend can, therefore, be identified, taking place not only in surface water management, as exemplified by the increasing number of river-basin committees and organizations worldwide, but also in groundwater management.

Given the alarming rate at which groundwater aquifers are being overdrafted and polluted in so many regions, the question is whether there is time for water users. They would have to slowly identify the deteriorating situation, start requesting data (this is often costly, especially when governments are not able or willing to provide the data), and go through a process of collective organization and of creating new institutional arrangements for groundwater management. This can take decades. In a number of cases, it may be too late to wait for this process. Instead, it would be advisable for existing water resources management institutions in those countries and regions affected to start identifying groundwater users, make information available and provide them with a framework for developing local management. This incremental approach could spark the beginning of new institutional arrangements that would provide incentives for behavioural change relatively quickly. While this would run counter to the notion of path dependence because it may require a bigger step away from 'business as usual' than many existing agencies are able to deal with, it is necessary to realize that the relative costs have changed. Further exploiting an already overdrafted aquifer is not the same thing as developing a relatively unused groundwater basin with stable yields. The transaction costs of developing approaches that provide water users with true incentives to manage their resource will, in many cases, be lower than the cost of continued overexploitation – in social, economic and environmental terms.

NOTES

1   The views expressed in this chapter are the author's alone and should not be attributed to the World Bank. In addition, the author wishes to acknowledge the comments of the Groundwater Management Advisory Team of the World Bank/Global Water Partnership, as well as the inspiration of team discussions for a number of the ideas put forward in the chapter.
2   This section draws on Kemper (1996).
3   Due to space limitations, this type of cost cannot be treated in detail. There exists extensive literature about these costs and their adverse effect on efficient contracting – for example, Stiglitz (1989); Akerlof (1970); Stevens (1993); Repetto (1986); Buchanan, Tollison and Tullock, (1980).
4   Part of the economics of groundwater use is that the poor will continue pumping as long as their pumps keep working, so the investment is amortized. In this sense, maintenance may be neglected due to lack of funds and the pump is simply used until the end of its lifetime. At that point, the pump may or may not be replaced.

REFERENCES

Akerlof, G A (1970) 'The market for "lemons": Quality uncertainty and the market mechanism', *Quarterly Journal of Economics*, vol 84, no 3, pp488–500

Blomquist, W (1992*) Dividing the Waters: Governing Groundwater in Southern California*, ICS Press, San Francisco

Bromley, D W and Cernea, M M (1989) *The Management of Common Property Natural Resources: Some Conceptual and Operational Fallacies*, World Bank Discussion Paper 57, The World Bank, Washington, DC

Brown, L R, Gardner, G and Halweil, B (1999) *Beyond Malthus: Nineteen Dimensions of the Population Challenge*, Worldwatch Environmental Alert Series, Earthscan, London/WW Norton, New York

Buchanan, J D, Tollison, R D and Tullock, G (eds) (1980) *Toward a Theory of the Rent-Seeking Society*, Texas A&M University Press, College Station, TX

David, P A (1985) 'Clio and the economics of QWERTY', *American Economic Review*, Papers and Proceedings, vol 75, May, pp332–337

DuMars, C T (undated) 'Conjunctive management of ground and surface water: New Mexico case law and policy issues' in Smerdon, E T and Jordan W R (eds) *Issues in Groundwater Management*, Water Resources Symposium Number 12, Center for Research in Water Resources, Texas

Foster, S et al (2002a) 'Groundwater quality protection: A guide for water service companies, municipal authorities and environmental agencies', World Bank, Washington, DC

Foster, S et al (2002b) 'Groundwater quality protection: Defining strategy and setting priorities', Groundwater Management Advisory Team Briefing Notes Series, No 8, World Bank, Washington, DC

Foster, S et al (1998) *Groundwater in Urban Development*, World Bank Technical Paper No 390, World Bank, Washington, DC

Furubotn, E G and Richter, R (1991) *The New Institutional Economics*, Texas A&M University Press, College Station, TX

Garduño, H et al (2002) 'Groundwater abstraction rights: From theory to practice', Groundwater Management Advisory Team Briefing Notes Series, No 5, World Bank, Washington, DC

Government of the People's Republic of Bangladesh, Department of International Development (UK) and British Geological Survey (2000) *Groundwater Studies of Arsenic Contamination in Bangladesh*, Final Report Summary

Hardin, G (1968) 'The tragedy of the commons', *Science*, vol 162, pp1243–1248

Kahnert, F and Levine, G (1993) *Groundwater Irrigation and the Rural Poor: Options for Development in the Gangetic Basin*, World Bank, Washington, DC

Kemper, K E (2001) 'Markets for tradable water rights', *Overcoming Water Scarcity and Quality Constraints* 2020 Focus 9, Brief 11 of 14, October, IFPRI, Washington, DC

Kemper, K E (1996) *The Cost of Free Water: Water Resources Allocation and Use in the Curu Valley, Ceará, Northeast Brazil*, PhD thesis, Department of Water and Environmental Studies, Linkoping University, Linkoping

Kemper, K and Alvarado, O (2001) 'Water' in Guigale, M et al (eds) *Mexico: A Comprehensive Development Agenda for the New Era*, World Bank, Washington, DC

Kemper, K E, Gonçalves, J Y and Bezerra, W (1999) 'Water allocation and trading in the Cariri Region: Ceara, Brazil' in Mariño, M and Kemper, K E (eds) *Institutional*

Frameworks in Successful Water Markets: Brazil, Spain and Colorado, USA, World Bank, Washington, DC

Kemper, K E and Simpson, L (1999) 'The water market in the Northern Colorado Water Conservancy District: Institutional implications' in Mariño, M and Kemper, K E (eds) *Institutional Frameworks in Successful Water Markets. Brazil, Spain and Colorado, USA*, World Bank, Washington, DC

Moench, M (2001) 'Ground water: Potential and constraints', *Overcoming Water Scarcity and Quality Constraints* 2020 Focus 9, Brief 11 of 14, October, IFPRI, Washington, DC

North, D C (1990) *Institutions, Institutional Change and Economic Performance*, Cambridge University Press, Cambridge

Ostrom, E (1990) *Governing the Commons: The Evolution of Institutions for Collective Action*, Cambridge University Press, Cambridge

Ostrom, E, Schroeder, L and Wynne, S (1993) *Institutional Incentives and Sustainable Development*, Westview Press, Boulder, CO

Postel, S (1992) *Last Oasis: Facing Water Scarcity*, WW Norton, New York

Repetto, R (1986) *Skimming the Water: Rent-Seeking and the Performance of Public Irrigation Systems*, Research Report No 4, World Resources Institute, Washington, DC

Schiffler, M (1998) *The Economics of Groundwater Management in Arid Countries*, DGI Book Series No 11, London

Shah, T et al (2000) *The Global Groundwater Situation: Overview of Opportunities and Challenges*, International Water Management Institute (IWMI), Colombo, Sri Lanka

Simon, H A (1982) *Models of Bounded Rationality*, vol 2, MIT Press, Cambridge

Stevens, J B (1993) *The Economics of Collective Choice* Westview Press, Boulder, CO

Stiglitz, J E (1989) 'Principal and agent' in Eatwell, J et al (eds) *Allocation, Information and Markets: The New Palgrave*, WW Norton, New York

Williamson, O E (1984) 'The economics of governance: Framework and implications', *Journal of Institutional and Theoretical Economics*, vol 140, pp195–223

World Bank (1999) 'Mexico: Policy options for aquifer stabilization', unpublished, World Bank, Washington, DC

Worldwatch Institute (2001) *The State of the World 2001*, Earthscan, London/WW Norton, New York

Chapter 8

Water rights and their management: A comparative country study and its implication for China

DAJUN SHEN[1]

INTRODUCTION

With the world's rapid population increase and the evolution of civilization during the 20th century, resulting in expanding cities, burgeoning industries and an increase in irrigating farms, more and more water resources are needed for economic development and living improvement. In the near future, this growth process is estimated to continue if changes are not made to our water resources management and development patterns. Thus, water resources will face extreme stress. At the same time, today's water crisis is, to a large extent, the result of poor water management, causing suffering to billions of people and the environment.

With the coverage of water issues extending worldwide, the current government-involved water resources management strategies are becoming increasingly incapable of dealing with water resources issues. Proven private-sector methods, including the participation of other stakeholders and the employment of different instruments, are becoming constructive methods for addressing social and economic development issues. With these alternatives, the market, rather than through government, is considered an efficient way of allocating water resources. However, water is not only an economic good. It is also a social good.

Perfect market operation is based on private ownership rights. Water, however, is a life-supporting resource that cannot be fully assigned to private property rights. This is the dilemma. A balance must be struck between the assignment of ownership rights and the development of market strategies to meet the social and environmental objectives of efficient water resources management.

Water is a universal necessity, thus making it difficult to assign rights of control over water resources management. In addition, water has multiple uses. The assignment of rights for one specific function may be in conflict with other uses. Due to the geographical characteristics of water, which normally originates in a river basin, connecting water rights to land rights would not be wise, even though many cases of this exist worldwide. Generally, the nation, state or public agency owns water resources.

In the resources allocation process, water rights are the most critical issue. Ultimately, the water market and water allocation methods depend on the definition of water rights. Therefore, discussing the issue of water rights will help guide water resources management.

LEGAL AND ECONOMIC ASPECTS OF PROPERTY RIGHTS

How producers and consumers use water resources depends on the property rights that are in place. Property rights refer to a bundle of entitlements defining the owner's rights, privileges and limitations to the resource. Property rights have evolved from the traditional relations between people. In fact, the assignment of property rights defines the rules that must be obeyed in human communication related to the management of goods, and those violating these rules will be punished. Thus, right has value and must be implemented through a way that is recognized by society.

Resources allocation, from a property rights viewpoint, is the distribution of rights among the economic participants. Property is an exclusive right to use goods. However, the property right is not unlimited. But, at the same time, the limit of the right is connected to the value of the right. If there were too many limits on a private right, the value of the rights to the owner and to others would decrease. There are four rights associated with property (Tietenberg, 1992):

1 *Ownership rights:* the rights to own the property or resources.
2 *Use rights:* the rights to use the property or resources.
3 *Beneficiary rights:* the rights to gain benefits from use of the property or resources.
4 *Disposal rights:* the rights to change the forms, contents or location of the property or resources.

In order to allocate resources efficiently in the market, the assignment of property rights requires specific conditions. Generally, an efficient rights system should have four main characteristics (Tietenberg, 1992):

1 *Universality:* all resources are privately owned and all entitlements completely specified;

2   *Exclusivity*: all benefits and costs accrued as a result of owning and using the resources should accrue to the owner, and only to the owner, either directly or indirectly by sale to others;

3   *Transferability*: all property rights should be transferable from one owner to another in a voluntary exchange.

4   *Enforceability*: property rights should be secure from involuntary seizure or encroachment by others.

An owner of a resource with a well-defined property right – exhibiting one of these four characteristics – has a powerful incentive to use that resource efficiently because a decline in the resource's value represents a personal loss. Otherwise, any weakening of the rights would decrease the owner's choices for, and value of, the property, thus resulting in the reduction of resource allocation efficiency.

The transferability of property rights is very important because it is the basis for developing a market, which would encourage the good flow from the low value to high value. The private rights, like group rights and common pool rights, may or may not be transferable. The transferable rights will have a market value. The competition in the market will make the rights move to the highest value. The high cost to hold this right compels the holder to use the right efficiently and to protect it.

If the right can be transferable, it must exclude someone who holds the right without transaction. If the 'free ride' cannot be prevented, or the implementation of exclusive methods is very complex, or the cost to exclude is very high, the market value of this right will be zero and it will not be exclusive. This is one of the problems of assigning water rights.

WATER RESOURCES AS COMMON POOL RESOURCES

To better understand water resources, we must separate the concepts related to resources and property rights. Water resources are common pool resources, which refers to resource systems regardless of the property rights involved. Water resources are also resources in which the exclusion of beneficiaries through physical and institutional means is especially costly, and exploitation by one user reduces resources availability for others. These two characteristics – difficulty of exclusion and subtractability – create potential dilemmas in which people who follow their own short-term interests produce outcomes that are not in anyone's long-term interests. When resource users interact without the benefit of effective rules limiting access and defining rights and duties, substantial free riding in two forms is likely: overuse without concern for negative effects on others, and a lack of contributed resources for maintaining and improving the water resource itself (Ostrom et al, 1999).

Specific characteristics of water resources affect the problems of devising governance regimes. These characteristics include the size and carrying capacity of the resource system, the measurability of the resource, the temporal and spatial availability of resource flows, and the amount of storage in the system.

Solving water resources problems involves two distinct governance elements: restricting access and creating incentives – usually by assigning individual rights to the resources – for users to invest in the resource instead of overexploiting it. At present, widely employed permit systems, such as abstracting permits and discharge permits, are methods of restricting access. Meanwhile, building water rights and trading markets, and the application of various environmental economics instruments, such as deposits and fines, are ways of creating incentives. Both governance elements are needed. Limiting access alone can fail if water resource users compete for shares. As well, the resources can become depleted unless incentives or regulations prevent exploitation.

Four broad types of property rights have been designed in relation to water resources (see Table 8.1). When water resources are left to open-access regimes, environmental degradation and potential destruction of the resources are the result. Both group property and individual property regimes are used to manage resources that grant varying individual rights of access to, and use of, water resources. The primary difference between group property and individual property is the ease with which individual owners can buy or sell a share of a resource. Government property regimes involve ownership by national, regional or local public agencies that have the power to grant or forbid an individual's use of the resource. Empirical studies show that no single type of property regime works efficiently, fairly and sustainably in relation to all common pool resources, including water resources.

From a historical perspective, the four types of water rights systems reflect the evolving nature of water from a plentiful resource to a scarce one. When water is plentiful, it is not considered a resource, so open access is appropriate. When water is scarce, it is considered a resource and is assigned property rights as needed. Because water is a public good, a government property regime is considered the best method of allocating water resources to meet the social needs. But water is becoming more and more scarce in some areas of the world, and it is evident that government property cannot adequately address the problems of resource allocation. Therefore, individual or group property rights systems are introduced. Water, then, becomes an economic good as well as a social good.

At the same time, this is also a development of water rights systems. A water right would not be necessary if water was abundant and anybody could use it as he or she wished. People once utilized water simply by taking it. But as local populations increased and development activities took place, water became a scarce natural resource. Water conflicts occurred frequently, especially during droughts; as a result, the concept of water rights as an institution of conflict was born. This is the origin of customary water rights (Teerink and Nakashima, 1992).

Unlike other common pool resources, assigning efficient property rights to water resources is difficult because of certain characteristics. These characteristics are as follows (Shen, 1999):

Table 8.1 *Types of property rights systems used to regulate water resources*

Property rights	Characteristics
Open access	Absence of enforced property rights
Group property	Resource rights held by a group of users that can exclude others
Individual property	Resource rights held by individual (or firms) that can exclude others
Government property	Resources rights held by a government that can regulate or subsidize use

- *Basic need for all life:* All life on Earth has depended on water since the first single-cell organisms appeared 3.5 billion years ago. Water is necessary for sustaining life. Water is the most active factor in the environment. It is not replaceable. Therefore, during the assignment of water resources, the basic needs of humans and the environment must be the first priority.
- *Movement:* The movement of water is controlled by gravity. Although there are some other mobile common pool resources, such as fish and wild animals, water is the only moving non-bioresource. Due to the movement of water, assigning efficient property rights is very difficult. Before 1950, when water was not a scarce resource, water rights were normally connected to land rights. This is still the case for many countries, including international river basins. But it has been proven that transaction costs for this system are too high, and water resource allocation efficiency is too low. Due to the movement of water, rights cannot be assigned to one individual if that person does not own the entire river basin. Furthermore, the development and management of water resources by one individual or group will affect others who hold rights upstream or downstream.
- *Locality:* Water is a local resource that cannot be transported elsewhere. Normally, water can only be traded in a local net, such as naturally occurring rivers, and human-made nets, such as channels, canals and urban water supply networks. Due to the locality, water markets are local markets.
- *Variable nature:* The variable nature of water flow, which makes it especially difficult and costly to achieve the necessary certainty in transferable rights, is affected by the hydrological phenomena. During droughts, water is very scarce and cannot meet the environment's basic needs. During periods of flooding, water can cause disaster, resulting in death and property damage. Therefore, if water is assigned to someone, that person must be responsible for both benefits and losses. At the same time, together with the movement of water, benefits and losses will affect the other water resource users.

TYPICAL WATER RIGHTS ASSIGNMENTS AND
THEIR CHARACTERISTICS

Chile[2]

The water rights reform in Chile is considered an innovative legal and institutional water allocation development. After the change of government in 1973, the new government shifted towards a market-oriented social and economic policy. With the shift to market-oriented policies, the fundamental policy reforms facilitating efficiency and flexibility in agricultural resource allocation were the redistribution of land and water resources to the private sector under the Agrarian Reform; the definition of clear and well-defined land and water property rights; and the market allocation of both of these resources. The water code, introduced in 1981, entitles secure transferable water rights expressed in volume. Water is considered a public good; but individuals can obtain private rights over water by receiving a grant from the state for new water sources by prescription, or by purchasing water rights. The constitution of Chile (passed in 1980 and modified in 1988) provides that 'the rights of private individuals, or enterprises, over water, recognized or established by law, grant their holders the property over them'. The water code establishes the basic characteristics of water rights. The right to utilize water is a real right that confers ownership to its holder. The owner is entitled to use water, obtain benefits from it and dispose of it. As well, water rights can be alienated from land and mortgaged. According to the water code, rights of use are either consumptive or non-consumptive. Their exercise can be permanent or contingent, continuous or discontinuous, or rights may alternate among several persons.

The rights to utilize water are originally granted by act of authority on available water (new or surplus) or, as in this case, on the basis of prescription. In 1975, the government, through administrative orders and transitory laws, froze the actual use of water at 1975 levels to establish a base for the assignment of water rights. Therefore, most new water users had a good basis for obtaining water rights that were established in 1979 through prescription. The second most common way of obtaining water rights, after state grants by prescription, has been through market transactions. Only a very small proportion of water rights has originated in grants over available water. There is no priority in Chilean law, with an equal sharing of shortages among rights holders.

To ensure the rights of third parties, any transfer of the use rights of natural watercourses requires authorization from the General Directorate of Water. With artificial watercourses, authorization comes from the respective water-user association. Those persons or organizations with hydraulic infrastructure that would be affected by a transfer of water rights to natural watercourses may file relevant motions before the respective user organization and the General Directorate of Water.

In Chile, any entity holding rights to water use must join a users' organization or association. These organizations are fundamental to the management of Chile's water. The general functions of these organizations are to distribute the water according to rights, and to build, administer, preserve and improve water infrastructure necessary to their members.

Active water markets have been developed in several regions both within and between agriculture and other sectors. The most frequent transactions in water markets are water rentals, or water swaps, between nearby farmers with different water requirements during different periods. Permanent water transactions between farmers also occur, motivated by shifts in cropping patterns. These shifts are in response to price changes in an open trade market economy, according to domestic and international demand. Other water sellers are highly intensive crop farmers who introduce more sophisticated techniques, such as drip irrigation, and sell water to finance the investment. One of the most important innovations of Chile's water policy is allowing cities to buy water without having to buy land or expropriate water. Today, growing cities buy rights from many farmers – usually buying a small portion of each farmer's total rights.

California[3]

In California, a water right is a legal entitlement authorizing water to be diverted from a specified source and put to beneficial, non-wasteful use. Water rights are property rights; but their holders do not own the water itself – they possess the right to use it.

The exercise of some water rights requires a permit or licence from the State Water Resources Control Board, whose objective is to ensure that the state's waters are put to the best possible use and that the public interest is served. In making decisions, the board must keep three major goals in mind:

1   Developing water resources in an orderly manner.
2   Preventing waste and unreasonable use of water.
3   Protecting the environment.

The state board's duties are limited to permits and licences. It may be called upon to adjudicate water for entire systems or to act as a referee or fact finder in court cases involving water rights.

Water right law in California and the rest of the West is markedly different from the laws governing water use in the eastern USA. Seasonal, geographic and quantitative differences in precipitation caused California's system to develop into a unique blend of two very different kinds of rights: *riparian* and *appropriative*. Other types of rights exist in California, as well, among them reserved rights – water set aside by the federal government when it reserves land for the public domain – and *pueblo* rights – a municipal right based on Spanish and Mexican law.

Riparian rights usually come with owning a parcel of land that is adjacent to a water source. With statehood, California adopted the English common law familiar to the eastern seaboard; such law also included the riparian doctrine. A riparian right entitles the landowner to use a correlative share of the water flowing past his or her property. Riparian rights do not require permits, licences or government approval; but they apply only to the water which would naturally flow in the stream. Riparian rights do not entitle a water user to divert water to storage in a reservoir for use in the dry season or to use water on land outside of the watershed. Riparian rights remain with the property when it changes hands, although parcels severed from the adjacent water source generally lose their right to the water.

Water right law was set on a different course in 1849, when thousands of fortune seekers flocked to California following the discovery of gold. Water development proceeded on a scale never before witnessed in the USA as these 'forty-niners' built extensive networks of flumes and waterways to work their claims. The water carried in these systems often had to be transported far from the original river or stream. The self-governing, maverick miners applied the same 'finders-keepers' rule to water that they did to their mining claims – it belonged to the first miner to assert ownership. To stake their water claims, the miners developed a system of 'posting notice', which signalled the birth of today's appropriative rights system. It allowed others to divert available water from the same river or stream; but their rights existed within a hierarchy of priorities. This 'first-in-time, first-in-right' principle became an important feature of modern water rights law.

In 1850, California entered the Union as the 31st state. One of the first actions taken by its law-makers was to adopt the common law of riparian rights. One year later, the legislature recognized the appropriative rights system as having the force of law. The appropriative rights system continued to increase in use as agriculture and population centres blossomed and ownership of land was transferred into private hands.

The conflicting nature of California's dual water rights system prompted numerous legal disputes. Unlike appropriative users, riparian rights holders were not required to put water to reasonable and beneficial use. This clash of rights eventually resulted in a constitutional amendment (Article X, Section 2 of the California Constitution) that requires all use of water to be 'reasonable and beneficial'. These 'beneficial uses' have commonly included municipal and industrial uses, irrigation, hydroelectric generation and livestock watering. More recently, the concept has been broadened to include recreational use, fish and wildlife protection, and enhancement and aesthetic enjoyment.

The Water Commission Act, 1914, established today's permit process. The act created the agency that later evolved into the state board and granted it the authority to administer permits and licences for California's surface water. The act was the predecessor of today's water code provisions governing appropriation.

The aforementioned hierarchy of priorities developed by the 'forty-niners' governs these post-1914 appropriation rights. In times of shortage, the most recent, or 'junior', right holder must be the first to discontinue such use; each right's priority dates to the time the permit application was filed with the state board. Although pre- and post-1914 appropriative rights are similar, post-1914 rights are subject to a much greater degree of scrutiny and regulation by the board.

Riparian rights still have a higher priority than appropriative rights. The priorities of riparian rights holders generally carry equal weight; during a drought, all share the shortage among themselves.

In most areas of California, overlying landowners may extract percolating groundwater and put it to beneficial use without approval from the state board or a court. California does not have a permit process for regulation of groundwater use. In several basins, however, groundwater use is subject to regulation in accordance with court decrees adjudicating the groundwater rights within the basins.

The California Supreme Court decided in the 1903 case, Katz versus Walkinshaw, that the 'reasonable use' provision that governs other types of water rights also applies to groundwater. Prior to this time, the English system of unregulated groundwater pumping had dominated, but proved to be inappropriate to California's semi-arid climate. The supreme court case established the concept of overlying rights, in which the rights of others with land overlying the aquifer must be taken into account. Later court decisions established that groundwater may be appropriated for use outside of the basin, although appropriators' rights are subordinate to those with overlying rights.

Permit holders run the gamut from water districts and electric utilities, to farmers and ranchers. Besides riparian rights holders and groundwater users, permits are not required for users of purchased water or those who use water from springs or standing pools lacking natural outlets on the land where they are located. However, unauthorized appropriation of water is against the law and can result in court action and fines.

Water right permits carefully spell out the amounts, conditions and construction timetables for the proposed water project. Before the board issues a permit, it must take into account all prior rights and the availability of water in the basin. The board considers, too, the flows needed to preserve in-stream uses such as recreation and fish and wildlife habitat. The state board's Division of Water Rights maintains records of water appropriation and use statewide.

To obtain a permit, the prospective appropriator must follow these seven steps:

1 File an application.
2 Accept the application.
3 Environmental review.
4 Public notice.
5 Protest resolution.
6 Permit issuance.
7 Licensing.

In recent years, temporary transfers of water from one water user to another have been increasingly used as a way of meeting statewide water demands, particularly in drought years. Temporary transfers of post-1914 water rights are initiated by petition to the state board. If the board finds that the proposed transfer will not injure any other legal user of water and will not unreasonably affect fish, wildlife or other in-stream users, then the transfer is approved. If the board cannot make the required findings within 60 days, a hearing is held prior to board action on the proposed transfer. Temporary transfers are defined for a period of one year or less. A similar review and approval process applies to long-term transfers in excess of one year.

Japan[4]

There is no statute in Japan that provides a definition of a water right in itself. However, the River Law of 1965 sets forth provisions regarding a formal allocation of water through administrative procedures. The law defines river water as public property, and a certain quantity of river water may be withdrawn for an exclusive use by obtaining permission. The Multipurpose Dam Law (Article 15) enables water users to obtain the Dam Usufructuary Right to use reservoir storage. This right is a property and similar to water right in nature. Water users with the purposes of municipal water supply, industrial water supply and hydropower generation may apply for this right by sharing the cost of dam construction.

After the Meiji Restoration in 1868, which was the beginning of modern Japanese history, the first statute dealing with river water was established in 1896. This law was the first statute to formally grant a water right. As a matter of fact, most water resources in natural streams had already been used up in Japan when this law was enacted. Since a water right was granted only when there was an excess quantity of water, reservoir storage had to be developed for flow augmentation in order to obtain a major water right.

In Japan, a water right is a right to use water exclusively for a long period of time. Since a river, including river flow, is public property, the 1965 River Law does not allow river water to be an object of private rights. Therefore, a water right is a usufructuary right and also a property right, which is bound by certain constraints. Such constraints include the following:

- A water right holder can take water with limited quantity for his or her own purpose.
- A water right holder cannot change his water-use purpose; but, if necessary, he or she may apply for a new water right with a different purpose after abandoning the original right.
- A water right transfer is permitted only when a corporate business is transferred with its property to another party and the water right is a part of the corporate property.

Water rights may be classified by the origin of their establishment, by the purpose of water uses and by security against drought or certainty of water intake during a drought. With regard to the origin of establishment, a permitted water right is a right obtained under the River Law. The customary water right is a right socially accepted before the enactment of the law.

Depending upon the purpose of water uses, several examples of water rights are irrigation water rights; industrial water rights; municipal water rights; hydropower water rights; and fish-farming water rights. With regard to the certainty or security of water intake, there is the stable water right; wet-year water right; tentative water right; or tentative wet-year water right.

River water had been used for hundreds of years before the River Law was enacted. Customary water uses were accepted by local societies. The customary rights were established and recognized by communities through investments by local people. The rights are now called customary water rights, which are also recognized by the 1965 River Law and looked upon as water rights permitted under the law:

- The customary water rights are mostly for irrigation purpose due to the long history where river water was developed for rice growing in paddy fields.
- Customary water uses are multipurpose in nature. Water has been utilized primarily for irrigation, but also for drinking, domestic uses, fire fighting, in-stream flow needs and all local needs.
- For water intake, there are local customs called upstream priority and old paddy priority. These are priority principles with respect to a location factor and a temporal factor, respectively. Local customs are different for each locality and the upstream priority is not always accepted, even where this principle prevails historically.
- The substance of customary water right is often expressed not by the quantity of water, but by the physical facility of water intake.

With regard to security against drought, there are four types of water rights. A water right is conferred only when there is excess in quantity of water after satisfying prior appropriations and in-stream flow needs with the ten-year return-period minimum flow. The stable water right is a right granted under the ten-year minimum-flow condition and is considered as a most secure water right. The remaining water rights are all conditional rights. A wet-year water right holder may withdraw river water only when there is more flow than the ten-year minimum flow, while a stable water right holder may withdraw river water even in the occurrence of the ten-year minimum flow. The tentative water right or tentative wet-year water right is granted under the condition that a storage facility is built in the near future and with a wet-year conditionality. This water right is tentative, since the right is terminated after a certain period, which is stated in permit terms and conditions.

In principle, a priority among various water rights should be determined based on the temporal order of granting a water right, which is essentially the same as the prior appropriation doctrine. This principle is indicated in the terms and conditions of a water right permit, which states that a permit holder should not disturb the prior appropriations and fishery activities. Exceptions to this general principle are allowed, which may be described in the following three cases:

1   There is a case where local customs prevail rather than the general principle of the prior appropriation doctrine.
2   Users who obtained the dam usufructuary right are not bound by the prior appropriation doctrine since they have the right to utilize certain storage capacity in a reservoir.
3   The tentative water right or tentative wet-year water right cannot enjoy the prior appropriation doctrine, since it is a conditional water right.

A water right is a property right. Therefore, it could be transferred to another person or party. River water is, however, a public property and the water must be treated as such. This implies that the water right is subject to certain constraints. According to a River Law statute, for example, an application must be made for a water right transfer and approved by a river administrator. By regulation, a water right transfer from one water-use purpose to another is not allowed. When a water right transfer is planned, a present water right holder and an intended water right recipient must file an application to a competent river administrator. The application must be accompanied by a description of the project, which necessitates the water use. The river administrator must consult with the concerned government agencies. These agencies are ministries and prefecture governments, depending on water-use purposes and river classes.

Comments on the three cases

The three water rights cases stated above demonstrate the great differences in implementing water rights systems. First, the three cases included two different legal systems. The Chilean system was adopted from the continental law, while the California system was adopted from the common law. These two systems are different from each other regarding the formulation and implementation of law. They also differ in their impact on water rights systems. Second, the difference in the legal definition of water rights would be the key factor in the water rights system. These differences showcase the disparity among social and legal systems in various countries, as well as the different water resources circumstances. Third, the complexity and development of water rights are different. The California case, because of historical reasons, might be the most complex water rights system in the world. The Chilean case may be the most recently developed. Fourth, the elements of water rights are different. The elements include the transferability, coverage and security factors related to water rights. As previously discussed, rights with less limitations have greater value. In the three cases, Chilean water rights could be transferred among sectors, while Japanese water rights could not. Fifth, the acquisition of water rights varies according to a region's conditions.

WATER RIGHTS REFORM IN CHINA: THEORETICAL AND PRACTICAL EXPLORATIONS TOWARDS EFFICIENT WATER RESOURCES MANAGEMENT

The basic principles of water rights in China

The 1982 constitution established the fundamental resources principles that must be compiled. The constitution contains three articles that specifically address natural resources. Article 9 provides that 'all mineral resources, waters, forests, mountains, grasslands, unclaimed land, beaches and other natural resources are owned by the state'. The 1988 Water Law is the 'umbrella' law for water management in China. Article 3 declares that water resources – both surface and groundwater – are property of the state, except when an agricultural collective owns water in ponds and reservoirs. Articles 14 to 23 identify priorities of use. Articles 32 and 33 establish a water permit system for diversion and extraction of water, except for small-scale household uses. But the 1988 Water Law did not develop the concept of usage rights for water resources. The amendment to the Water Law, currently under way, proposes that 'water resources are property of the state, and the State Council, on behalf of the state, implements the ownership rights'. Article 40 identifies that 'the state permits systems for drawing water directly from ground aquifers, rivers and lakes; the acquisition of water drawing permits means withholding water-use rights. Approved by the original licensing agencies, the water-use rights can be transferred according to regulations.' So, the new Water Law will develop a water rights system in China; but it needs time to be approved.

Although the water rights issue has been widely discussed within and outside of the Chinese water sector, since the foundation of the People's Republic of China, in practice there are no water rights implemented in China. With deepening economic reforms in China, including reforms to the water sector, water-sector managers and administrators in China recognize the need for market mechanisms in water resources management. But in the process of implementing a new water rights system, too many issues must be addressed, including legal, institutional and constitutional problems.

Priority in water uses

Article 14 of the 1988 Water Law established this water resources development priority: 'the water resources development should first satisfy the domestic water demand, and comprehensively consider the requirements of agriculture, industry and navigation'. Article 5 of 'Regulations for the Implementation of the Water Drawing Permit System' (State Council Decree 119, 1993) declares in more detail that:

> ...*in the implementation of the water drawing permit system, the domestic water demands of urban and rural inhabitants shall be satisfied first, while agricultural and industrial demands, as well*

> as navigation and environmental protection requirements, shall also be considered. The people's governments at the provincial level may specify priorities in water drawing in light of site-specific conditions in designated water bodies or areas.

The amendment to Article 17 proposed that:

> ...the water resources development should first satisfy the domestic water demand, and comprehensively consider the requirements of agriculture, industry, environment and the ecological system. In the environmentally fragile regions, the water requirements should be specially considered.

In the meantime, Minister of Water Resources Wang Sucheng developed ideas for prioritizing water rights assignments (Department of Legislation, 2001):

- First, basic human water demands must be satisfied. Everyone has the right to use water for basic domestic needs. This water must be clean and available.
- Factors affecting priority:
  - *Water source area priority:* In dealing with the relation between down stream and upstream, water source area should be prioritized. Host water area should be first.
  - *Food security priority:* In China, food security is the most important factor maintaining social stability.
  - *Water-use efficiency priority:* The water should be used where it is of highest value.
  - *Investment capacity priority:* The water should be allocated to those with the investment capacity on water resources projects.
  - *Current water-use priority:* This priority considers the present water resources development.
  - *Changing priority:* This priority varies with social and economic development, as well as water resources development.

But Wang does not mention the priority of the environmental water use. Perhaps environmental water usage was not included in the water rights assignment, or perhaps it is a low priority.

Analysis of China's first water rights transaction case

Although a definition regarding water rights laws and regulations is unclear, with support for implementing water rights in China, a water rights transaction case occurred in 2000. This case triggered a water rights debate.

This case happened in the two neighboring counties of Dongyang and Yiwu in Eastern China's Zhejiang Province. The counties are located in a subtropical zone with plentiful precipitation; however, because of high population density and fast economic development in Yiwu County, the local water resources cannot meet demand. Therefore, after negotiations with Dongyang County, the two counties signed a water rights transaction contract. The contract states that:

- Yiwu County purchases the right to use 50 million cubic metres (m³) of water at a price of 200 million yuan from the Hengjin Reservoir located in, and managed by, Dongyang County.
- After the transaction of water-use rights, the responsibility for managing the reservoir will not change. Yiwu County should pay a tariff of 0.1 yuan per m³ of water.
- The engineering to convey water from Hengjin Reservoir to Yiwu should be designed and paid for by Yiwu County, while the engineering in Dongyang County should be consulted on and built by Dongyang County, but paid for by Yiwu County.

This is the first case regarding water trading in China. There is no doubt that it is a milestone in China's water-sector reform. Its importance is outlined below:

- It is a new form of water resources allocation. This form, employing market mechanism, reflects the value of water resources and will be helpful in managing water resources efficiently.
- A mechanism to regulate the water transfer was constructed. Generally, inter-basin or inter-region water transfers are very difficult to regulate and always result in large transaction costs. This mechanism will save those costs.

But most importantly, this case reveals many issues that must be addressed in order to gradually implement and improve water rights systems. The following are some of these issues:

- Who can own the water rights on behalf of the state? In China, water law only declares that water resources are state owned. Did the seller, in this case, own the water rights and have the right to sell?
- The third-party effect: because the water sold does not fully come from the seller's territory, did the seller have the right to sell the water that does not originate in its territory? If not, how can one deal with the upper stream?
- This case features an issue facing historical water transfer projects, as well as future water transfer projects. For example, in China, before this case happened, there were many inter-region water transfer projects. If water rights systems are implemented in China, how should one cope with these cases? And how should compensation for the past water supplies – especially inter-region and inter-river basin – that are provided at almost no cost be handled? In the future, if China attempts to build the South-to-

North Project while applying a water rights system, doing so will be nearly impossible, according to this case. The water-importing region would have to pay a large amount of money to buy the water rights, even without considering the infrastructure investment. Moreover, the price for this water rights transaction would be much higher since water is more valuable in these areas than in the case area.

- The contract was signed by two governments, rather than by individuals or companies. Therefore, the contract is a governmental document, rather than a business contract. If violated, there would be complex legal problems.
- The water (rights) traded is not the raw water rights that would be transferred from the reservoir directly. As a result, a question arises concerning the water rights in the reservoir. Is it legal for transaction? If it is legal, who owns the water drawing permit? Does the holder of the permit agree to let the government sell it?
- This is a case between the regions. What about water rights trading among different sectors in and around regions?

A proposal for implementing a water rights system in China

Regarding water rights assignments, other countries have formulated rules that may no longer be appropriate, though they are difficult to change. China is a relatively untapped land that does not have any experience of implementing water rights systems. During the design of a Chinese water rights system, the external environment, such as the economic and social systems, must be considered. In the water sector, the rights systems should be designed to meet the efficient property rights system in order to improve resources allocation and to reduce the transaction cost.

In China, water resources must be treated as a public good. But the use rights, the beneficiary rights and the disposal rights could be assigned as private rights, on par with efficient property rights and market allocation demands. Therefore, an initiative can be developed in China (see Table 8.2) that will increase the resources allocation efficiency, especially in regions where water is owned by the public agency.

Table 8.2 *The proposed efficient assignment of water rights in China*

Characteristics	Ownership	Use rights	Beneficiary rights	Disposal rights
Universality	No	Yes	Yes	Yes
Exclusivity	No	Yes	Yes	Yes
Transferability	No	Yes	Yes	Yes
Enforceability	No	Yes	Yes	Yes

Note: 'Yes' for meeting the condition; 'no' for not meeting the condition.

Table 8.2 shows that, aside from ownership rights, the other three rights – use rights, beneficiary rights and disposal rights – can, through appropriate assignments, be as efficient in allocating resources. This means that use rights, beneficiary rights and disposal rights can be universal, exclusive, transferable and enforceable, while ownership rights cannot.

From proposal to realization

To realize the proposal, the basic works, such as water resources assessment, environmental water requirement assessment and basic human demand, should be conducted before the system's implementation. In terms of water rights, the following steps are critical:

- *Acquisition of water rights:* Acquisition of water rights would separate the use rights, together with the beneficiary rights and disposal rights, from the property rights. Through the application of water rights, the owner of the resources (generally, the government) can regulate the water resources development by controlling the water resources quantity and development measures. In China, the water-drawing permit system has been implemented to authorize the water transfer to the users. If a water rights system is developed, the reform can be based on the current water-drawing permit system.
- *Water resources fee/tax:* To realize the transfer of the beneficiary rights from the owner to the user, the water resources fee/tax system is necessary to avoid monopoly profits from the holding of the permits or the rights. This can be regarded as the transfer of the user rights from the owner to the user, as well. But from the property rights viewpoint, it is the beneficiary rights transfer from the owner to the user.
- *Water rights trading market:* In order to expedite the resources allocation efficiency, market mechanisms are needed. Therefore, concerning the transfer of disposal rights from the owner to the user, the public agency should build a water rights trading market and ensure that water resources are directed to a place where it is needed and most valued.

CONCLUSIONS

There is no correct method of assigning water rights. Because of the different water resources management systems worldwide, a considerable theoretical exploration is needed to effectively address the new water resources issues that are being faced. Allocation of water through tradable water rights offers a number of potential advantages, including the empowerment of water users by requiring consent to any reallocation of water and compensation for any water transferred; security of water rights tenure, which improves incentives for investment in water-saving technology; the establishment of water users to consider the potential cost of water, including its value in alternative uses; the provision of incentives for water users to take account of some of the external costs imposed by their water use, reducing the pressure to degrade resources; and flexibility in responding to change in crop prices and water values as demand patterns change and diversification of cropping proceeds (Schleyer and Rosegrant, 1996). But the most important advantage is that by employing market mechanism and releasing governmental pressures in water resources management, the efficiency of water resources allocation will be improved and water resources will not be as badly managed as before.

However, a number of possible problems with applying market principles to water rights systems have also been identified. They include high transaction costs for water trades that could limit the scope of trading; the variable nature of water flow, which could make it especially difficult and costly to achieve the necessary certainty in transferable rights; the costly investment in technology and management to implement improved conveyance for the on-demand delivery of water, water metering and enforcement of contracts; the high demands on institutional capabilities to regulate markets; and the presence of significant externalities imposed on third parties. This includes, for example, the spillover effects of water trade on other people's welfare (Schleyer and Rosegrant, 1996). Water rights management is affected by the following key factors.

Cost of water rights

In the market, price should reflect the value of the goods. But a water rights market is not perfect. If price was not properly developed, the function of the water rights market would be misleading. Considering the public good of water resources, the price of water rights always demonstrates some policy direction. For example, the domestic water rights should give special attention to basic human needs, as well as to the poor's ability to pay for water.

The transfer of water rights

Water rights must be transferred if rights are assigned. Otherwise, there will be no incentive for improving water resources management. Due to the multifunctionality and locality of water resources, it is necessary to define compensation mechanisms for the transfer of water rights among sectors.

Priority uses in sectors and users

From a sustainable development viewpoint, the environmental water requirement should be given second priority, just after the domestic water requirements. Other sectors, such as industry, agriculture, hydropower and navigation, are based on the consideration of regional objectives for developing water resources. In the meantime, the priority of water rights for these sectors will vary. In addition, different users within the same sector will have different priorities.

Third-party effects

Due to the complex connection with other factors in the environment, the third-party effects of water resources activities are always profound, yet not immediately identifiable. Thus, trying to evaluate third-party effects during the assignments is very critical. It needs thorough investigation from the licensing agency before water resources can be allocated.

Conflict resolution mechanism

Due to the nature of water resources, water management cannot avoid conflict during the allocation of rights. Therefore, the conflict resolution mechanism is a very important supplement to the market. Regardless of the type of mechanism in place, whether it is a water-user association, water administrative agency or court, conflict resolution mechanisms should be effective and less costly.

Crisis management mechanism

Crisis management is used to manage water rights when there is a drought. When a drought occurs, the specific regulatory procedure is active, and the regulator should be fully responsible for the allocation of water according to the rules of water rights assignment during crises.

At the same time, the following lessons are learned in water rights management practices:

- *The legal aspects of water rights:* The water rights system falls within the scope of the legal system. The real estate rights law should first define the water rights or natural resources property rights, and then water law could be formulated from the water rights articles. At the same time, the different legal systems of the regions and/or countries decide a legal frame to formulate the laws and/or regulations related to water rights. All water rights systems must fit into this frame.
- *The initial assignment of water rights:* The initial assignment of water rights is a redistribution of wealth among users. Therefore, it must be fair and equitable. In Chile, the establishment of tradable water rights in 1976 was linked to the reprivatization of land that had been collectivized in 1966. Farmers and other water users saw the new assignment of tradable water rights as a significant improvement in equity. On the other hand, in California, the traditional assignment of water rights cannot be considered fair today. In China, while facing water rights reform, equally allocating the initial water rights will become the key problem because water resources are owned by the state.
- *Traditional ethics on water:* Until now, most people thought that water should be free to use, and that it is a common property, even though this resulted in bad water resources management. The traditional thinking on water is very difficult to change, and therefore it will be more difficult to

design a proper water rights system. Thus, when reforming the water rights system, public awareness and education will be very important, especially in China.

- *The transaction costs of water rights:* From an institutional economics viewpoint, the assignment of water rights aims to decrease the transaction costs of water allocation and to improve the water resources efficiency. If the transaction costs of implementing water rights systems are too high, efficiency cannot be achieved.
- *The clear, secure water property rights:* This is the basic principle of property rights. Only clear and secure water rights can be allocated by the market to generate the full benefits.

NOTES

1   The author would like to thank Naser Faruqui and Liam Gerofsky at the International Development Research Centre in Ottawa, Canada, for their editing work.
2   The Chilean case is abstracted from Schleyer and Rosegrant (1996).
3   The Californian material is cited from www.waterrights.ca.gov.
4   The Japanese case is abstracted from Teerink and Nakashima (1992).

REFERENCES

Department of Legislation (2001) *Collection of Water Rights and Water Market,* Ministry of Water Resources, Beijing

Food and Agriculture Organization (FAO) (2001) 'Water rights administration: Experience, issues and guidelines', FAO, Rome

Furubotn, E G and Richter, R (1991) *New Institutional Economics,* JCB Mohr, Tubingen

Ostrom, E et al (1999) 'Revisiting the commons: Local lessons, global challenges', *Science,* vol 284, pp278–282

Schleyer, R G and Rosegrant, M W (1996) 'Chilean water policy: The role of water rights, institutions and markets', *Water Resources Development,* vol 12, no 1, pp33–48

Shen, D (1999) *Water Pricing Theory and Practices,* Science Press, Beijing

Teerink, J R and Nakashima, M (1992) 'Water allocation, rights, and pricing: Examples from Japan and the United States', World Bank Technical Paper No 198

Tietenberg, T (1992) *Environmental and Natural Resources Economics,* HarperCollins, New York

Zhang, J (1996) *Modern Property Rights Economics,* Shanghai Sanlian Press, China

Chapter 9

The present and future of transboundary water management

AARON T WOLF

INTRODUCTION

A closer look at the world's international basins gives a greater sense of the magnitude of the issues. First, the problem is growing. There were 214 international basins listed in 1978 (United Nations, 1978), the last time any official body attempted to delineate them, and there are 261 today. The growth is largely the result of the 'internationalization' of national basins through political changes, such as the break up of the Soviet Union and the Balkan states, as well as access to today's better mapping sources and technology.

Even more striking than the total number of basins is a breakdown of each nation's land surface that falls within these watersheds. A total of 145 nations include territory within international basins. Twenty-one nations lie in their entirety within international basins; including these, a total of 33 countries have greater than 95 per cent of their territory within these basins. These nations are not limited to smaller countries, such as Liechtenstein and Andorra, but include such sizable countries as Hungary, Bangladesh, Belarus, and Zambia (Wolf et al, 1999).

A final way to visualize the dilemmas posed by international water resources is to look at the number of countries that share each international basin. Nineteen basins are shared by 5 or more riparian countries: 1 basin – the Danube – has 17 riparian nations; 5 basins – the Congo, Niger, Nile, Rhine and Zambezi – are shared by between 9 and 11 countries; and the remaining 13 basins – the Amazon, Ganges-Brahmaputra-Meghna, Lake Chad, Tarim, Aral Sea, Jordan, Kura-Araks, Mekong, Tigris-Euphrates, Volga, La Plata, Neman and Vistula (Wista) – have between 5 and 8 riparian countries.

Development on waters crossing political boundaries has additional complexities brought on by strains in riparian relations and institutional limitations. Recent studies, particularly in the field of environmental security, have focused on the conflict potential of these international waters. Some stress the dangers of violence over international waters (see, for example, Gleick, 1993; Homer-Dixon, 1994; Remans, 1995; Westing, 1986; and Samson and Charrier, 1997), while others argue more strongly for the possibilities and historic evidence of cooperation between co-riparians (see Libiszewski, 1995; Wolf, 1998; and Salman and Boisson de Chazournes, 1998). The fortunate corollary of water as an inducement to conflict is that water, by its very nature, tends to induce even hostile co-riparians to cooperate, even as disputes rage over other issues.

Much of the recent thinking about the concept of 'environmental security', though, has moved beyond a presumed causal relationship between environmental stress and violent conflict to a broader notion of 'human security' – a more inclusive concept focusing on the intricate sets of relationships between environment and society, and encompassing issues of internal stability and sub-acute tensions (those that fall short of violence). It is important to understand in this context there *is* a history of water-related violence – it is a history of incidents at the sub-national level, generally between ethnic, religious or tribal groups, water-use sectors, or states/provinces. In fact, there are many examples of internal water conflicts, ranging from interstate violence and death along the Cauvery River in India, to California farmers blowing up a pipeline meant for Los Angeles, to much of the violent history in the Americas between indigenous peoples and European settlers. There is also an extensive history of sub-acute tensions between, for example, Arabs and Israelis, Indians and Pakistanis, and even between non-contiguous nations, such as Egypt and Ethiopia.

THE TRANSBOUNDARY FRESHWATER DISPUTE DATABASE

To aid in assessing the process of water conflict resolution, we have been working over the past five years to develop the transboundary freshwater dispute database, a project of the Oregon State University Department of Geosciences, in collaboration with the Northwest Alliance for Computational Science and Engineering. The database currently includes a digital map of the world's 261 international watersheds; a searchable compilation of 300 water-related treaties, along with the full text of each; an annotated bibliography of the state of the art of water conflict resolution, including approximately 1000 entries; negotiating notes (primary or secondary) from 14 detailed case studies of water conflict resolution; a comprehensive news file of all reported cases of international water-related disputes and dispute resolution (dating from 1950 to 2000); and descriptions of indigenous/traditional methods of water dispute resolution.

Within the context of the database project, Wolf, Yoffe and Giordano (2003) attempted to assess the indicators of settings with a high potential for water disputes. By correlating each of the incidents of water conflict and cooperation against the biophysical, geopolitical and socio-economic setting that existed when each event occurred, they made a preliminary identification of those international basins that are at the greatest risk for potential dispute in the near future. It is to be hoped that the appropriate international agencies might then be able to focus energy and resources on these 'basins at risk' for activities of preventative diplomacy in order to ameliorate the potential for conflict.

The hypothesis of the study was as follows: 'The likelihood of conflict rises as the rate of change within the basin exceeds the institutional capacity to absorb that change.'

This suggests that there are two sides to the dispute setting – the rate of change in the system and the institutional capacity. Clearly, one of the most rapid rates of change within a basin, with an attendant risk for conflict, occurs when a dam or major development project is constructed (the other is the 'internationalization' of national systems, as will be explored below). The likelihood of dispute over such a development rises with low institutional capacity – for example, when there is no treaty or other regional agreement, or when relations are especially bad over other issues.

To cut through the prevailing anecdotal approach to the history of water conflicts, the study attempted to compile a dataset of *every* reported interaction between two or more nations, whether conflictive or cooperative, that involved water as a scarce and/or consumable resource, or as a quantity to be managed – where water is the *driver* of the events – over the past 50 years.[1] The study documents a total of 1831 interactions, both conflictive and cooperative, between two or more nations over water during the past 50 years and found the following:

- First, despite the potential for dispute in international basins, the record of cooperation historically overwhelms the record of acute conflict over international water resources. The last 50 years have seen only 37 acute disputes (those involving violence) while, during the same period, 157 treaties were negotiated and signed.[2] The total number of water-related events between nations of any magnitude are likewise weighted towards cooperation: 507 conflict-related events versus 1228 cooperative, implying that violence over water is neither strategically rational, hydrographically effective, nor economically viable.
- Second, nations find many more issues of cooperation than of conflict. The distribution of cooperative events is shown below and indicates a broad spectrum of issue types, including quantity, quality, economic development, hydropower and joint management. In contrast, almost 90 per cent of the conflictive events relate to quantity and infrastructure. Furthermore, if we look specifically at extensive military acts – the most extreme cases of conflict – almost 100 per cent of events fall within these two categories.
- Third, at the sub-acute level, water acts as both an irritant and as a unifier. As an irritant, water can make good relations bad and bad relations worse.

Threats and disputes have raged across boundaries, with relations as diverse as those between Indians and Pakistanis and between Americans and Canadians. Water was the last and most contentious issue resolved in negotiations over a 1994 peace treaty between Israel and Jordan, and was relegated to 'final status' negotiations – along with other difficult issues, such as Jerusalem and refugees – between Israel and the Palestinians.

Equally, international waters, despite their complexities, can also act as a unifier in basins where relatively strong institutions are in place. The historical record shows that international water disputes *do* get resolved, even among bitter enemies, and even as conflicts erupt over other issues. Some of the most vociferous enemies around the world have negotiated water agreements or are in the process of doing so, and the institutions they have created frequently prove to be resilient over time and during periods of otherwise strained relations. The Mekong Committee, for example, has functioned since 1957, exchanging data throughout the Vietnam War. Secret 'picnic table' talks have been held between Israel and Jordan since the unsuccessful Johnston negotiations of 1953 to 1955, even as these riparians, until only recently, were in a legal state of war. The Indus River Commission survived through two wars between India and Pakistan. And all ten Nile riparians are currently involved in negotiations over cooperative development of the basin.

In the absence of institutions, however, changes within a basin can lead to conflict. To avoid the political intricacies of shared water resources, for example, a riparian, generally the regional power, may implement a project that impacts at least one of its neighbours.[3] This might be to continue meeting existing uses in the face of decreasing relative water availability – for example, Egypt's plans for a high dam on the Nile or Indian diversions of the Ganges to protect the port of Calcutta – or to meet new needs and associated policies, such as Turkey's Southeastern Anatolia Project (GAP) on the Euphrates. When projects such as these proceed without regional collaboration, they can become a flash point, heightening tensions and regional instability, and requiring years or, more commonly, decades to resolve. Evidence of how institutions can diffuse tensions is seen in basins with large numbers of water infrastructure projects. Co-riparian relations have been significantly more cooperative in basins with treaties and high dam density than in similarly developed basins without treaties. Thus, institutional capacity, together with shared interests and human creativity, seem to ameliorate water's conflict-inducing characteristics, suggesting that an important lesson of international water is that, as a resource, it tends to induce cooperation and incite violence only in the exception.

The choice for the international community, then, is one between a traditional chronology of events, where unilateral development is followed by a crisis and, possibly, a lengthy and expensive process of conflict resolution, on the one hand, or, on the other, a process where riparians are encouraged to get ahead of the crisis curve through crisis prevention, preventive diplomacy and institutional capacity building. It feels both counter-intuitive and precarious that the global community has often allowed water conflicts to drag on to the extent that they often do. The Indus Treaty took 10 years of negotiations, the Ganges, 30 and the Jordan, 40 – while all the while water quality and quantity degrade to where the health of dependent populations and ecosystems are damaged or destroyed. A reread through the history of international waters suggests that the simple fact that humans suffer and die in the absence of agreement apparently offers little in the way of incentive to cooperate; even less so the health of aquatic ecosystems. This problem gets worse as the dispute gains in intensity; one rarely hears talk about the ecosystems of the lower Nile, the lower Jordan or the tributaries of the Aral Sea – they have effectively been written off to the vagaries of human intractability.

INTERNATIONAL INSTITUTIONS AND INDICATORS OF CONFLICT

International institutions

Just as the flow of water ignores political boundaries, so, too, does its management strain the capabilities of institutional boundaries. While water managers generally understand and advocate the inherent powers of the concept of a watershed as a unit of management, where surface and groundwater quantity and quality are all inexorably connected, the institutions which have developed to manage the resource have historically followed these tenets only in the exception.

Frederiksen (1992), for example, describes the principles and practices of water resources institutions from around the world. He argues that while, ideally, water institutions should provide for ongoing evaluation, comprehensive review and consistency among actions, in practice, this integrated foresight is rare. Rather, he finds a rampant lack of consideration of quality considerations in quantity decisions, a lack of specificity in rights allocations, disproportionate political power-by-power companies, and a general neglect for environmental concerns in water resources decision-making. Buck, Gleason and Jofuku (1993) describe an 'institutional imperative' in their comparison of transboundary water conflicts in the USA and the former Soviet Union. Feitelson and Haddad (1995) take up the particular institutional challenges of transboundary groundwater.

To address these deficiencies at the international level, some have argued that international agencies might take a greater institutional role. Lee and Dinar (1995) describe the importance of an integrated approach to river-basin planning, development and management. Young, Dooge and Rodda (1994) provide guidelines for coordination between levels of management at the global, national, regional and local levels. Delli Priscoli (1989) describes the importance of public involvement in water conflict management. In other work (1992), he makes a strong case for the potential of alternative dispute resolution (ADR) in the World Bank's handling of water resources issues. Trolldalen (1992) likewise chronicles environmental conflict resolution at the United Nations (UN), including a chapter on international rivers.

Despite decades of institutional risk aversion and a general lack of leadership in international waters, there appears to be some recent momentum at the global level, at least as judged by public proclamations and political awareness. One result of the United Nations Conference on Environment and Development (UNCED or Earth Summit) held in Rio de Janeiro in 1992, and its adopted action plan *Agenda 21*, has been a tremendous expansion of international freshwater resource institutions and programmes. The World Water Council, a self-described 'think tank' for world water resource issues, which was created in 1996, has organized three World Water Forums – gatherings of government, non-government and private agency representatives to discuss and collectively determine a vision for managing water resources over the next quarter century. The first two forums led to the creation of the World Water Vision, a forward-looking declaration of philosophical and institutional water management needs. The Second World Water Forum also served as the venue for a ministerial conference in which the leaders of participating countries signed a declaration concerning water security in the 21st century. Continued momentum of these recent global water initiatives is supported by a number of interim appraisal meetings to review actions taken since the Earth Summit. Progress towards the objectives outlined in *Agenda 21* were evaluated in 2002, for example at the World Summit on Sustainable Development (WSSD) in Johannesburg, and implementation of the World Water Vision was assessed during the Third World Water Forum held in Japan in 2003.

None of these statements or declarations, however, focuses exclusively on international freshwater sources. Additionally, despite the efforts over the past decade to expand global institutional capacity over freshwater resources, no supra-national agency exists to manage transboundary resources globally. Thus, while many of the principles of national water management apply to international rivers and lakes, the political, social and economic dynamics associated with transboundary waters can require special consideration.

Yet, during recent years, there is movement on the ground, as well. The World Bank and the United Nations Development Programme (UNDP) have collaborated to facilitate the Nile Basin Initiative, which looks close to establishing a treaty framework and development plan for the basin, and the World Bank is taking the lead on bringing the riparians of the Gurani Aquifer in Latin America to dialogue. The US State Department, a number of UN agencies and other parties have established a Global Alliance on Water Security aimed at identifying priority regions for assistance, which may help countries get ahead of the crisis curve. The South African Development Community (SADC) and Economic and Social Commission for Asia and the Pacific (ESCAP) have been taking the lead in establishing transboundary dialogues within their respective regions.

Getting beyond the imperative of 'integrated international basin management', a concept practiced, in actuality, only in the exception, has been an important step in some basins. Even friendly states often have difficulty relinquishing sovereignty to a supra-legal authority, and the obstacles only increase along with the level of suspicion and rancour. At best, in many regions, one might strive for coordination over integration. Once the appropriate benefits are negotiated, it then becomes an issue of 'simply' agreeing on a set quantity, quality and timing of water resources that will cross each border. Coordination, when done correctly, can offer the same benefits as integration and be far superior to unilateral development, but does not threaten the one issue all states hold dear – their very sovereignty.

Indicators of conflict

Traditional parameters often cited as indicators of conflict were assessed by Wolf et al (2003) in an effort to help identify tomorrow's areas of potential tensions; but most of the parameters commonly identified were found actually to be only weakly linked to dispute. These parameters include climate, water stress, dependence on hydropower, dams or development per se, or level of development. In fact, our study suggests that institutional capacity within a basin, whether defined as water management bodies or treaties or generally positive international relations are as important, if not more so, than the physical aspects of a system. As mentioned earlier, it is when the rate of change within a basin exceeds the institutional capacity to absorb that change that tensions occur.

If institutional capacity were a driver, then it would stand to reason that the most significant indicators would be related to extremely rapid changes, either on the institutional side or in the physical system. The most rapid changes institutionally are associated with 'internationalized' basins – a basin whose management institution was developed under a single jurisdiction, but was shattered as that jurisdiction suddenly became divided among two or more nations. On the physical system side, the most rapid change is typically the development of a large-scale dam or diversion project. But here, too, the institutional capacity makes a difference. In other words, high levels of animosity and/or the absence of a transboundary institution can exacerbate the setting, while positive international relations and/or the presence of transboundary institutions can mitigate the negative effects of such projects.

By taking these parameters of rapid change as indicators – internationalized basins and major planned projects in hostile and/or institutionless basins – the basins with settings that suggest the potential for dispute in the coming five to ten years were identified. These basins include the Ganges-Brahmaputra, Han, Incomati, Kunene, Kura-Araks, Lake Chad, La Plata, Lempa, Limpopo, Mekong, Ob (Ertis), Okavango, Orange, Salween, Senegal, Tumen and Zambezi.

Almost more important than helping to identify the basins at risk themselves, these indicators allow us to monitor for 'red flags' or markers that may suggest new basins at risk as they arise – among them, tenders for future projects and nations with active nationalist movements.

BASKETS OF BENEFITS[4]

One productive approach to the development of transboundary waters has been to examine the benefits in the basin from a regional approach. This has regularly required the riparians to get past looking at the water as a commodity to be divided – a zero-sum, rights-based approach – and to develop an approach that equitably allocates not the water, but the benefits derived from them – a positive-sum, integrative approach. The boundary waters agreement between the USA and Canada, for example, allocates water according to equal benefits, usually defined by hydropower generation. This results in the seemingly odd arrangement that power may be exported out of basin for gain, but the water itself may not. In the 1964 treaty on the Columbia, an arrangement was worked out where the USA paid Canada for the benefits of flood control and Canada was granted rights to divert water between the Columbia and Kootenai for hydropower. Likewise, the 1975 Mekong Accord defines 'equality of right' not as equal shares of water, but as equal rights to use water on the basis of each riparian's economic and social needs. The relative nature of 'beneficial' uses is exhibited in a 1950 agreement on the Niagara, flowing between the USA and Canada, which provides a greater flow over the famous falls during 'show times' of summer daylight hours, when tourist dollars are worth more per cubic metre than the alternate use in hydropower generation.

In many water-related treaties, water issues are dealt with alone, separate from any other political or resource issues between countries – water *qua* water. By separating the two realms of 'high' (political) and 'low' (resource economical) politics, or by ignoring other resources that might be included in an agreement, some have argued that the process is either likely to fail, as in the case of the 1955 Johnston accords on the Jordan, or, more often, to achieve a sub-optimum development arrangement, as is currently the case on the Indus Agreement, signed in 1960. Increasingly, however, linkages are being made between water and politics, and between water and other resources. These multi-resource linkages may offer more opportunities for creative solutions to be generated, allowing for greater economic efficiency through a 'basket' of benefits. Some resources that have been included in water negotiations are as follows:

- *Financial resources:* An offer of financial incentives is occasionally able to circumvent impasses in negotiations. World Bank financing helped to resolve the Indus dispute, while UN-led investments helped to achieve the Mekong Agreement. Cooperation-inducing financing has not always come from outside of the region. Thailand helped to finance a project in Laos, as did India in Pakistan, in conjunction with their respective watershed agreements. A provision of the Nile Waters Treaty has Egypt paying Sudan outright for water, to which they both agreed Sudan had rights, but that it was not able to use the water.

- *Energy resources:* One increasingly common linkage being made is that between water and energy resources. As noted above, in conjunction with the Mekong Agreement, Thailand helped to fund a hydroelectric project in Laos in exchange for a proportion of the power to be generated. In the particularly elaborate 1986 Lesotho Highlands Treaty, South Africa agreed to help finance a hydroelectric/water diversion facility in Lesotho – South Africa acquired rights to drinking water for Johannesburg, and Lesotho receives all of the power generated. Similar arrangements have been suggested in China on the Mekong, Nepal on the Ganges tributaries, and between Syria and Jordan on the Yarmuk.

- *Political linkages:* Political capital, like investment capital, might likewise be linked to water negotiations, although no treaty, to date, includes such provisions. This linkage might be done implicitly – as, for example, the parallel but interrelated political and resource tracks of the Middle East peace talks – or explicitly – as talks on Turkish acquiescence on water issues have been linked in a quid pro quo with Syrian ties to Kurdish nationalists.

- *Data:* As water management models become more sophisticated, water data is increasingly vital to management agencies. As such, data itself can be used as a form of negotiating capital. Data sharing can lead to breakthroughs in negotiations – an engineering study allowed circumvention of an impasse in the Johnston negotiations when it was found that Jordan's water needs were not as extensive as had been thought, allowing for more room in the bargaining mix. Conversely, the lack of agreed-to criteria for data in negotiations on the Ganges has hampered progress over the years. Data issues, when managed effectively, can also allow a framework for developing patterns of cooperation in the absence of more contentious issues, particularly water allocations. For one, data gathering can be delegated to a trusted third party or, better, to a joint fact-finding body made up of representatives from the riparian states. Perhaps the best example of this internationally is on the Mekong, where the Mekong Committee's first five-year plan consisted almost entirely of data-gathering projects, effectively both precluding data disputes in the future and allowing the riparians to get used to cooperation and trust.

- *Water-related 'baskets':* Some of the most complete 'baskets' were negotiated between India and Nepal in 1959, on the Bagmati and the Gandak, and in 1966 on the Kosi (all tributaries of the Ganges). These two treaties include provisions for a variety of water-related projects, including irrigation/hydropower, navigation, fishing, related transportation and even afforestation – India plants trees in Nepal to contain downstream sedimentation. While Nepal has expressed recent bitterness towards both of these accords, the structures of these treaties are good examples of how broader 'baskets' can allow for more creative solutions.

WHY MIGHT THE FUTURE LOOK NOTHING LIKE THE PAST?

The entire basis of this study rests on the not unassailable assumption that we can tell something about the future by looking at the past. It is worth stopping at this point, then, and challenging the very foundation of that assumption. Why might the future look nothing at all like the past? What new approaches or technologies are on the horizon to change or ameliorate the risk to the basins that we have identified, or even to the whole approach to basins at risk?

By definition, a discussion of the future cannot have the same empirical backing as an historical study – the data just is not there yet. However, there are cutting-edge developments and recent trends that, if one examined them within the context of this study, might suggest some possible changes in store for transboundary waters in the near future. What follows, then, are four possibly fundamental changes in the way in which we approach transboundary waters, the results of several brainstorming sessions among the Basins at Risk Team at Oregon State University.

New technologies for negotiation and management

Our event dataset goes back to 1948. In some ways, water management is still very similar (and, for that matter, still resembles the way it was 5000 years ago). But some fundamental aspects are profoundly different. Institutions are getting better and more resilient, management and understanding are improving, and these issues are increasingly on the radar screen of global and local decision-makers. But, most importantly, the 21st century has access to new technology that could not be dreamed of in 1948, and that adds substantially to the ability both to negotiate and to manage transboundary waters more effectively:

- Modular modelling systems (MMSs) such as STELLA, Waterware, and Riverware can now be used for comprehensive modelling of hydrologic and human systems. Because of their modular design, they can also act as a facilitation tool by allowing managers/negotiators to cooperatively build the model, increasing the joint knowledge base and communications.
- Geographic information systems (GIS) and remote sensing allow several spatial data layers, encompassing biophysical, socio-economic and geopolitical parameters, to be viewed and analysed graphically.
- Real-time monitoring tools, such as radio-controlled gauging stations, add new options for real-time management, as well as allocations based on existing hydrologic settings rather than fixed quantities.
- Graphical user interfaces (GUIs) allow for each component to be brought together into an intuitive, user-friendly setting.

While new technologies and data cannot replace the political goodwill necessary for creative solutions, nor are they widely available outside of the developed world, they can, if appropriately deployed, allow for more robust negotiations and greater flexibility in joint management.

Globalization: private capital, WTO and circumvented ethics

Very little of the recent attention on globalization and the World Trade Organization (WTO) has centred on water resources; but there is a definite water component to these trends. One of the most profound is the shift of development funds from global and regional development banks, such as the World Bank and the Asia Development Bank, to private multinationals, such as Bechtel, Vivendi and Ondeo (formerly Lyonnaise des Eaux). Development banks have, over the years, been susceptible to public pressures and ethics and, as such, have developed procedures for evaluating social and environmental impacts of projects, and incorporating them in decision-making. On international waters, each development bank has guidelines that generally prohibit development unless all riparians agree to the project, which in and of itself has promoted successful negotiations during the past. Private enterprises have no such restrictions, and nations eager to develop controversial projects have been increasingly turning to private capital to circumvent public ethics. The main construction projects of the most controversial developments of the day – Turkey's GAP project, India's Sardar Sarovar project on the Narmada River and China's Three Gorges Dam – are all proceeding through the studied avoidance of development banks and their mores.

There is a more subtle effect of globalization, though, which has to do with the WTO and its emphasis on privatization and full-cost recovery of investments. Local and national governments, which have traditionally implemented and subsidized water development systems to keep water prices down, are under increasing pressure from the forces of globalization to develop these systems through private companies. These large multinational water companies, in turn, manage for profit and, if they use development capital, both push and are pushed to recover the full cost of their investment. This can translate not only into immediate and substantial rises in the cost of water, disproportionately affecting the poor, but also to greater eradication of local and indigenous management systems and cultures. If there is to be water-related violence in the future, it is much more liable to resemble the 'water riots' against a Bechtel development in Bolivia in 1999, where eight people were killed, than 'water wars' across national boundaries.

As WTO rules are elaborated and negotiated, real questions remain concerning how much of this process will be *required* of nations in the future simply in order to retain membership in the organization. The 'commodification' of water as a result of these forces is a case in point. Over the last 20 years, no global water policy meeting has neglected to pass a resolution which, among other issues, defined water as an 'economic good', setting the stage at the Second World Water Forum in 2000 for an unresolved showdown against those who would define water as a human or ecosystem *right*. The debate looms large over the future of water resources. If water is a commodity, and if WTO rules disallow obstacles to the trade of commodities, will nations be forced to sell their water? While far-fetched now (even as a California company is challenging British Columbia over precisely such an issue under North American Free Trade Agreement – NAFTA – rules), the globalization debate between market forces and social forces continues to play out in microcosm in the world of water resources.

The geopolitics of desalination

Twice during the last 50 years – the 1960s nuclear energy fervour, and in the late 1980s, with 'discoveries' in cold fusion – much of the world briefly thought that it was on the verge of having access to free energy supplies. 'Too cheap to meter' was the phrase during the Atoms for Peace Conference. While neither the economics nor the technology finally supported these claims, it is not far-fetched to picture changes that could profoundly affect the economics of desalination.

The marginal cost of desalinated water (between US$0.80 and US$1.00 per m^3) currently makes it only cost-effective in the developed world, where the water will be used for drinking water, the population to whom the water will be delivered lives along a coast and at low elevations, and there are no alternatives. The only places not so restricted are where energy costs are especially low, notably the Arabian Peninsula. A fundamental shift either in energy prices or in membrane technology could bring costs down substantially. If either happened to the extent that the marginal cost allowed for agricultural irrigation with sea water (around US$.08 per m^3, on average), a large proportion of the world's water supplies would shift from rivers and shallow aquifers to the sea (an unlikely, but plausible, scenario; for more realistic opportunities, see Chapter 6).[5]

Besides the fundamental economic changes that would result, geopolitical thinking of water systems would also need to shift. Currently, there is inherent political power in being an upstream riparian and, thus, controlling the headwaters. In the scenario for cheap desalination described above, the spatial position of power would shift from mountains to the valleys, and from the headwaters to the sea. Many nations such as Israel, Egypt and Iraq, who currently depend on upstream neighbours for their water supply, would, by virtue of their coastlines, suddenly find roles reversed.

The changing sources of water and the changing nature of conflict

Both the worlds of water and of conflict are undergoing slow but steady changes that may obviate much of the thinking in this report. As surface water supplies and easy groundwater sources are increasingly exploited throughout the world, two major changes result: quality is steadily becoming a more serious issue to many than quantity, and water use is shifting towards less traditional sources. Many of these sources – such as deep fossil aquifers, wastewater reclamation and inter-basin transfers – are not restricted by the confines of watershed boundaries, our fundamental unit of analysis in this study. Moreover, population-driven food demand will grow exponentially in coming years, putting unprecedented pressures on water demand (for a more thorough discussion of water and food, see Chapter 5).

Conflict, too, is becoming less traditional, increasingly being driven by internal or local pressures, or more subtle issues of poverty and stability. The combination of changes (in water resources and in conflict) suggests that tomorrow's water disputes may look very different from today's.

CONCLUSION: WHAT TYPES OF POLICY RECOMMENDATIONS CAN ONE MAKE?

Given these lessons, what can the international community do?

International institutions

Water dispute amelioration is as important, more effective and less costly than conflict resolution. Watershed commissions should be developed for those basins that do not have them, and strengthened for those that do.

Three characteristics of international waters – the fact that conflict is invariably sub-acute, that tensions can be averted when institutions are established early, and that such institutions are tremendously resilient over time – inform this recommendation. Early intervention can be far less costly than conflict resolution processes. In some cases, such as the Nile, the Indus and the Jordan, as armed conflict seemed imminent, tremendous energy was spent getting the parties to talk to each other. In contrast, discussions in the Mekong Committee, the multilateral working group in the Middle East and the working group on the Danube have all moved beyond the causes of immediate disputes to actual, practical projects that may be implemented in an integrative framework.

Funding and development-assistance agencies

Water-related needs must be coordinated and focused, relating quality, quantity, groundwater, surface water, and local socio-political settings in an integrated fashion. Funding should be commensurate with the responsibility that assistance agencies have for alleviating the global water crisis.

Ameliorating the crux of water security – human suffering – often rests with agencies which, given the size of the crisis, are extraordinarily underfunded. One can contrast the resources spent on issues such as global change and arms control, laudable for their efforts to protect against potential loss of life in the future, to the millions of people now dying because they lack access to clean freshwater. Agencies such as the United States Agency for International Development (USAID), the Canadian International Development Agency (CIDA) and Japan International Cooperation Agency (JICA) have the technical expertise and experience to help, yet are hindered by political and budgetary constraints. Funding agencies are often hamstrung by local politics.

A powerful argument can be made that water-related disease costs the global economy US$125 billion per year, while ameliorating the diseases would cost from US$7 billion to US$50 billion in total (Gleick, 1998). Programmes such as USAID's Project Forward, which integrates water management with conflict resolution training, offer models for the future.

Universities and research agencies

Universities and research agencies can best contribute to alleviating the water crisis in three major ways:

1   Acquire, analyse and coordinate the primary data necessary for good empirical work.
2   Identify indicators of future water disputes and/or insecurity in regions most at risk.
3   Train tomorrow's water managers in an integrated fashion.

The internet's initial mandate is still one of the best: to allow communication between researchers around the world in order to exchange information and enhance collaboration. The surplus of primary data currently threatens an information overload in the developed world, while the most basic information is often lacking in the developing world. Data availability not only allows for greater understanding of the physical world, but – by adding information and knowledge from the social, economic and political realms – indicators showing regions at risk can also be identified.

Private industry

Private industry has historically taken the lead in large development projects. As the emphasis in world water shifts to a smaller scale, and from a focus on supply to one on demand management and improved quality, private industry has much to offer.

Private industry has three traits that can be harnessed to help ameliorate the world water crisis: their reach transcends national boundaries, their resources are generally greater than those of public institutions, and their strategic planning is generally superb. Historically, private companies such as Bechtel and Lyonnaise des Eaux have been involved primarily in large-scale development projects, while the smaller-scale projects have been left to development-assistance agencies. Recently, a shift in thinking has taken place in some corporate boardrooms. Bank of America, for example, was not involved in the California-wide process of water planning until recently, when its president noticed that practically *all* of the bank's investments relied on a safe, stable supply of water. This was true whether the investments were in microchip manufacturing, mortgages or agriculture. When the bank became involved in the Cal-Fed Plan, it brought along its lawyers, facilitators and planning expertise, as well as its financial resources. Subsequently, progress was made in several areas where previously there had been an impasse.

Civil society

Inherent in our recognition that the most serious problems of water security are those at the local level is the attendant recognition that civil society is among the best suited to address local issues.

One recurrent pattern in water resources development and management has been a series of projects or approaches in opposition to local values, customs and other cultural processes. Examples of these include large projects such as dams that have displaced hundreds of thousands of people and wiped out sites of cultural and religious heritage; projects promoting water markets among religious groups for whom the idea is sacrilege; or activities as seemingly minor as cutting down a tree sacred to a village djinn. In recent years, as a consequence, those affected by a project have been increasingly involved in the decision-making process, and such efforts must be strongly encouraged.

ACKNOWLEDGEMENTS

Early versions of this chapter were prepared and distributed for the UNESCO–Green Cross International programme From Potential Conflict to Cooperation Potential: Water for Peace, in collaboration with the Organization for Security and Cooperation in Europe. The author owes a debt of thanks to these organizations.

NOTES

1   Excluded are events where water is incidental to a dispute, such as those concerning fishing rights, access to ports, transportation or river boundaries. Also excluded are events where water is not the driver, such as those where water is a tool, target or victim of armed conflict.

2   The only 'water war' on record between nations occurred over 4500 years ago, between the city states of Lagash and Umma in the Tigris-Euphrates basin (Wolf, 1998).

3   'Power' in regional hydropolitics can include riparian position, with an upstream riparian having more relative strength vis à vis the water resources than its downstream riparian, in addition to the more conventional measures of military, political and economic strength. Nevertheless, when a project is implemented that impacts one's neighbours, it is generally undertaken by the regional power, as defined by traditional terms, regardless of its riparian position.

4   This section draws from Wolf (1999).

5   While the shifts described here are very dramatic, current trends suggest that desalinated water is becoming more attractive in the developing world, as well. It should also be noted that desalinated drinking water also becomes available as wastewater, which can be treated for agricultural and industrial uses (Asit Biswas, 2001, pers comm).

REFERENCES

Biswas, A (2001), personal communication

Buck, S, Gleason, G and Jofuku, M (1993) 'The institutional imperative: Resolving transboundary water conflict in arid agricultural regions of the United States and the Commonwealth of Independent States', *Natural Resources Journal*, vol 33, pp595–628

Delli Priscoli, J (1992) 'Collaboration, participation, and alternative dispute resolution: Process concepts for the World Bank's role in water resources', Unpublished mimeo

Delli Priscoli, J (1989) 'Public involvement, conflict management: Means to EQ and social objectives', *Journal of Water Resources Planning and Management*, vol 115, no 1, pp31–42

Feitelson, E and Haddad, M (1995) *Joint Management of Shared Aquifers: Final Report*, The Palestine Consultancy Group and the Harry S Truman Research Institute, Jerusalem

Frederiksen, H (1992) *Water Resources Institutions: Some Principles and Practices*, Technical Paper No 191, World Bank, Washington, DC

Gleick, P H (1998) *The World's Water: The Biennial Report on Freshwater Resources 1998–1999*, Earthscan, London/Island Press, Washington, DC

Gleick, P H (1993) 'Water and conflict: Fresh water resources and international security', *International Security*, vol 18, no 1, pp79–112

Homer-Dixon, T (1994) 'Environmental scarcities and violent conflict', *International Security*, vol 19, no 1, pp5–40

Lee, D and Dinar, A (1995) *Review of Integrated Approaches to River Basin Planning, Development and Management*, 1446, World Bank, Washington, DC

Libiszewski, S (1995) *Water Disputes in the Jordan Basin Region and their Role in the Resolution of the Arab-Israeli Conflict*, Occasional Paper 13, Center for Security Studies and Conflict Research, Zurich

Mandel, R (1992) 'Sources of international river basin disputes', *Conflict Quarterly*, vol 12, no 4, pp25–56

Remans, W (1995) 'Water and war', *Humantäres Völkerrecht*, vol 8, no 1, pp4–14

Salman, M A and Boisson de Chazournes, L (eds) (1998) 'International watercourses: Enhancing cooperation and managing conflict', Technical Paper No 414, World Bank, Washington, DC

Samson, P and Charrier, B (1997) 'International freshwater conflict: Issues and prevention strategies', *Green Cross Report*, May

Trolldalen, J (1992) *International Environmental Conflict Resolution: The Role of the United Nations*, World Foundation for Environment and Development, Washington, DC

United Nations (1978) *Register of International Rivers*, Pergamon Press, New York

Westing, A H (ed) (1986) *Global Resources and International Conflict: Environmental Factors in Strategic Policy and Action*, Oxford, New York

Wolf, A (1999) 'Criteria for equitable allocations: The heart of international water conflict', *Natural Resources Forum*, vol 23, no 1, February, pp3–30

Wolf, A (1998) 'Conflict and cooperation along international waterways', *Water Policy*, vol 1, no 2, pp251–265

Wolf, A et al (1999) 'International river basins of the world,' *International Journal of Water Resources Development*, vol 15, no 4, pp387–427

Wolf, A T, Yoffe, S B and Giordano, M (2003) 'International waters: Identifying basins at risk', *Water Policy*, vol 5, no 1, pp29–60

Young, G, Dooge, J and Rodda, J (1994) *Global Water Resource Issues*, Cambridge University Press, Cambridge, MA

Chapter 10

Forgetting political boundaries in identifying water development potentials in the basin-wide approach: The Ganges-Brahmaputra-Meghna issues

ZAHIR UDDIN AHMAD[1]

INTRODUCTION

One of the major stumbling blocks in water resources planning for co-basin and co-riparian countries is that adherence to the political boundary may be to derive political benefits. As we all know, water simply flows from a higher elevation to a lower elevation. For delta regions, the upper riparian countries are at a higher elevation and in an advantageous position in terms of large-scale interventions. The lower riparian countries suffer from water shortages if a dam is built by an upper riparian to divert the flow to their benefit without having a proper sharing arrangement to meet various demands for drinking, agriculture, fisheries, navigation and the environment. This kind of unilateral diversion without proper consultation, negotiation and sharing arrangements may lead to a long-term dispute and environmental hazard such as desertification. Sometimes, politicians gain by politicizing the issues linking it to the national interest 'in an over-inspired patriotic feeling'. In the long run, these kinds of short-sighted national-interest oriented plans fall apart. Unique examples are some of the barrages that have raised the bed levels of the upstream rivers to a threatened level. Had there been an integrated approach towards water resources planning among the co-basin and co-riparian countries, these kinds of hazards could have been avoided to a large extent.

The concept of fully integrated water resource management (IWRM) which has emerged from *Agenda 21*[2] and the Dublin Principles[3] suggest that there should be an integrated approach in water resources planning among co-basin and co-riparian countries. We are familiar with the common saying, 'water knows no boundary'. The water resources planners of a region must ignore the political boundary to harness and explore the resources in an integrated manner, making sure that it strikes a balance between the drinking, agricultural, fisheries, navigational and environmental needs, not only for the nation, but most optimally for the region. It requires a strong political will and wisdom to really forget the political boundary. It is only possible if the process of integrated planning is patronized with proper techno-political backing and spirit. The whole process should ultimately be linked to the sustainable development framework of a region.

The additional complexities of shared-water development created by strains in riparian relations and institutional limitations are discussed at the start of Chapter 9. On the one hand there is the potential for conflict between co-riparians, and on the other there is the possibility for – and historic evidence of – cooperation. There are 19 basins in the world shared by five or more riparian countries (Wolf et al, 1999). The Ganges-Brahmaputra-Meghna (GBM) is such a basin. The GBM region is a unique and opportune region to identify water development potentials in an integrated manner beyond the limits of its political boundary to derive a win–win scenario. The GBM region river systems constitute the second largest hydrologic region in the world. The total drainage area is about 1.75 million square kilometres (km^2), stretching across five countries: Bangladesh, Bhutan, China, India and Nepal. While Bangladesh and India share all three rivers, China shares the Brahmaputra and the Ganges, Nepal only the Ganges, and Bhutan the Brahmaputra.

The region is rich in natural resources, including water; but the irony is that over 600 million people who live in this region are still struck by endemic poverty. The development and utilization of the region's water resources had never been sought in an integrated manner by the regional countries due to past differences, legacies of mistrust and lack of goodwill. An integrated and holistic approach to the development of the region, considering water resources as a point of departure, is the crying need for the region. The abundance of water in the GBM region as a shared resource can serve as a principal agent of development for millions of people living in the region to achieve a win–win scenario (see Chapter 3).

A number of options and opportunities exist for collaborative efforts in such sectors as hydropower development, flood management, dry-season flow augmentation and water sharing, water quality improvement, navigation, and catchment/watershed management.

The policy environment in the region is now favourable for such cooperation. For example, India recently entered into two water-sharing treaties; one with Nepal, which is known as the Mahakhali Treaty, and the other with Bangladesh, which is known as the Ganges Treaty. Although the treaties had been signed in a bilateral mode, this may be considered a major ice-breaking event for the region within the context of water sharing. As mentioned earlier, water and energy could be the entry points in the regional cooperation, among other issues. The large multipurpose dams built in Nepal can generate huge amounts of hydroelectric power and, at the same time, can augment flows during the dry season. The current issue is how to move out from bilateralism towards multilateralism, and how to share the cost and the benefit in an equitable manner among the regional countries.

However, identification of the water development potentials beyond the limit of the political boundary will help the policy-makers and politicians to have a common ground for negotiation. Indications are there that the techno-political atmosphere in the region is congenial for ice melting, if not ice breaking, towards harnessing and exploring the water development potentials in an integrated manner. Flood damage mitigation through improved flood forecasting and warning systems in the region could be a non-conflicting starting point through which the technocrats may sit together in a common forum. The other development options can build on this non-conflicting regional development of flood forecasting and warning systems. The whole collaborative approach to water resources development should ultimately be linked to the sustainable development framework of the GBM region.

REGIONAL WATER-BASED DEVELOPMENT CONTEXT

The GBM region (see Figure 10.1) has high water development potential if planned in a basin-wide approach, which may again be characterized as a water-rich region. Although hydrological data for the region is not available, the enormity of the water resource potential can be gauged in general terms. It is the single most important natural resource of the GBM regional countries, and it is widely recognized that water would be the most important sector of development towards shaping the future of millions of people living in this region.

The average annual water flow in the GBM region is estimated at roughly 1350 billion cubic metres (m^3) (BCM), of which nearly half is discharged by the Brahmaputra. The three rivers constitute an interconnected system – discharging into the Bay of Bengal. Compared to an annual average water availability of 269,000m^3 per km^2 for the world, the availability in the GBM region is 771,400m^3 per km^2 – which is nearly three times the world average. In addition to surface water, the GBM region has an annually replenishing groundwater resource of about 230 BCM.

Water is abundant during the monsoon but scarce during the dry season. Harnessing the bounty of the GBM rivers requires that the monsoon flows be stored and redistributed over space and time when and where required within a framework of sustainable development. The real challenge is to utilize this resource in an integrated manner. It offers the most promising entry point for achieving a social and economic transformation in Nepal, northern, eastern and north-eastern India, Bangladesh and Bhutan. At the advent of a new

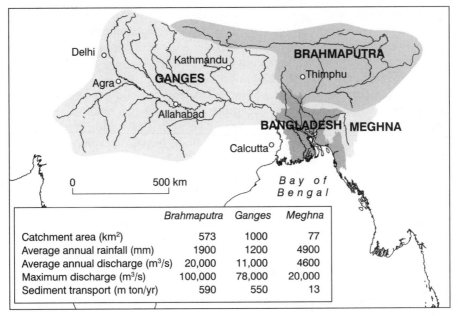

The following table appears within the map figure:

	Brahmaputra	Ganges	Meghna
Catchment area (km²)	573	1000	77
Average annual rainfall (mm)	1900	1200	4900
Average annual discharge (m³/s)	20,000	11,000	4600
Maximum discharge (m³/s)	100,000	78,000	20,000
Sediment transport (m ton/yr)	590	550	13

Source: EGIS

Figure 10.1 *Map of the Ganges-Brahmaputra-Meghna basin*

century and a new millennium, the vision concerning the development of the GBM countries should focus on options for collaborative harnessing of water resources in the region, and should formulate a framework for multidimensional cooperation in related sectors, such as energy, ecological health, flood management, water quality, navigation and trade and commerce. Cooperation in developing the huge water resources of the GBM river systems is not a zero-sum game. Instead, all of the regional partners can and should overcome the current mindset to construct the future scenarios on a win–win dispensation for all by working on all relevant perspectives, concerns, options and trade-offs, with the aim of achieving optimal benefits for all. In the absence of such a long-term vision, the GBM region will continue to stagnate, and millions of people will remain in a state of deprivation while other parts of the developing world march ahead towards prosperity. Water resources development can play a catalytic role in bringing about wider changes and promoting sustainable development in the GBM region.

Fortunately, a climate of goodwill and confidence has been created over the past few years through the signing of the Mahakali Treaty between India and Nepal in January 1996 and the Ganges Water Sharing Treaty between Bangladesh and India in December 1996. These treaties are acclaimed as landmark events, offering a window of opportunity for water-based collaborative development endeavours in the region. The time is, therefore, conducive to formulating a broad framework of regional cooperation among the GBM regional countries for the optimal, integrated development of the region. At the same time, one should not remain complacent and euphoric in the wake of these landmark treaties. It is necessary to strengthen the process through renewed commitments to a wider vision of sustainable regional development and commensurate collaborative efforts.

The Male (1997) and the Colombo (1998) South Asian Association for Regional Cooperation (SAARC) Summit Declarations endorsed sub-regional cooperation within SAARC by accepting the idea of two or more countries collaborating in project-based cooperative activities within the SAARC framework, which consists of India, Bangladesh, Nepal, Pakistan, Sri Lanka, Bhutan and Male. Therefore, the efforts of GBM countries to forge a common water-based development vision are consistent with SAARC principles. It may be noted that in the report of the SAARC Group of Eminent Persons, entitled *SAARC Vision beyond the Year 2000*, it has been envisioned that the enhancement of the quality of life and welfare of the peoples of South Asia should be pursued through 'the creation of dynamic complementarities transcending national boundaries, development of managerial and productive capacity so as to exploit the internal and external economies of scale, resource complementarity and cost reduction'.

Entry through water should trigger wider development in the region. As opportunities unfold, emphasis will shift from more irrigation to sustainable agricultural productivity, from electricity production to energy grids and industrialization, from flood control to flood management, and from inland navigation to inter-modal transport. The ultimate goal is to attain a mutually beneficial synergy between national interests, people's well-being and regional prosperity, initiated through the best possible utilization of the huge potential of the region's water resources.

REGIONAL WATER-RESOURCE UTILIZATION ISSUES

Floods, riverbank erosion and sedimentation

The GBM countries are severely handicapped by recurrent floods, which damage life, property and infrastructure. It is the poor who occupy the more flood-prone areas and constitute the bulk of the victims. The general flooding pattern is similar in all three countries, characterized by 80 per cent of annual rainfall occurring in four to five months of monsoon, often concentrated in several days of heavy spells.

In Nepal, the runoff generated by heavy precipitation cannot quickly drain out, often because of the high stage of the outfall river. Flooding in hill valleys occurs due to sudden cloudbursts that are localized in nature but may be heavy for several days. In the higher mountains, floods induced by glaciers, or glacier lake outburst floods (GLOFs), are also experienced. The Nepalese *terai* region is prone to flash floods, which also produce spill-over effects in northern India.

Floods have become an annual feature in the GBM plains of India. Of the total estimated flood-prone area in India, about 68 per cent lies in the GBM states, mostly in Assam, West Bengal, Bihar and Uttar Pradesh. The Ganges in northern India, which receives waters from its northern tributaries originating in the Himalayas, has a high flood-damage potential, especially in Uttar Pradesh and Bihar. Likewise, the Brahmaputra and the Barak (headwaters of the Meghna) drain regions of very heavy rainfall, and produce floods from over-bank spilling and drainage congestion in north-eastern India.

Bangladesh, being the lowest riparian, bares the brunt of flooding in the GBM region. Even in a normal year, up to 30 per cent of the country is flooded and up to about 80 per cent of the land area is considered flood prone. Flooding in Bangladesh is caused by a combination of factors such as flash floods from neighbouring hills, inflow of water from upstream catchments, over-bank spilling of rivers from in-country rainfall, and drainage congestion. The conditions could be disastrous if flood peaks in all of the three rivers synchronize.

A natural corollary of flooding is riverbank erosion, especially in the Brahmaputra system. Large seasonal variations in river flows and the gradual loss of channel depth cause banks to erode and river courses to change. Wave action during the high stage further accelerates the process. Riverbank erosion is manifested in channel shifting, the creation of new channels during floods, bank slumping due to undercutting, and local scour from turbulence caused by obstruction. Riverbank erosion is responsible for the destruction of fertile agricultural lands, homesteads and, sometimes, entire clusters of villages.

The GBM rivers convey an enormous amount of sediment load from the mountains to the plains, which compound the adverse effects of floods. The Kosi and some tributaries of the Brahmaputra are particularly notable in this regard. Bangladesh is the outlet for all of the major rivers and receives, on average, an annual sediment load varying between 0.5 billion and 1.8 billion tonnes. Most of this sediment load passes through the country to the Bay of Bengal; but a part of it is deposited on the floodplain during over-bank spilling. This process gradually changes the valley geometry and floodplain topography, often reducing the water conveyance capacity and navigability of the drainage channels.

Water quality

During the past, the emphasis in water resource planning largely related to water supply or quantity, rather than to quality. Meanwhile, water quality has progressively deteriorated due to increasing withdrawals for various uses, progressive industrialization and insufficient stream flows to dilute the pollutants during lean flow periods. The increased use of agrochemicals and the discharge of untreated domestic sewage and industrial effluents into rivers have aggravated the problem. Given that water flows down the river systems and across countries and that there are interactions between surface and groundwater, water pollution in the region has been spreading across water sources, rivers and countries and has already reached alarming proportions.

In Nepal, water quality has deteriorated primarily due to industrial pollution. The volume of effluents generated by most industries is not large; but the concentration of pollutants is remarkably high. India had initiated an elaborate water-quality monitoring programme under the Ganga Action Plan during the late 1980s. This has recently been incorporated into a larger National Rivers Conservation Programme. In Bangladesh, the magnitude of water quality deterioration from the above-mentioned causes is further compounded by salinity intrusion in the south-western region. The reduced flow of the Ganges in the dry season, coupled with the silting of distributary mouths, has exacerbated the process of northward movement of the salinity front, thereby threatening the environmental health of the region. An additional problem is the detection of high concentrations of arsenic in the groundwater in 59 of the 64 districts of Bangladesh and in some adjoining districts of West Bengal. Since the detection of arsenic and the recognition of the potential hazard of ingesting arsenic-contaminated water, water resource planners have realized that a radical shift in the strategy is necessary to ensure affordable safe domestic water supply.

Climate change

The impact of climate change due to global warming on the water resources of tropical Asia could be very significant. General circulation models have revealed that mean annual rainfall in the north-eastern part of the South Asian subcontinent could increase with higher temperatures. The 'best-estimate' scenario for 2030 is that monsoon rainfall could increase by 10 to 15 per cent. It is believed that increased evaporation (resulting from higher temperatures), in combination with regional changes in precipitation characteristics, has the potential to affect mean runoff, frequency and intensity of floods and drought, soil moisture, and surface and groundwater availability in the GBM countries.

Climate change-related increases in temperatures could also increase the rate of snowmelt in the Himalayas and reduce the amount of snowfall if winter is shortened. In the event of climate change altering the rainfall pattern in the Himalayas, the impacts could be felt in the downstream countries of (northern) India and Bangladesh. The impact of any change in the length of the monsoon would also be significant. If the monsoon is shortened, soil moisture deficits in some areas might get worse, while prolonged monsoons might cause frequent flooding and increase inundation depths. By and large, any change in the availability of water resources as a consequence of climate change could have a substantial effect on agriculture, fishery, navigation, industrial and domestic water supply, salinity control, and reservoir storage and operation. Besides, the anticipated sea-level rise in the Bay of Bengal would further compound the problem in Bangladesh through coastal submergence and enhanced drainage congestion in the floodplain.

Gender dimension

The status of women in the GBM region has special significance with respect to water supply and sanitation because women are the principal managers of domestic water use and family health care. Women play a vital role as water collectors and water managers. It is the women who possess the knowledge of the location, dependability and quality of the local water resources, and their indigenous knowledge of local water conditions is passed on to successive generations. Collecting water for the family is an arduous and tiring task, especially in the hilly and semi-arid regions, and not only adult women but girls, as well, are involved in this life of hard labour and drudgery. Women are also the worst sufferers due to floods.

Despite such a responsibility performed by women in relation to water, they enjoy little or no authority in decision-making in water management. The knowledge and perceptions of women can be gainfully utilized in planning the water distribution network, designing and locating the water pumps, and organizing community management of water supply facilities. The ultimate goal concerning the gender dimension in water management is to attain and ensure equitable participation of both men and women in the allocation and use of water.

Demand management

Sustainable water management calls for a comprehensive, cost-effective, market-oriented and participatory approach to water demand management. Nepal has formulated liberal policies for strengthening the economy and made corresponding changes in the role of the state and the market in its water resources policy. The National Water Policy of India, adopted in 1987, defines priorities for different water-using sectors, treats water as an economic good and proposes the use of water pricing in a manner that would cover the costs of investment, operation and maintenance. The National Water Policy of Bangladesh, approved in January 1999, emphasizes the principle of accessibility of water to all, and proposes to develop sustainable public and private water delivery systems, including delineation of water rights (see Chapter 8) and guidelines for water pricing (see Chapters 4 and 11).

Two types of demand-side approach are feasible. The first is entirely market-based and depends upon a market-determined price mechanism for the economic use of water. This requires certain prerequisites such as an efficient water distribution system, full dissemination of information relating to water demand and supply, and an appropriate regulatory framework – conditions that are lacking, at present, in the GBM regional countries. The second approach, which is more realistic and partly in operation in the region, is through a system of administered control that determines water allocation and pricing according to given or chosen social, economic and environmental criteria. An administered system has the advantage of laying down the priorities concerning access to water resources, especially of the poor and underprivileged, involving the users in conservation and quality monitoring, and determining the charges or prices to be borne by different categories of users.

Institutions and governance

Institutions and the manner in which they foster good governance determine the long-term ability of a country to manage its water resources. Institutions that are responsible for implementing water policies and strategies suffer from serious deficiencies and drawbacks in the region. They lack efficiency or perform sub-optimally with respect to such components as legal and regulatory aspects, implementation of rules, accountability and responsiveness to user needs.

Water-sector planning is now changing from a top-down technocratic approach to a bottom-up grassroots approach. The goal is to establish a genuine participatory water management environment. Along with the participatory approach come the steps to develop a nexus between public and private sectors in water development and management. Public-sector water institutions have a poor record of cost recovery. The involvement of the private sector under the build-own-operate (BOO) mode may help to reduce public-sector deficiencies, improve the level of governance and attract investment in infrastructure.

REGIONAL WATER-BASED DEVELOPMENT POTENTIALS

General

The enormity of the development potential of the huge water resources of the GBM region stands out in stark contrast to the region's socio-economic deprivation. It is a direct reminder for all of us to formulate a long-term vision to develop a sustainable framework for water utilization. It has been already alluded to in the preceding section that, owing to the seasonal availability of water in the Himalayan rivers, harnessing the resource requires that it be stored for meeting year-round demands. Run-of-the-river projects may produce valuable energy, but they do not store water. Flood control benefits cannot also be ensured without storage. In principle, there is no conflict between small, medium and large projects since each has its unique place depending upon the discharge, valley traits and other technical, socio-economic and environmental considerations. Storage reservoirs are custom built, and each can be designed to meet specific parameters.

The terrain of the northern and middle belts of Nepal offers excellent sites for storage reservoirs. One study in Nepal, based on available information and past studies, has identified 28 potential reservoir sites in the country. Nine of them are classified as large, with an aggregate gross storage capacity of 110 BCM, and each site has a gross storage capacity of over 5 BCM. The Brahmaputra Master Plan of India (1986) has identified 18 storage sites in north-eastern India, five of which are classified as large, having a total gross storage capacity of 80 BCM. In the Meghna (Barak) system, one large storage site (Tipaimukh) with a gross storage potential of 15 BCM has been identified.

The potential sites referred to above provide the opportunity to construct dams for storing excess water in the Himalayas for a variety of downstream uses. Hence, by definition, they are multipurpose in nature, providing benefits (beyond national borders) in such areas as power generation, flood moderation, dry-season flow augmentation, irrigation and navigation. The hydropower potential of these reservoir sites is the most significant aspect of water development in the GBM region, especially since per-capita energy consumption in the region is among the lowest in the world. However, the construction of such storage dams involves high costs and has a long gestation period.

High dams and other large water resource development programmes have encountered severe criticism and opposition in recent years on a variety of technical, social, and environmental considerations. This sensitivity ranges from concerns for seismic hazards, submergence, population displacement, loss of farmland, forests and biodiversity, and downstream physical impacts. At its extreme, the opposition to large projects is rooted in a subjective belief that they are like demons and wicked artefacts – a belief in which the long-term benefits of development and prosperity, as well as potentials for transborder cooperation, are ignored. Some environmental activists are so zealously opposed to large dams that they evoke a vision of perpetually stagnating pre-industrial society. The movement against large dams is obviously motivated by sympathy for the displaced population due to submergence. No one denies the rights of the displaced or affected people to appropriate rehabilitation and compensation packages or their right to claim and enjoy equitable shares of the accrued benefits. However, blind opposition to each large water development project demonstrates a subjective appraisal psyche and a failure to appreciate that development and environment are complementary aspects of the agenda for poverty eradication. In the past, things have gone wrong in certain instances due to lack of knowledge, experience and coordination, the use of wrong technology, inefficient/poor implementation and management, corruption, and insensitivity towards project affected persons (PAPs). The key does not lie in doing nothing, but doing differently and wisely. Lessons learned from past mistakes could serve as one of the building blocks in the context of promoting sustainable development.

With respect to dam construction in the Himalayas, which is a dynamic tectonic region, the seismology issue deserves serious consideration. The GBM regional countries should monitor seismicity and understand the Himalayan tectonics comprehensively. This would help in identifying the potential zones of seismic activity. Careful and rigorous geological and geophysical investigations are now done prior to the designing of high dams. Earthquake-resistant high dams, in terms of both design and construction, especially rockfill dams with greater strength against seismic forces, are now attainable.

Similarly, the socio-economic and environmental impacts of large dams and water projects must also be addressed adequately (see Chapter 2). The national guidelines of the GBM regional countries and the norms of international funding agencies are both specific and stringent in matters of resettlement and rehabilitation of the PAPs, as well as mitigation of potential negative impacts on the environment. The basic rule for the resettlement and rehabilitation exercise is that the PAPs should, preferably, be better off after the project. As a compensation measure, 'land for land' is not always realistic in the GBM region, where the population pressure on land has been rapidly increasing. Employment creation, capability improvement to shoulder new responsibilities in work places and self-employment (income-generating) opportunities, with an emphasis on education and skill development, may therefore constitute the areas of crucial focus as the means of rehabilitating the PAPs. Resettlement and rehabilitation could also be accomplished above or near the submerged area, and the programme could be a part of a broader community and area development concept. It would relieve the PAPs from the cultural trauma of relocation in alien surroundings. Besides, the dam sites that are generally remote and inaccessible would witness the development of transport routes and other infrastructure that would open up the area and, in turn, foster mobility, market access and all-round development. Large water resource projects could thus find their image transformed from apparent monsters to harbingers of economic growth, social change and improvement of the quality of life.

A long-term regional water vision for the GBM region should be built on the premise that the supply is likely to remain more or less finite, while the demand will continue to rise rapidly in the coming decades and centuries. In order to develop a framework for water utilization as a transboundary challenge, it is essential for the GBM regional countries to identify sectors and issues with respect to which cooperative strategies and action plans can be formulated, using water as the focal take-off point (see Chapter 3).

A number of options and opportunities exist for collaborative efforts in such sectors as hydropower development, flood management, dry-season flow augmentation and water sharing, water quality improvement, navigation, and catchment/watershed management. Policy environment in the region is now favourable for such cooperation, and the remaining roadblocks should be cleared through mutual confidence-building measures.

Hydropower development

Energy consumption is often a useful index of a country's level of development and standard of living. The GBM region's consumption of energy is very low. The energy economy of the region's countries is highly dependent upon non-commercial sources, mainly biomass. This is not a sustainable situation, especially in view of the growing energy demands of a rising population and expanding economic activity. Yet, the hydropower potential of the region is vast. In the past, efforts have been made by each of the regional countries to develop hydropower within its own borders to meet domestic needs. But cooperative efforts to produce and trade hydropower have not been pursued.

Nepal's theoretical hydropower potential is estimated at about 83,000 megawatts (MW). However, the identified economically feasible potentials are about 40,000 MW. Given its modest load curve, Nepal's energy market lies in the northern and eastern regions of India, as well as in Bangladesh and possibly in Pakistan. Nepal's hydropower could serve as valuable peaking power to the adjacent thermal-based load in India. The country's three-pronged approach to hydropower development envisages small, decentralized projects to meet local needs, medium-scale projects for national needs and large-scale multipurpose and mega projects for transborder regional demands. The installed capacity of hydropower generation in India is about 22,000 MW – which is only 25 per cent of the country's total installed power capacity. The demand for electricity in India is growing at an annual compound growth rate of 8 to 9 per cent. In order to reduce the current imbalance in the hydro–thermal mix and the general consensus to go more for environment-friendly water-based power, the future planning would incorporate a need to exploit maximally the GBM region's hydro potential through a regional grid. Bangladesh had an installed power capacity of about 3000 MW as of 1997 to 1998. Its flat terrain limits the country's hydropower potential. The lone Hydel plant in the south-eastern hills (Kaptai), which is outside of the GBM catchment areas, has an installed capacity of only 230 MW.

It is sometimes argued that Nepal, India and Bangladesh are inefficient consumers of electricity owing to system loss through transmission/distribution anomalies and pilferage; hence, production of more power from large hydroelectric projects is both socially and economically undesirable. Yet, the per-capita electricity consumption in these countries is minuscule in comparison to countries such as Canada, the USA, Norway, Sweden or Switzerland. It is also difficult to accept the contention that Nepal, India and Bhutan should refrain from undertaking large storage schemes to produce electricity, when all the identified future storage would together harness little more than 10 per cent of the annual flows. A more striking comparison relates to the proportion of the installed hydropower to total hydro potential, which is only 0.6 per cent in Nepal compared to 56 per cent, 73 per cent and 87 per cent, respectively, in the similar mountainous countries of Norway, Sweden and Switzerland.

Hydropower has many advantages. It is clean and does not emit greenhouse gases. It is a renewable source of energy without any recurring fuel cost that also obviates uncertainties relating to future costs of inputs. It exhibits a declining unit cost of generation over time with amortization of the initial capital expenditure. Above all, a hydropower generation plant can, and usually does, generate other benefits, and it fosters a development process through opening up remote and outback areas. In view of the likely financial constraints on the development of large projects, there is a clear need to promote private investment in the hydropower sector through joint ventures and foreign direct investment (FDI). Interconnecting the various national power systems through a regional grid could open up the power market and enable Nepal and Bhutan to export surplus electricity to India and Bangladesh.

Flood management

The recurrent floods in the GBM region demand an integrated approach involving cooperation among all of the co-basin countries. Both India and Bangladesh have undertaken certain in-country measures for flood mitigation during the past four decades. These include embankments, river training and channel/drainage improvement. Upstream storage reservoirs can play a vital role in flood management. Multipurpose reservoirs on the Ganges and Brahmaputra systems, with provision for a dedicated flood cushion and well spelled-out reservoir operation and regulation instructions, will be beneficial in moderating floods in northern, eastern and north-eastern India (particularly Uttar Pradesh, Bihar, West Bengal and Assam), as well as in Bangladesh.

Among the non-structural flood management approaches, the greatest potential for regional cooperation lies in flood forecasting and warning. Currently, bilateral cooperation exists between Nepal and India and between India and Bangladesh for transmission of flood-related data, which needs to be further strengthened. More reliable forecasts with additional lead time would be possible in Bangladesh if real-time and daily forecast data are available from additional upstream points on the three rivers. Such effective flood data-sharing arrangements are also necessary with upper riparians, Nepal and Bhutan, for providing Bangladesh with greater lead time to undertake disaster preparedness measures. A review of the current status of flood forecasting methods in India and Bangladesh shows that both countries are using similar technologies for data observation and transmission. This provides an excellent opportunity to exchange expertise and experiences between the two countries for mutual benefit.

As a broader vision, the flood forecasting and warning system needs to be integrated with the overall disaster management activity – both nationally and regionally. The co-riparians should agree on free flow of data relevant to flood forecasting among them on a real-time basis. The importance of satellite observation, especially for early warning of heavy rainfalls, should be recognized; for that purpose, the installation of adequately equipped satellite ground stations throughout the region could be considered.

Flow augmentation and water sharing

The dry-season flows of the GBM rivers, particularly of the Ganges, are inadequate to meet the combined needs of the GBM countries. As early as 1974, the prime ministers of India and Bangladesh had recognized the need for augmentation of the dry-season Ganges flows. The Ganges Water Sharing Treaty of 1996 also includes a provision for the two governments 'to cooperate with each other in finding a solution to the long-term problem of augmenting the flows of the Ganga/Ganges during the dry season'. With Uttar Pradesh, Bihar and West Bengal in India also seeking additional water to meet their requirements, the issue of augmentation deserves serious attention. The Calcutta port authorities are concerned that the Ganges Treaty has diminished lean-season diversions into the Bhagirathi, which would affect draughts requiring increased dredging.

One possible option for substantial augmentation of the Ganges flows, which could benefit Nepal, India and Bangladesh, would be to construct large storages on the Ganges tributaries originating in Nepal. A highly favourable project from this perspective is the Sapta Kosi High Dam in Nepal, the revived third phase of the original Kosi project. It is likely that the Indo-Nepalese detailed project report of the high dam will soon start moving forward. The Kosi Dam will have a significant storage capacity that should provide both north Bihar (India) and Bangladesh with flood cushion and augmented dry-season flows after meeting Nepal's full irrigation requirements.

One other option for augmenting dry-season flows could be the proposed Sunkosh Dam in Bhutan, with a power potential of 4000 MW. It is proposed that water stored behind the dam could be released into a canal, designed to provide a two-stage link to the Teesta and Mahananda barrages in West Bengal. Augmentation of about 12,000 cusec (340 cumec) is expected – a part of which could supplement the water needs of the two Teesta barrages (one in West Bengal and the other in Bangladesh), and a part could reach the Ganges at Farakka. This option still awaits full environmental assessment and Bhutan's concurrence.

The issue of augmentation has direct relationship with concerns for transboundary water sharing among the co-riparians. The Ganges Treaty of 1996 calls on India and Bangladesh to make efforts to conclude water-sharing agreements with regard to other common rivers. One river that has received priority in the water-sharing negotiations is the Teesta – especially because the lean-season flows are inadequate to meet the requirements of both countries while each country has constructed a barrage on the river. Although some ad hoc sharing ratios were proposed earlier, it may be useful to seriously examine the option for Teesta augmentation, as well as whether some arrangements could be arrived at to operate the two barrages in tandem. In such a case, parts of Bangladeshi land lying outside of its barrage's command area could be irrigated by extending canals from the barrage in India.

In the same track of regional cooperation, various other arrangements for augmentation and sharing could be conceived in the backdrop of probable trade-offs between the two countries. One such possibility is a westward diversion link (through Indian territory) between the Brahmaputra and the Ganges, with provisions for diversion along a lower alignment to augment Teesta waters in Bangladesh, or a further alignment southward to revive derelict streams and link up with the Ganges above the proposed barrage site at Pangsha. Some of these options are futuristic in nature, yet they deserve consideration within a long-term time frame for the region.

Linked to the issues of water sharing, lean-season water availability and augmentation options is the state of the ecological health of the rivers. The environment is now recognized as a stakeholder in the water demand nexus. Hence, apart from meeting the requirements of irrigation, power generation, domestic supply and other consumptive uses, a reasonable quantity of water must be available in the rivers in order to sustain the channel equilibrium, as well as to maintain acceptable water quality standards. This question of setting aside a proportion of water in the river received attention in past Indo-Bangladesh negotiations relating to the sharing of the Brahmaputra and Teesta waters. All future planning for water resource development needs to take special note of this aspect.

Following the 1996 Ganges Treaty, Bangladesh now has the opportunity to plan for environmental regeneration of its south-western hydrological system. One option is to construct a barrage on the Ganges at Pangsha to pond the river and force its backwaters into the Gorai River (the principle distributary of the Ganges in Bangladesh). India has offered to assist in the feasibility study for such a venture and extend whatever technical support it can towards its construction. However, several international funding agencies have expressed reservations about such an intervention and stressed that Gorai resuscitation through dredging, with the aim of helping rejuvenate a network of moribund channels, ox-bow lakes and other wetlands in the south-west, could be sufficient. Work on Gorai restoration and associated studies are now in progress. An options study for the best utilization of the water available as a result of the Ganges Treaty, including a barrage on the Ganges, has just been initiated. In spite of Gorai dredging, siltation proneness at its intake point from the Ganges necessitates additional measures such as the Ganges Barrage to supplement the flows in the Gorai and other channels in order to achieve long-term environmental sustainability.

Water quality

In all the GBM countries, the deterioration of both surface and groundwater quality is now a matter of serious concern. Water is essential to sustain agricultural growth and productivity; it is also more vital for life and healthy living. More than half of the morbidity in the GBM region stems from the use of impure drinking water. Safe water supply and hygienic sanitation are basic minimum needs that the GBM countries are yet to meet in both rural and urban areas. A holistic approach is required to monitor the water quality in each country, together with regional initiatives to prevent further deterioration and bring about improvement in the quality of water.

The mitigation of the additional problems of salinity and arsenic in Bangladesh involves special action plans. Saline intrusion in coastal areas could be addressed through dry-season flushing of channels by means of such methods, cited earlier, as storing monsoon water and resuscitating moribund channels. The Bangladesh Arsenic Mitigation Water Supply Project (BAMWSP) funded by the World Bank/Swiss Development Corporation is currently engaged in assessing the extent, dimensions and causes of the arsenic problem with a view to developing a long-term strategy for supplying arsenic-free water.

The monitoring of water quality in the GBM rivers is not as extensive as it should be except in the case of the Ganges in India and the Buriganga in Bangladesh. The GBM countries need to set uniform standards relating to water quality parameters, along with establishing an effective water-quality monitoring network. The countries should review their existing water quality/pollution laws, and make efforts to enforce the polluter pays principle. At the regional level, they should also coordinate their actions to deal with transboundary transmission of pollution, and evolve a mechanism for real-time water-quality data exchange.

Inland navigation

The Ganges, the Brahmaputra, the Meghna and their principle tributaries had served as major arteries of trade and commerce for centuries. However, during recent years, their importance has diminished as traffic has moved away from waterways to road and railway nodes. Yet, even today, the lower part of the GBM system depends upon waterways, especially in Bangladesh and north-eastern India.

For landlocked Nepal, Bhutan and north-eastern India, an inland water outlet to the sea is of great significance. The establishment of links with the inland water transport networks of India and Bangladesh would provide Nepal access to Calcutta (India) and Mongla (Bangladesh) ports. Potentials exist for the development of water transport in Nepal in all of the three major rivers (Karnali, Gandaki and Kosi), which are tributaries of the Ganges. Construction of high dams on these rivers would improve navigability in these channels.

The Karnali (known as the Ghagra in India) has the maximum potential for navigation – all the way from the Indo-Nepalese border to the confluence with the Ganges. The Gandaki is an important waterway serving central Nepal and has the navigation potential to serve eastern Uttar Pradesh and eastern Bihar in India if it is linked with India's National Waterway No 1 in the Ganges – running from Allahabad to Haldia, below Calcutta. The upper reaches of the Kosi River are too steep for navigation; but river training works could facilitate the operation of shallow draught barges. Among the multiple benefits to be derived from the proposed Sapta Kosi High Dam is the provision for a navigational channel with a dedicated storage. The principle focus for Nepal's navigational development would be to gain exit to the sea through the Ganges, and obtain linkages with the inland ports of India en route. The strategy should be to ensure that structures constructed under water-development projects do not impede the development of inland water routes.

With a view to reviving the past significance of inland water routes, India has already designated the Ganges between Allahabad and Haldia (1629km) as the National Waterway No 1, and the Brahmaputra between Sadiya and Dhubri (891km) as the National Waterway No 2. The maintenance and further development of the requisite minimum navigable width and depth, coupled with provision of navigation aids and terminal facilities, would enhance the navigation potential in the GBM region. India and Bangladesh have a bilateral protocol, renewed every two years, for India to use the Ganges-Brahmaputra-Meghna riverway for water transit between West Bengal and Assam. The potentials of these routes – not optimally used, at present – could expand through channel improvement, better pilotage and navigation aids, and simplification and standardization of rules and regulations. A dedicated willingness to integrate the waterways network in the GBM regional countries would benefit all of the countries in the long run.

Catchment management

The geographically interlinked character of the major rivers in the GBM region warrants an integrated regional approach to the care and management of the catchments. Sound basin-wide catchment management is an essential long-term strategy to combat the threat of floods and erosion and to preserve the ecosystem. The sediment load in the rivers, which is largely the consequence of geomorphologic processes in the upper catchment areas, tends to increase with the progressive removal of vegetative cover on slopes.

Soil conservation and reforestation in the upper catchments of Nepal and India, and also within Bangladesh, could help in substantially reducing sedimentation. In most instances of water-resource development programmes at higher elevations, soil conservation practices are initiated as a follow-up step. This need not be so. Soil conservation and management programmes could be taken up independently in vulnerable sites, as well as through integrating them in the environmental management plans for water-related interventions. Soil conservation strategies should be both rehabilitative and preventive, and could only succeed with people's participation in the whole process of strategy formulation and implementation.

In the context of the fragility of the Himalayan ecosystem and the burgeoning population pressure on hilly slopes, an integral part of water resource planning should be to adopt rational land-use and cropping patterns, including contour ploughing, in the upper catchments. Measures to conserve soil quality and improve the ecological health of the land might be highly desirable in the context of area development programmes in upland regions that tend to be neglected or are less accessible.

BROAD-BASED CONCLUSIONS AND RECOMMENDATIONS

In the previous three sections, the water-based development contexts, issues and potentials have been presented and briefly described, reflecting vast scopes and opportunities for the future implementation of the water-based regional projects. The true spirit of regional cooperation lies in moving out from bilateralism towards multilateralism. The congeniality in the political atmosphere may lead to a visionary approach among the politicians of the regional countries to create an enabling environment of multilateralism. Civil societies of the regional countries have a vital role to play in this context. They should voice the need for the integrated basin-wide approach in water resources planning in their respective countries and, eventually, across the region. Various institutions and think tanks of the region should structurally try to link up with each other with a long-term commitment to cooperate and collaborate.

After succeeding in creating a multilateralistic environment in the region, the water-based projects should be implemented with a clear attachment of the issue of prioritization and institutional arrangement. For example, non-conflicting and non-structural issues such as technically and regionally improving the flood forecasting and warning system could be a point of departure, both in terms of piloting the institutional linkages and institutional arrangements.

Under the purview of the institutional arrangements, all of the relevant regional countries should be involved in the detailed feasibility studies of the regional projects, which has a bearing both on cost sharing and the benefit sharing of the regional countries. Linked to these, institutional arrangements for long-term cost recovery by the regional countries is also crucial. The above-mentioned issue is the crux of the matter in terms of attaining and ensuring sustainability in the integrated water resources management of the region. The active donors in the water sector of the region have an important role to play in this regard.

Bilateral funding examples are there. World Bank financing helped to resolve the Indus dispute, while UN-led investments helped to achieve the Mekong Agreement. Cooperation-inducing financing has not always come from outside of the region. Thailand helped to finance a project in Laos, as did India in Pakistan, in conjunction with their respective watershed agreements. A provision of the Nile Waters Treaty has Egypt paying Sudan outright for water to which they both agreed that Sudan had rights, but that it was not able to use the water.

As a general recommendation, proposition and thesis towards improvement, it may be put forward that the active water-sector donors of the region should persuade and promote this agenda of water-based regional cooperation. As development partners of the region, the donors may be involved in the cost-sharing arrangements. A more coordinated, harmonized and synchronized approach may be adopted from the donors' side to maintain the long-term vision. As a proposition, the donors may create regional funds for the regional projects and attach a general condition that all relevant countries in the region should act together in a joint spirit, both in terms of cost and benefit sharing, in order to realize the funds.

NOTES

1   The views expressed in this chapter are the author's alone and should not be attributed to the Dutch embassy, the Dutch government or any other government.
2   The plan of action agreed at the United Nations Conference on Environment and Development (UNCED) in Rio de Janeiro in 1992.
3   The four principles of water resource management that came out of the International Conference on Water and Environment in Dublin in 1992.

REFERENCES

Adhikari, K D et al (2000) *Cooperation on Eastern Himalayan Rivers: Opportunities and Challenges*, Konark Publishers, Delhi

Ahmad, Q K, Rangachari, R and Sainju, M M (2001) *Ganges-Brahmaputra-Meghna Region: A Framework for Sustainable Development*, University Press, Dhaka

Ahmad, Q K et al (eds) (1994) *Converting Water into Wealth: Regional Cooperation in Harnessing the Eastern Himalayan Rivers*, Academic Publishers, Dhaka

ICID–CIID (1994) *Management of International River Basins and Environmental Challenges*, Academic Publishers, Dhaka

Malla, S K (1989) *Three-Country Study on Water Resources Development of the Ganges-Brahmaputra-Barak River Basins: Nepal Country Report*, IIDS, Kathmandu

Shrestha, A P (1991) *Hydropower in Nepal: Issues and Concepts in Development*, Resources Nepal, Kathmandu

Verghese, B G (1998) *Water of Hope: From Vision to Reality in Himalaya-Ganga Development Cooperation*, 2nd edition, CPR, New Delhi

Wolf, A et al (1999) 'International river basins of the world,' *International Journal of Water Resources Development*, vol 15, no 4, pp387–427

Chapter 11

Let's pump money into the water sector!

CAROLINE M FIGUÈRES

INTRODUCTION

The World Water Vision and the associated Framework for Action presented during the Second World Water Forum held in The Hague in March 2000 estimated that the cost of required water services in developing countries during the period between 2000 and 2025 was around US$180 billion per year. This estimate refers to investment in new works alone, and takes no account of the ongoing costs of maintenance, rehabilitation and replacement. Broken down by sector, the required investments will be about US$30 billion for agriculture, US$75 billion for the environment and industry, and US$75 billion for water supply and sanitation (Cosgrove and Rijsberman, 2000; GWP, 2000).

At present, the largest investors in water services in developing countries are governments (the traditional public sector), which contribute around US$50 billion per year. The domestic private sector contributes US$15 billion, international donors a further US$9 billion (of which the World Bank Group accounts for about US$4 billion) and the international private sector around US$4 billion. The total amount currently being invested in water services is therefore only US$78 billion per year (Cosgrove and Rijsberman, 2000; GWP, 2000). The annual shortfall between demand and present resources is unimaginably huge: some US$100 billion per year for new works alone.

These amounts, especially how they have been calculated, have been the subject of many debates. While it is undoubtedly necessary to obtain more precise data at both national and regional levels on which to base new calculations, it is clear that the gap between what is needed and the resources currently available is enormous and has to be filled as soon as possible.

The World Water Vision document suggests some ways in which resources could be mobilized to meet the financial challenge facing the water sector (GWP, 2000):

- Encourage new investments from the international private sector.
- Integrate service development with the local consumer economy.
- Develop pricing and charging schemes that will ensure the financial sustainability of water investments.
- Gain recognition for water investments from the ethical investment community (so-called 'blue' funds).
- Facilitate poor countries' access to water funds and develop micro-credit mechanisms.
- Encourage local development banks to invest in water.
- Enable developing countries to attract and benefit from private-sector funding.
- Make concessional multilateral funds available for investment in water supply and sanitation.
- Ensure that improved water services would contribute to the goal of poverty reduction.
- Enable governments to use the funds released by debt relief for water services.

This chapter analyses the present situation and tries to explain why it is proving so difficult to meet the financial challenge in the water sector. It also suggests some concrete actions to complement and improve the proposals presented in the Framework for Action. As the financial shortfall needs to be met as soon as possible, we need to speed up progress towards meeting the targets, and to find new ways of pumping money into the water sector as soon as possible. For this reason, it is essential to improve communication between financial specialists and the users of financial services in the water sector. This chapter aims to improve understanding on both sides, and to facilitate the decision-making process.

TODAY'S FOUR MAJOR CHALLENGES

Making money available for the water sector

Money as such is not a problem. There is obviously enough money in the global economy to finance development and reduce poverty. As noted above, in the coming years, the annual shortfall in investments in the water sector is likely to be about US$100 billion per year for new works alone. This amount is unimaginably huge; but, at the same time, it is relatively modest compared with the turnover of some of the companies listed on *The Economist* world ranking 2001. Exxon Mobil, for example, had a turnover of US$210.4 billion in 2000. This is more than the gross national product of Denmark (US$175 billion), which is the world's 24th largest national economy (*The Economist*,

2000). Also in 2000, Vivendi Water had a turnover of about US$10.8 billion (Vivendi Water, 2001). The total volume of transactions on international financial markets is colossal. In 1998 it averaged around US$1500 billion *per day* and has been rising steadily ever since (Chauvin, 2001). In this context, the annual needs of the water sector are mere chicken feed.

The following organizations/institutions are currently financing activities in the water sector in developing countries:

- International financial institutions, such as (regional) development banks.
- Foreign private foundations.
- Bilateral funding/aid agencies.
- Foreign private investors
- Multinationals (private water utilities).
- Government (including government agencies).
- Local private-sector companies.
- Non-governmental organizations (NGOs).
- Local communities.

Their contributions to the water sector are presented in Table 11.1.

Table 11.1 *Major investors in the water sector in developing countries*

Type of investor	Contribution	
	US$ billion	Percentage
Traditional public sector	50	64
Domestic private sector	15	19
International donors	9	12
International private sector	4	5

Table 11.2 presents a simple categorization of the sources of funds invested in the water sector in developing countries (after Hall, 2001); general comments are added below.

Table 11.2 *Sources of funds invested in the water sector in developing countries*

	Sources of funds	
	Domestic	International
Internal resources	Surplus of undertaking	–
State	Government, national funds	Aid agencies
Bank loans	Domestic banks	International banks
Bonds	Domestic bonds	International bonds
Intermediate funds	Municipal development funds	–
International financial institutions	–	Development banks
Equity finance	Private shareholders	Private shareholders

In the case of water supply, the simplest way for a country to raise finance for water undertakings is to use internal resources (surpluses that can be reinvested in operations and maintenance). In The Netherlands, for example, consumers have to pay for water. Some Dutch municipalities, as owners of the water supply companies and as public authorities, are not obliged to maximize profits or distribute them. They may decide, as a matter of policy, that the surpluses are reinvested in the water system itself and are not used, for example, to reduce taxes for other services. In most developing countries, on the other hand, water undertakings for various reasons often have no surpluses to reinvest.

In many countries, the national government provides some or all of the finance for investment in the water sector (see Table 11.1), either in the form of grants or loans to local authorities or through special environmental/water funds. This method of financing investments compares favourably with the cost of private finance (Hall, 2001).

According to a recent World Bank report, *Global Development Finance* (World Bank, 2001), the cyclical slow-down in the global economy that began during the second half of 2000 suddenly intensified towards the end of the year. The tragic events of 11 September 2001 will certainly slow economic growth in the USA and elsewhere, and this will affect developing countries. In a harsher economic environment, countries with severe domestic imbalances, often concealed during the 1990s by an exceptionally favourable external environment, may face closer scrutiny from financial markets. As a consequence, developing countries will find it even more difficult to mobilize new investments from international financial sources.

As the availability of money appears not to be a problem, the challenge is, in fact, to make the water sector more attractive for investors or donors, especially in a less favourable economic environment. The Framework for Action document (GWP, 2000) suggests various ways to improve the situation, such as encouraging new investments from the international private sector; but it gives no firm suggestions about how to make the water sector more attractive. For developing countries, therefore, it is essential to make clear the purposes for which the money is needed.

Formulating the need for water infrastructure and the adequate answer

Today's greatest challenge is water development for the provision of safe water supplies and sanitation and to enhance food security, especially in countries with water shortages and stagnating economies. The water needs of the population are related to their uses: drinking, washing, cooking, growing crops, producing electricity, etc. At this point, it is important to distinguish between the terms 'water needs' and 'water demands'. The demand for water is highly dependent on its price or, more specifically, on the willingness to pay for water. Paying for water makes people more responsible for their demand, as they often ask for more than they really need. If water is free of charge, people will tend to claim and use more than if it has a price or is subsidized by the government. For this reason, we refer to water needs rather than demands.

To make available or improve access to water to meet the realistic water needs of a population requires the development of (small-scale and large-scale) water infrastructure. In the case of drinking water supply and sanitation systems, the scale of the infrastructure can range from a single borehole with a hand pump and pit latrines (for a small community) to large water supply schemes and wastewater treatment plants (for large communities).

In the short term, the task is to identify and formulate water projects and programmes that will meet the water needs of the population. In general, people at the grassroots know empirically how much water they need for a specific purpose, when to use it and how. But this does not mean that they are able to quantify the total amount of water needed by their community, as a whole, or to determine whether the water is being used as efficiently as possible. Furthermore, the need of water infrastructure for a community, as a whole, is not just the sum of individual needs. A translation is required to identify the most suitable solution, taking into account the variability of needs and resources in space and time.

In addition, it is also necessary to place local demand in a broader context, whether a regional, national or river-basin framework (see Chapter 10) when suitable new technology and techniques that have proven successful elsewhere have to be introduced (see Chapters 5 and 6). For these reasons, identification and formulation of water infrastructure projects and programmes must be based not only on knowledge of the local situation, but also on the experience and expertise of experts with international background.

The financing of water infrastructure schemes depends not only on the availability of funds. In order to obtain funding from international sources for the construction of water infrastructure, projects and programmes have to satisfy certain criteria, which can vary considerably from one donor agency or lender, beneficiaries, etc to another. An environmental impact assessment study is mostly required (see Chapter 2). Such criteria include economic efficiency, social justice and political acceptability and environmental sustainability. Even if these criteria are strictly defined and universally agreed, projects will still have to be identified and formulated in order to obtain funding. Donors more and more often require projects to be demand driven – identified and formulated by the beneficiary government to ensure national ownership.

At present, however, in the identification and formulation of water infrastructure projects and programmes to meet local needs, many developing countries face a number of constraints:

*   Shortages of local personnel with the capacity to identify and formulate good projects: as noted above, local people have to indicate what they need; but they are often unable to formulate their needs in terms that lenders can understand, or they are unable to place the project in a broader context.

- Water is often accorded lower priority than other sectors; for example, in most developing countries the electricity coverage is greater than the water supply coverage.
- Governments may lack the financial resources needed for identification and formulation missions and to obtain help from experts with international background specializing in identification and formulation missions to support them.

For projects to meet today's criteria, participation by all stakeholders is essential. Addressing environmental issues and moving towards sustainability requires the joint efforts of all stakeholders. The different stakeholders are all organizations/institutions active in the water sector: they may be water-related ministries or national agencies, knowledge institutions, NGOs, local municipalities, international or local private companies, trade unions, consumers organizations, churches, etc.

Local stakeholders – the project owners – need to be supported in the process of identifying and formulating sustainable projects and programmes. The formulation of a project is a difficult task, demanding not only a considerable capacity to analyse and synthesize information, but preferably also extensive experience in developing countries and knowledge of the local situation. It is therefore important to increase human capacity at the national level to support local people in identifying and formulating their water needs.

International experts can give local people access to new technology and new approaches that have proven successful elsewhere. For example, in many areas the development of ecological sanitation systems could offer a promising technical alternative to piped sanitation. Managing rainwater is also a promising means of increasing food production, as indicated by Johan Rockström in Chapter 5. In addition, marketing strategies can be used in campaigns to raise awareness of the need to reduce water demand.

Finally, many donors' project/programming cycles are far too long and must be speeded up. The World Bank and the European Commission, for example, may require a long period (sometimes two years or more) between the identification and preparation of large projects and their approval and implementation. One of the main reasons for the delay is that lenders (donors and foreign governments) are now emphasizing the need for country ownership. Another reason is the need to follow official procedures to get the project financed. These procedures are necessary to ensure transparency and to avoid corruption; but very often they are bureaucratic and slow down the project cycle.

Matching water infrastructure demand and financial resources efficiently

Assuming that money is available (first challenge) and that a suitable water infrastructure project/programme has been formulated (second challenge), the next challenge is to obtain adequate financing to make the project a reality.

The demand (the individual project) has to be matched to the resources (money). However, there are a number of inherent risks in the water and sanitation sector, which is why private investment is so much lower than in the power, telecommunications and transportation sectors.

Identifying risks

Matching water infrastructure projects and sources of finance is mainly a matter of identifying the right combination of risks for all parties. The development of the right financing construction basically depends upon a good risk assessment that identifies all of the possible risks. The risks will depend upon the type of water project under consideration, which could be an urban or a rural water supply system, a sewage treatment plant, a hydropower plant, an irrigation and/or drainage system, etc. They will also depend upon the scale of the project (for example, the size of the population or area involved) and the country or region where the project will be carried out. The point of view of the partners involved in a project is a major factor in evaluating risks. The risks perceived by the lender will be very different from those of the user of the grant or those who will be affected by the project. Risk also depends upon circumstances; for example, multinational companies are more likely to be willing to take risks when international markets are depressed than during an economic boom, when they will have enough work in their home markets and will be able to satisfy their shareholders without risk-taking abroad.

There are various kinds of risk: completion risk, technological risk, risk relating to the supply of raw materials, economic risk, financial risk, currency risk, political risk, environmental risk and risk of catastrophe (Finnerty, 1996). Figure 11.1 presents an overview of the possible risks involved, some of which are explained in more detail in the following subsections.

Economic risk For international water utilities, the major risk is economic. Even if a project proves to be technologically sound and is completed on time and operating satisfactorily at or near capacity, there is still a risk that the demand for its products or services may be insufficient to generate the revenue needed to cover the project's operating costs, service its debts and provide a fair rate of return to investors. Depending upon the economics of the particular project, there may be very little margin for raising water prices to achieve a return on equity (Finnerty, 1996).

The water and sanitation sector is characterized by high levels of uncertainty about the condition of the assets and thus the investment required. Private investors have only limited information about the state of the existing physical infrastructure (pipelines) and the customers' base (the number of illegal connections). The condition and value of the water and sanitation infrastructure are often difficult to determine because many of the assets are underground. This problem has significant implications for the risks faced by private investors. Underinvestment and inadequate maintenance can go unnoticed for years at a time. This makes it difficult both for the government and any water utility company to agree on a contract, taking into account the

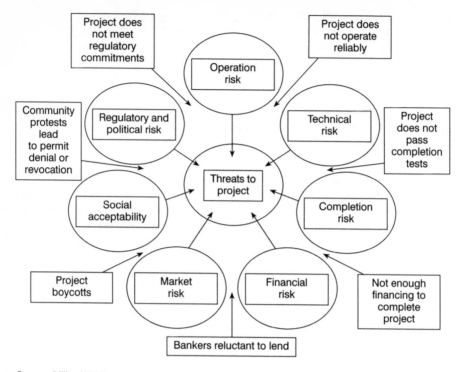

Source: Miller (2001)

Figure 11.1 *Overview of the possible risks involved in a water project*

value of the assets. Furthermore, it makes it difficult for governments to control the efficiency of operators, who are also highly risk averse (Haarmeyer and Mody, 2000).

International water and wastewater utilities that take over existing water and wastewater systems may have difficulty in estimating the costs of rehabilitation, so that tariff setting and adjustment can be subject to considerable uncertainty. Fixed water charges that have been set too low are known to discourage investment. An important element in economic risk is the operating efficiency of project facilities, so that many lenders will insist that the project sponsors arrange to employ a competent operator/manager.

The Dolphin Coast project north of Durban in South Africa provides a good illustration of the economic risk. The 1999 contract envisaged a 40 to 50 per cent increase in the number of customers over the first five years. In fact, growth over the first two years has been no more than 5 per cent, making it highly unlikely that the forecast will be realized. Much of the blame has been laid at the door of local property developers, who overestimated the demand from nearby holiday homes. The original contract between the local council and the private utility company was flexible, in that it provided for renegotiation in the event that the return on investment fell either above or below a predetermined band. The result has been a fundamental revision of the contract, including a 15 per cent increase in water tariffs, a transfer of the bulk of the local council's debt, a stringent austerity programme and reduced investments in the local water and sewerage system. The political and labour reaction to the new agreement, especially the tariff hikes, remains to be seen (Global Water Report, 2001).

Financial risk Lenders do not like to take financial risks. As a rule, lenders will not agree to fund a project unless they are convinced that it will be viable once in operation. Most of the risks are business (as opposed to credit) risks, which are not normally knowingly accepted by lenders. However, guarantees, contractual arrangements and other supplementary credit-support measures can be used to spread the project's business risks among the various parties involved. It may also be possible to cover the risks by means of security arrangements: passive investors (passive equity investors as well as lenders) are only interested in receiving a return on their financial investment. They will usually be prepared to bear certain credit risks, but are extremely reluctant to bear significant operating risks or other risks that are not premised on the ability of the project to meet its financial obligations.

If a significant portion of the debt financing for a project is at a floating rate, there is a risk that rising interest rates may jeopardize the project's ability to service its debt (Finnerty, 1996). In the water and sanitation sector, capital intensity is high and large sunk costs are involved. Water assets often last 30 to 50 years, with depreciation rates of only 3 to 5 per cent per year. To keep tariff levels low, the payback period for water investments is usually amortized over 15 to 30 years. Long-term financing is needed to finance such investments, which is why the water sector is not very attractive for investors. A simple way to avoid risk would be to arrange fixed-rate loans; but not every lender will accept this without a trade-off concerning other risk exposures. Is it possible to say that, even in the water sector, cover for risks can always be bought? The question is how much it will cost and who will pay for it.

Political risk Lenders and/or international water utilities do not like political risk – that is, the risk that political authorities may disrupt the development of the project and/or its long-term economic viability. For example, they could make retroactive changes in water and environmental laws. Or they could make new popular (short-term) decisions to improve their chances of re-election without considering the effects on ongoing (long-term) projects. The price of water, for example, should not become a populist cause.

Environmental risk Environmental risk for the lender is the risk that the environmental impacts of a project may delay or prevent its completion, or they may necessitate a costly redesign. In the past, changes in environmental regulations and actions by environmental pressure groups have created significant risks for environmentally sensitive projects, such as big dams or large irrigation canals. To the extent that environmental objections are voiced through the political process, they also create a political risk. Because of the growing influence of environmental activists, it is increasingly important that the environmental risks are thoroughly evaluated in an environmental impact assessment, especially since the environment is not regarded as a beneficiary of a project (see Chapter 2).

Managing risks

A good understanding of risks is fundamental to finance water infrastructure. In the business world, several rules are observed when drawing up contacts. Firstly, the risk has to be taken by the partner who is best able to manage and limit it. Secondly, if several partners can manage one specific risk, it has to be shared. Thirdly, the risk has to be taken by the partner who can deal with it at the lowest cost. Fourthly, risks that are difficult to identify are to be taken by the partner who creates them (Van de Vijver, 2001).

For example, in the case of donor-financed projects, many of the above-mentioned risks are relevant even if the donor is not a business organization. In particular, donors are sensitive to political and environmental risks, even if projects do not need to be economically viable to be financed. The project cycle needs to be speeded up, and international organizations must be able to make funds available more quickly at the right time, in the right place and to the right people. The decision processes within these organizations should be adapted where needed to increase efficiency.

One way to increase efficiency could be to identify existing national organizations or to create some facilitating ones that would be able to channel the demands within their countries to financing organizations, and to coordinate and channel flows of funding back to the local project owners. Such national organizations could play a major role in improving the coordination of foreign aid and in speeding up the project cycle.

In this respect, eight donors and international financial institutions (including The Netherlands government and the World Bank) have recently launched an interesting initiative in Mozambique, aimed at improving collaboration in the agricultural and rural development-specific sectors. The eight organizations have created a joint financial mechanism in which they all transfer funds to a special bank account of the Ministry of Finance, which are included in the annual national budget. The government has agreed to use the funds for projects in the agricultural and rural-development sectors, following the national development plan, and to prepare common reports for the eight financial backers on a regular basis. This pilot experiment in the pooling of financial assistance looks very promising.

In many developing countries, an additional problem is the presence of many different development and aid organizations (as many as 500 in attractive countries!). This means that local managers have their hands full simply writing progress reports on projects that have already been funded or are receiving identification/formulation/evaluation missions. There is an urgent need to improve the coordination of international and national aid in order to free local civil servants from the burden of routine tasks so that they can concentrate on risk management and the development of new projects.

Financing projects and programmes

To be attractive to investors, projects have to be demonstrably both technically feasible and environmentally and socially sustainable in the long term. Private companies are driven by the desire for short-term profit. The challenge is to make the water sector attractive enough that the private sector will be interested in investing billions of dollars in building the infrastructure that is needed to solve the long-term sanitary and social problems caused by shortages of water. From the private sector's point of view, a major incentive would be if the long-term risks could be reduced through specific measures or mechanisms such as guarantees.

In the case of economically viable projects, the private sector (foreign private investors or international water utilities) is ready to play a financial role provided that the risks are clear cut. In addition to several conventional means of financing investments in water infrastructure, some years ago the concept of project financing was introduced. Project financing is already used in various other sectors, but is a new and promising means of financing water infrastructure projects (Finnerty, 1996).

Project financing Project financing involves raising funds to finance an economically separable capital investment project that is capable of generating a cash flow sufficient to service the loans, as well as to repay and provide a return on the investment. This needs to be distinguished from conventional direct financing, or what may be termed financing on a firm's general credit. The special feature of project financing is that the project is a distinct legal entity: project assets, project-related contracts and project cash flows are segregated to a substantial degree from the sponsoring entity. At the time of initial debt financing, a project has no operating history. Consequently, guarantees of technical feasibility and economic viability are very important for the providers of funds. Lenders require assurances that the project will actually go into service and will then constitute an economically viable undertaking.

In the financial world, the term 'project financing' is widely misused and, perhaps, even more widely misunderstood, so that it is important to clarify what it does *not* mean. It is *not* a means of raising funds to finance a project that is so economically weak that it may not be able to service its debt or provide an acceptable rate of return to equity investors. In other words, it is *not* a means of financing a project that could not be financed on a conventional basis. At the heart of project financing there is always a discrete asset, such as a single facility or a related set of assets with a specific purpose. In the case of the water sector, it could be a water supply or sewerage network, a drinking water or wastewater treatment plant, or an irrigation scheme. The operation, supported by a variety of contractual arrangements, must be organized so that the project has the unquestioned ability to generate sufficient cash flow to repay its debts. Project financing is well adapted to financing water infrastructure.

From the point of view of major water operators, the ideal candidates for project financing are capital investment projects that are capable of functioning as independent economic units, can be completed without undue uncertainty, and will be worth demonstrably more than they cost to complete.

Many believe that the shift to private-sector participation in the water sector could generate large benefits for the local population; but effective private involvement requires governments to play a new facilitating and regulatory role in order to create a credible (and, hence, low-risk) contracting and operating environment. Such private-sector involvement may bring substantial benefits for consumers, as well as significant improvements in production efficiency. However, the sustainability of the benefits and improvements will generally depend upon the implementation of complementary water pricing, financing and regulatory reforms.

In countries where the financial resources are limited and specific facilities such as water and wastewater treatment plants for large cities are urgently needed, public–private partnerships (PPPs) may offer a means of obtaining financing (Blom, 2000). If the regulatory framework is adequate, build-own-operate (BOO) or build-operate-transfer (BOT) contracts could offer quick and effective ways of channelling private investment and initiatives to provide new water facilities. However, to ask the private sector to play a role in financing water infrastructure is implicitly to accept that water is subject to the profit motive. In some situations, such as major cities without efficient water supply systems, the privatization process may be the only way to obtain the resources needed to remedy the situation in the *short term*. In such critical situations, the choice appears to be simple: either invest immediately using (sometimes expensive) private money, or wait (perhaps for a very long time) until a donor makes money available for such a project through gifts or soft loans. In some cases, public–public partnerships (PUPs) could present a valuable alternative (Hall, 2001; Blokland et al, 1999).

The issue here is not whether privatization is good or bad, although many believe that the involvement of private financing in the water sector will solve all of its problems. Even experts at the World Bank are adopting a more balanced position in this field. As already noted, the international private sector already contributes around US$4 billion, and it is clear that this sector will not be able to bridge the US$100 billion gap. It is also clear that the private sector will not be willing to take uncalculated risks for such an amount, even in the case of economically viable projects. The challenge is, therefore, to find financial arrangements that fit the local/regional/national framework without conditionality. Mixed credits or cluster financing should be such an alternative.

Mixed credits or cluster financing Water projects are not always economically viable, especially if they involve water supplies in rural areas or small cities. This does not mean that they are not worthwhile or urgently needed, but that there will be no commercial funding available for them. Such projects are usually donor financed and many of them have to wait a long time for donors such as the World Bank or the European Commission to provide gifts, grants or soft loans to finance them. But in some cases, remote industries (mines) need water and a win–win situation can be created by combining the industrial and the small-city supplies. As an alternative, financial constructions known as 'mixed credits' or 'cluster financing', combining donor funds and private-sector money, are in the process of financing such projects (NEDECO, 2001).

Considerable skills are required to set up these complex financial constructions, which are still in the experimental phase. And as the concept is new, it takes time to persuade international donors or foreign governments that they can be useful for financing projects that may not be economically viable, but address urgent social or environmental problems. Real commitments on the part of national governments, donors, international financial institutions and private-sector partners are fundamental to start such projects.

In general, once the risks are well understood it is possible to draw up contracts that cover the risks in an acceptable way for the different contractors. New kinds of contracts are needed, covering all aspects of the partnerships between private organizations, donors or financial institutions. However, there is an acute shortage of financial experts and lawyers capable of handling such complex financing structures in the highly specialized water sector.

One of the major challenges in this area is to formulate procedures that will be acceptable to both private and public actors. A private company investing money in the development of a new project (such as a feasibility study) is likely to lose interest in taking the risks of development if the public actor or the donor stipulates that the company must follow its own tendering procedures in the later stages of the project. For this reason, standard procedures between public and private actors need to be established to simplify and speed up the process. Some multinationals are already addressing this issue and have proposed some new procedures to limit the risks for the client.

To illustrate how these proposals would work, consider the case of a national or local government (GOV, for the purpose of this example) and a water utility company (Water-Int). The principle is simple. Water-Int invests in a pre-feasibility study. This means that GOV accepts that Water-Int carries out the feasibility study, including the preparation of tender documents, for a large-scale water supply or sanitation project. When the study has been completed, GOV launches the tender at its convenience. Water-Int and other companies submit their proposals. If Water-Int wins the contract, GOV pays nothing for the feasibility study. If Water-Int does not win then GOV has to refund Water-Int for the costs of the feasibility study, which may be about 5 to 10 per cent of the contract value. The terms of the contract between GOV and Water-Int are discussed and agreed upon before Water-Int begins work on the feasibility study (the percentage to be refunded). Such an arrangement creates a win–win situation for both parties. GOV does not need to find financing for the feasibility study and obtains tender documents that are ready to be used. Water-Int creates the opportunity to take a calculated risk, since part of the investment will be refunded if the company does not win the contract.

Implementing the planned water infrastructure project and managing it wisely

Even if a good financial deal has been struck, and money is available, the project still has to be implemented and the infrastructure will have to be maintained over many years. This represents an enormous challenge, which would need a chapter to itself. However, some points for reflection are summarized below.

During the African Capacity Building Forum, held in Bamako, Mali, in October 2001, Eveline Herfkens, The Netherlands minister for development cooperation, stated that effective institutional development and capacity building would require a radical break with outdated ideas and practices. Three key changes are needed: a new way of thinking, a new way of seeing and a new way of working (Herfkens, 2001).

In many developing countries, even if the money is available, one of the greatest bottlenecks is the lack of local capacity. Not only are there shortages of technically qualified local personnel to implement and maintain water infrastructure projects, but there is a lack of efficient and reliable project managers who will be able to perform their primary task: management.

Over the years, capacity-building programmes in the water sector have tried to address the problem of the lack of management capacity; but this is likely to be resolved only in the long term. Many national water managers are technically skilled to deal with the water infrastructure, but very often lack the skills necessary to manage complex projects. Good water governance has everything to do with the availability of skilled and capable personnel (Figuères, 2001; see Chapter 12 in this volume). In particular, the relationship between water managers and the political authorities is not always clearly spelled out, and very often managers are not able to take the necessary actions because of political interference (Allan, 2003). For this reason, it is very important to define clearly what decisions are to be taken by the authorities, and for what and to whom the management is accountable. Water pricing is such a decision (Hall, 2001).

SUGGESTED ACTIONS TO IMPROVE THE SITUATION

Financing water infrastructure is obviously a complicated problem. It is often claimed that there is no money, and that is both true and false. In itself, money is not really the problem. There is enough money, just as there is enough water; but it is not always available at the right time and in the right place. With money, as with water, the challenge is to match resources with demand, taking into account both short- and long-term factors, global and local levels and a range of other complex considerations, ranging from social justice and politics to the needs of the environment. Money needs to be channelled into the water sector, and simplifying and speeding up existing processes should allow using the available money more efficiently. Finally, the risks involved need to be better understood to improve the relationship between the financial world and the water sector. A number of possible actions that could help to channel money into the water sector are described below.

Encourage governments, traditional lenders and existing actors in the water sector to finance more water infrastructure

Firstly, decision-makers of all kinds need to change their attitudes to risk in the water sector and to take new kinds of decisions that are more favourable to it. The process has already begun, and much has been done at both international and national levels to raise awareness of the need for a change in attitudes. The creation of the World Water Council, the Global Water Partnership and the World Water Forums has had a positive effect.

Environmental activists, NGOs, trade unions and civil society organizations of various kinds are playing a major role in raising awareness about water issues and informing the public. In recent years, however, there have been more and more protests against the construction of large-scale water infrastructure, such as dams or pipelines. This clearly creates a complex situation. For example, a government authority proposes to build a facility, which for many reasons arouses protest from interest groups. In a democratic country/process, the opponents of a water infrastructure project may prove to be in the majority and will, therefore, win and the project will not go ahead. In some cases, however, even if the opponents cannot muster a democratic majority, they may continue to protest. By doing so, these interest groups indicate both that they disagree with the political decision and that they do not recognize that the elected decision-makers are truly representative of the population. This kind of protest may become so widespread and vehement that it can endanger the decision because the politicians fear that they may not be re-elected and so change their minds. In this way, interest groups may prevent the construction of large infrastructure that is needed for the development of the country. In non-democratic countries, it may be difficult for interest groups to have their say; yet, their protests can endanger the decision if international organizations/multinationals/institutions are involved and fear for their own image.

National authorities may insist that the infrastructure is needed for the good of the whole community, while the interest groups argue that the adverse effects on local people will outweigh the benefits. Both are convinced they are in the right: the authorities, perhaps, because they see the benefits and disadvantages on a national or even international scale, and the interest groups because they are looking at the potentially adverse effects at the local level. It is clear, however, that the two scales need to be seen in relation to one another. For example, what are 300,000 people to be resettled in the context of a country with a population of 300 million? For the interest groups, 300,000 people is too many (it is a very large number); but for the government they represent only 0.1 per cent of the population (it is a low percentage). In this discussion, the scientific community should develop objective arguments and inform the public. This way, democracy can work and the interests of the majority are clearly defined and the opposition of a minority understood (see Chapters 2 and 10).

In some cases, the reasons used to justify an infrastructure project have nothing to do with water. The real reason, which may never be officially announced, may be internal politics (such as ethnic control). For example, a government may launch a land reclamation project in a desert area to discourage migration to the capital, even though in terms of the use of water resources the project is not really sustainable.

By raising awareness, it may be possible to encourage existing investors in developing countries (local governments; the private sector, both domestic and international; and international donors) to increase their contributions to fill the financial gap. In reality, however, water awareness (for instance, due to protests) are causing many organizations to rethink their policies and re-evaluate the risks involved in financing major infrastructure works. Because of their caution, the decision-making processes related to large water infrastructure projects take more time, and the availability of money to finance them decreases. It seems that many foreign governments and donors now prefer to finance institutional capacity building in the water sector rather than to finance the water infrastructure itself, in line with the principle of country ownership. Most donors and foreign governments indicate clearly that the recipient countries have to decide for themselves what they want to build, how and where. For this reason, the trend is to provide assistance for capacity building, leaving it to the national government to finance infrastructure building from its own budget.

It seems that as soon as the national government takes full political responsibility for building the water infrastructure in their own country, donors no longer need to be afraid to give money. But, at the same time, handing over responsibility means that these donors will have to give up some of their influence on the internal political processes in these countries. For example, in line with the principle of country ownership, The Netherlands government wants the beneficiary countries themselves to decide in which sectors the Dutch aid should be spent. The European Commission's policy is moving in the same direction, with the slogan 'all but arms' (Richelle, 2001). In contrast, the World Bank Group offers loans and grants for funding water projects, subject to certain conditions. The International Bank for Reconstruction and Development (IBRD) provides loans to public authorities, and the International Finance Corporation (IFC) invests exclusively in the private sector. In the water supply and sanitation sector, some of the IBRD's loans (to Ghana, for example) are conditional on privatization. In some countries, International Monetary Fund (IMF) loan agreements include conditions such as water privatization or full-price recovery (Grusky, 2000).

Reassuringly, water and sanitation appear to be key outcomes of the World Summit on Sustainable Development (WSSD) held in Johannesburg in September 2002:

- Halve, by the year 2015, the proportion of people without access to safe drinking water (reaffirmation of Millennium Development Goal).
- Halve, by the year 2015, the proportion of people who do not have access to basic sanitation.

This should give governments that are board members of these international organizations the willingness and the power to use their position and request more investments in the water sector.

For years, the United Nations target for aid from rich countries to poor has stood at 0.7 per cent of their gross domestic product (GDP). Today it stands at 0.22 per cent. It is time for governments to reach the 0.7 per cent target and eventually increase it to 0.8 per cent or more.

For these reasons, the amount of money available from lenders and others already active in the water sector is not enough to fill the gap in the short term, although that does not mean that it is not possible to do anything in the long term. In the first challenge, we identified the different investors in the water sector. In reality, who actually pays for these investments? It is not the investors themselves but, ultimately, us, of course, as we are water users and/or taxpayers! If and when these water users and taxpayers organize themselves, they could become a powerful force and may influence decision-makers in the future. In the short term, however, because such a huge amount of money is required to finance water infrastructure, new sources of funding need to be found, and/or the available money needs to be used more effectively.

Develop new ways to finance water infrastructure

General

Taxes and charges are introduced at the national or the regional level. This is already the case in developed countries, where many water-related services and polluting activities are taxed. Developing countries should improve the efficiency of the collection and should use a greater proportion of their tax revenues to finance their own water infrastructure, since access to water underlies many of the goals that need to be addressed to combat poverty.

In *A Better World for All*, the first report ever issued jointly by the IMF, the Organisation for Economic Co-operation and Development (OECD), the United Nations (UN) and the World Bank, the report begins: 'Poverty in all its forms is the greatest challenge to the international community... Setting goals to reduce poverty is an essential part of the way forward' (IMF et al, 2000). The report sets seven goals to be achieved by 2015:

1 Halve the proportion of people living in extreme poverty.
2 Enrol all children in primary school.
3 Empower women and eliminate gender disparities in education.
4 Reduce infant and child mortality rates by two-thirds.
5 Reduce maternal mortality rates by three-quarters.
6 Provide access to reproductive health services for all who need them.
7 Implement national strategies for sustainable development.

Although each of these seven goals addresses a different aspect of poverty, they are all mutually reinforcing. The report also reflects the general lack of awareness of the importance of water in combating poverty. Water is referred to only seven times: twice in general terms, twice in relation to the goal of reducing infant and child mortality rates, and three times in relation to the environment goal (Figuères, 2001).

The report does not mention (as it is too obvious) the common feature underlying the various goals – they are all directly or indirectly dependent on water. For this reason, developing countries should collect taxes and give priority on the long term – that is to say, to the need to finance the water infrastructure.

Tax on international monetary transactions

Another way of increasing the amount of money available to finance water infrastructure is to impose national or international taxes that should be used to finance water infrastructure. It is estimated that 80 per cent of all international monetary transactions (totalling an average of US$1500 billion per day) involve 'round trips' of five days or less. Most of these transactions are purely speculative in nature; in other words, they have no productive purpose other than the pursuit of financial gain. The economist James Tobin was the first to suggest that a tax on these international monetary transactions would generate a significant amount of revenue. Exactly how much is difficult to assess, since the number of transactions liable to such a tax would naturally decline in proportion to the severity of the tax (Chauvin et al, 2001).

There are several ways of estimating the prospective revenue from such a tax. One way is as follows. Assuming that some US$1500 billion change hands every day on the international money market, and that the market operates 240 days a year, a minimum tax of 0.05 per cent might be expected to yield between US$113 billion and US$122 billion each year (Chauvin et al, 2001). This amount is comparable to the financial gap in the water sector.

Implementing this tax would certainly be a major political challenge, however. For many years, several organizations have promoted such a tax, but so far without success. Many governments acknowledge that the idea is interesting, but consider it unacceptable and unworkable. In reality, it is just a question of political will and courage. It would be sufficient for the few countries that host these exchange markets (which are highly centralized) to adopt the tax and impose a penalty rate on transactions originating from a non-tax zone. The computerization of transactions means that collecting the tax would be a simple matter: taxing every operation on settlement would suffice to raise an income for the central banks. This tax would have a number of benefits. First, it would allow governments and public institutions to regain some control over the international money market, and would signify a return to international financial cooperation. Second, the tax revenues could be used specifically for development and poverty reduction, such as by improving access to water (Chauvin et al, 2001).

Debt-relief arrangements

Last but not least, another opportunity to raise funds for water infrastructure in developing countries is to use the funds made available under debt-relief arrangements. The Highly Indebted Poor Countries (HIPC) Initiative was launched in 1996 as the first comprehensive effort to eliminate the unsustainable burden of debt for the world's poorest, most heavily indebted countries. Debt-relief packages are now in place for 23 countries, most of which are in sub-Saharan Africa. Debt service payments are cut almost in half, creating room for additional public expenditures on poverty reduction. Debt service as a percentage of government revenue is reduced from 23 per cent to an average of less than 10 per cent over the decade of 2000 to 2010. The resources made available by debt relief under the HIPC Initiative are to be allocated to key anti-poverty programmes, as outlined in the country's 'Poverty Reduction Strategy Paper' (PRSP), in particular to water-related infrastructure.

In Mozambique, for example, as a result of HIPC assistance and bilateral debt relief already committed, the total external debt has been reduced by some 73 per cent, and possible additional bilateral relief could raise this figure. Debt-service relief under the HIPC Initiative from Mozambique's creditors will amount to approximately US$600 million. Including assistance provided under the earlier HIPC Initiative, this brings the total estimated debt service relief to about US$4.3 billion. Bolivia, Mozambique and Uganda are the first three countries to reach this point (World Bank, 2001). Mozambique's eligibility for debt relief under the HIPC Initiative underscores the international community's recognition of its continued progress in implementing sound macro-economic and structural policies, and of the overall quality of its PRSP.

Building water infrastructure is certainly needed to reduce poverty and could be included as such in the HIPC agreement to make funds available. This should be done in all countries preparing a poverty reduction strategy. In some countries, however, it is questionable whether any of the resources made available by debt relief under the HIPC Initiative is available for allocation to the water sector.

Create an enabling environment to invest at the local level

Securing property laws

The local private water sector could play a role at both the national and the local level. In many developing countries, it is common for people to have no formal title to prove their ownership of the assets they undoubtedly possess. For this reason, they cannot use those assets as collateral to raise loans. This restricts the growth of the private sector and favours the informal economy. Economists and financial experts tend to think of the informal economy as a marginal phenomenon; but in many countries it is actually larger than the formal economy. It is regarded as marginal only because it is the sum of innumerable small initiatives. In such situations, the involvement of the local private sector, particularly in water, is limited to small-scale activities. Money can only be raised from the local private sector on a larger scale if all citizens have secure property rights, allowing them to use their assets as collateral. This means secure property laws (see Chapter 8).

Valuing water

Another issue related to the prospect of raising funds at the local level is water pricing. Giving water a value and asking a price for it is a way of making money available to help finance water services. At present, a lot of research is done in this way. For example, a joint United Nations Educational, Scientific and Cultural Organization–IHE Water Education Institute (UNESCO-IHE) research project is currently ongoing to develop a methodology for water valuation that addresses the socio-economic, cultural and environmental values of different types of water stocks and flows (IHE, 2000). The question of water pricing is a major issue and cannot be considered in detail in this chapter; but some general comments are presented below.

Depending on the objectives, there are certain principles that can be adopted in designing a national water pricing policy. These include marginal-cost pricing, ability-to-pay principle, net-benefit principle and full-cost pricing. These broad principles are put into practice through a variety of pricing/charging methods (such as volumetric pricing, two-part tariffs, crop/area/time-based pricing and water wholesaling) that vary from country to country.

Although the effects of water pricing on efficiency and equity are questionable, pricing is regarded as a potentially powerful means of generating revenues. Some argue that it could make a substantial contribution to increasing the efficiency of water use, the equity of water-sharing arrangements and the sustainability of water resources. In many countries, however, water-pricing policies have been ineffective and have failed to achieve even their financial objective, often because of a lack of political will and the unwillingness on the part of users to pay for water (see Chapter 7).

In various parts of the world, initiatives are being launched that are intended to give a realistic value to water. In South Africa, for example, the 1999 National Water Act introduced a new national pricing system for raw water use. The act has four objectives, all of equal national importance: social equity, ecological sustainability, financial sustainability and economic efficiency. This act is a demonstration of political will, even if it has been very difficult to implement. In Europe, in July 2000, the European Commission adopted a communication on pricing policies to enhance the sustainability of water resources. In spring 2001, the Canadian federal government launched a study to establish the value of national water reserves.

Although water pricing can affect the amount of money available from the private sector, the revenue will not, in itself, provide all of the funding required for financing the necessary infrastructure. However, it will surely give an incentive to investors, and will improve water demand management by reducing water use.

Supporting micro-finance

The time has come to consider local water needs and to try to find local solutions, taking into account the broader context. This approach has a number of benefits. First, it will enhance the sense of local ownership that is essential to increase the efficiency of water projects. Second, projects are small in scale, making it easier to find local funds to finance them. Third, small- and medium-sized enterprises (SMEs) are often the driving force behind economic development in developing countries. Micro-finance is not simply banking; it is a development tool. It has been estimated that there are 500 million economically active poor people running their own micro-enterprises and small businesses. Most of them do not have access to adequate financial services. As indicated earlier, the development of micro-finance schemes that would play a major role in poverty alleviation could also become a major trend in the water sector. Local small-scale financing can be used to support the development of water initiatives at the grassroots level. For example, the World Bank has proposed bringing together in a single handbook all of the guiding principles and tools that will promote sustainable micro-finance and create viable institutions. In Africa, 400 organizations are proposing micro-finance products and in the Côte d'Ivoire only about 2 million Euros are borrowed through 25 organizations.

The support given by international donors to micro-finance initiatives has already reached its maximum. The public perception is that micro-finance programmes have been the success story of development finance. Although this may not be the whole truth, as a critical analysis has revealed (Schmidt and Zeitinger, 1997), it is nonetheless legitimate to say that some successful micro-finance institutions have emerged over the last decade. They may be few in numbers, but their achievements have been spectacular. These success stories have to be replicated and, for this reason, it is obvious that funds to finance small-scale water projects must be increased in the coming years to continue this positive development.

Develop country water partnerships to enhance the environmental and social sustainability of water infrastructure projects

The development of water resources to provide safe water supplies and sanitation and to ensure food security will be an enormous task, especially in countries with water shortages and stagnating economies. For this, long-term cooperation between the different stakeholders is vital to ensure that environmental issues are addressed and to move towards sustainability. Each stakeholder has a distinct role to play; but it is equally important that they coordinate their efforts, ensuring that they are complementary and mutually reinforcing, and that they share responsibility and work together. Cooperation is vital if we are to achieve results as efficiently, effectively and quickly as possible. By acting together, we can achieve our goals quicker and better.

It is now accepted that people at the grassroots level have the best understanding of their local situation and are in the best position to identify the most appropriate solutions to their problems. Accordingly, most donor or government policies are based on the idea that development actions must be demand driven. But driven by whose demand? Not everyone has the same goal or the same needs, which is why partnerships are essential as a framework for dialogue through which all stakeholders can reach agreement that is acceptable to all members. Water partnerships already exist, even though they have different names. For example, the stakeholder water committees in some African villages can be regarded as local water partnerships. Through their representatives on these committees, local people are able to articulate what they want and how they want it done.

It may be reasonable to assume that actions identified, planned and carried out at the local level will have a better chance of ensuring the efficiency of water development. But the most appropriate solution at the local level may have negative effects on a larger scale. Local solutions have to be seen in a broader context – for example, a water development for one village has to take into account other demands and resources throughout the entire river basin, both upstream and downstream. Actions identified by a local partnership must fit within the regional, national or even international framework. This means that country and international partnerships also have an important role to play in disseminating information, best practices and available knowledge and expertise in such a way that local partnerships can have access to, and benefit from, experiences gained in other regions or countries. By learning from best practices elsewhere, mistakes can be avoided and projects can be more effective. For this purpose the Global Water Partnership has developed a toolbox on integrated water management (GWP, 2001).

Long-term cooperation between the different stakeholders is essential; yet, experience has shown that cooperation cannot be forced. Cooperation starts only when people come together to address a clearly defined common need or a shared goal. The various stakeholders need to engage in dialogue in order to develop a trusting relationship. They need to develop an independent platform where they can meet and exchange views in order to improve communication. Based on such a trusty relationship, the stakeholders can discuss their ideas and translate them into projects that will benefit them. In each country concerned, the centralization of information would help to avoid inefficiency or duplication of efforts.

In other words, developing country partnerships (being essentially demand driven) can identify and articulate the needs and demands of the stakeholders, which can be made known to the international community. Developed country and/or international water partnerships (being essentially supply driven) can play a vital role in the transfer of knowledge, making resources available to other partnerships. The bottom-up approach of 'demand-driven' water partnerships and the top-down approach of 'supply-driven' national and/or international water partnerships are both essential to water development.

Furthermore, the creation of a global network of national and/or regional water partnerships could improve the transfer of knowledge to a specific country by allowing the relevant information to be selected for the local situation.

Experience has shown that partnerships involving disadvantaged and marginalized sections of society can play a vital role in advancing their point of view and ensuring that their fundamental rights are respected. As democratic organizations, local water partnerships can serve to empower people living in poverty by providing opportunities and access to the political arena.

The purpose of developing country water partnerships is to improve communication between the different stakeholders and to centralize national information about water activities, with the aim of avoiding inefficiency and duplication of efforts. True partnership relies on ownership, real communication, morality, transparency, fairness, democracy and trust.

As the different stakeholders are represented in the national partnership, they can also guarantee that projects meet the required criteria (especially with regard to social and environmental aspects). The partnership could award a kind of 'certificate of sustainability' for water infrastructure projects, facilitating their financing. Even more important, such partnerships could recommend financial analyses to identify the most appropriate financing construction for a project. To ensure that criteria are observed in the same way worldwide, national water partnerships would gain from the support of an organization such as the Global Water Partnership (GWP), an international network of organizations and institutions. The members of the GWP are equal partners, interested in water resources development and management, and are committed to the Dublin Principles.[1] As a reinforced network, the GWP fosters interactions among its members by promoting cross-sectorial and multi-stakeholder dialogues at the global, regional and national levels. The GWP also aims to improve communications within the water sector and to promote high-quality services. Its four major objectives are to establish country and regional partnerships and mobilize political will; to build strategic alliances for action; to promote good practices in international water resources management; and to develop and implement regional actions.

The country water partnerships are the best platform from which to make the process of matching national demand and external resources simpler, faster and more efficient.

Concentrate on capacity building and education

Good water governance has everything to do with skilled and capable water managers. Every country, in the North and South, has capacity, though not always in the amount or form that it would like. And every country, in the North and South, needs more capacity (Herfkens, 2001).

Even more important than the infrastructure projects in the water sector are the capacities of its individuals, organizations and others institutions.

Capacity building is the process of providing individuals, organizations and the other relevant institutions with the capacities that allow them to perform in such a way that the water sector, as a whole, can perform optimally, now as well as in the future. Individuals are the often underused resources who are the key to sustainability (Alaerts et al, 1999; see Chapter 3 in this volume).

Identifying and formulating needs and supply is part of integrated water management (IWM). For example, today the common understanding continues to be that IWM activities require multidisciplinary teams of technical specialists, ecologists, economists, sociologists, communicators, and managers. This is both true and false. We do need to take all of those aspects into account and involve the experts; but simply rounding up a few good experts does not guarantee us a winning team. As mentioned above, we need water professionals to identify and formulate needs in an integrated manner. These professionals are able to understand the local needs, to put them in the local, regional, national and even international perspective, to define the most suitable solution and translate and make it attractive for financial organizations. Furthermore, these water professionals have a fundamental role to fulfil in creating synergy by integrating all of these fields and in managing the process involving the actors. I call these water professionals 'integrating water managers' (Figuères, 2002). There are too few of them, but they will be better able to cope with the water challenges of today and tomorrow. Education and training still has a major role to play in developing the water sector.

This emerged as a priority from the Second World Water Forum; certainly, this means capable and skilled water professionals. Water education and training at all levels are needed, from school children to adults, and from generalist to highly specialized technicians/engineers. Two examples of activities supported by the United Nations Human Settlements Programme (UN-HABITAT) are, firstly, the water education projects for primary and secondary schools, and mainstreaming water awareness in the national education programme (successful examples occur in Ghana, the Ivory Coast, Zambia and Kenya). The message is obvious: teach children to manage water wisely and they will become the wise water users/managers of the future. The Water for African Cities Programme is another good example of improving the available capacity. During the programme, the staff of seven African cities (about 200 individuals, ranging from middle-level management to executives and politicians) are trained in the field of water demand management, prevention and pollution control, and public awareness activities. They are coached during the preparation/formulation/realization of personal action plans. These plans aim to increase the water supply and sanitation situation in the different cities by wisely using the available means. Furthermore, the capacity-building part of the programme aims to increase the national training capacities (UNCHS, 2001; UNESCO-IHE, 2002). Both cases illustrate the importance of education and training for citizens and professionals.

Build a trusting relationship between the financial world and the water sector and develop adapted financial products

Just as donors or lenders can identify projects that meet the set quality criteria, so more simple procedures can be introduced for allocating funds to projects. But changing the financial world's perception of risk related to water infrastructure could be a very long process if we wait until enough water projects are proven less risky than supposed. Improving communication between the financial world and the water sector is an important way of enhancing mutual understanding. Financial specialists require detailed information about the risks in the water sector, and water specialists need to understand what the 'bankers' mean by risks. Once the risks are better known, it is possible that the cost of borrowing money could be reduced. Skilled and capable water professionals and organizations will contribute to increasing investor confidence in the water sector.

During the 11th Water Symposium, held in Stockholm, Sweden, in 2001, the Global Water Partnership and the World Water Council announced a common initiative, and the creation of a high-level panel of financial experts. Acting as chairperson is Michel Camdessus, former director of the IMF. The panel was set up to investigate ways of increasing the water market and of preparing a report for the Third World Water Forum in 2003. This is an interesting first step.

A second step could be the creation of a Global Water Bank, as suggested in a recent report by Leclerc and Raes (2001), with the aim of increasing the financial world's understanding of the challenges faced by the water sector. The Global Water Bank would be composed of institutions that finance water activities, ranging from donor agencies and government representatives, to multinationals (banks and insurance companies), foreign private investors and contributing agencies from developing countries. For the private sector, such a bank should provide guarantees needed to operate in countries with high political or economic risks. In any case, the creation of national water facilities will be a valuable first step in the short term, as the creation of a global bank should probably take several years.

In some countries (such as The Netherlands and The Philippines) such national banks already exist (Blokland et al, 1999). For example, the Dutch Bank for the water boards, fully owned by the public sector, was created as a response to the severe floods in 1953. This bank provides long-term funding to provinces, municipalities, water boards and water supply companies. The provision of long-term finance to small water boards (which were not considered creditworthy at the time) is a key business of the bank (van Dijk and Schwartz, 2002).

In developing countries, the way is now open to create within ministries of finance a department responsible for funds that are earmarked for water projects (following the initiative in Mozambique). These departments would coordinate the financing of water projects. The following step should be that projects must be 'cleared' by an external independent organization, such as the national water partnership (giving a guarantee that the projects are demand driven with a multi-stakeholder approach). Within these departments, national experts specializing in water activities would be able to assess the risks more accurately. The professionalism of risk experts who work for lending institutions in water activities would help to reduce the financial risks and make projects more attractive to lenders.

CONCLUSIONS

This chapter has analysed the present situation and given some explanations of why it is so difficult to meet the financial challenge in the water sector. The purpose of this chapter has not been to make a catalogue of all areas where the water and finance sectors interact, but to highlight four of the major challenges.

The first major challenge is to make money available for the water sector. There is enough money in the global economy to finance development and reduce poverty. But the question is how to bridge the annual shortfall in investment – about US$100 billion per year – in the water sector.

The second major challenge is to formulate the need for water infrastructure and to identify adequate answer to it. This means:

- Give water the highest priority in development.
- Give national governments the financial resources for identification and formulation.
- Reduce the shortages of capable and skilled national staff to identify and formulate good projects (through institutional capacity building and education and training of water professionals).
- Give local stakeholders a say in the identification and choice of water activities.
- Make use of relevant international expertise.
- Simplify the donor procedures.

The third major challenge is to match water infrastructure demand and financial resources in the most efficient way. Assuming that money is available (the first challenge) and that a suitable water infrastructure project/programme has been formulated (second challenge), the next challenge is to obtain adequate financing to make the project a reality. This means identifying and managing risks in a proper way. This entails making a linkage between the global level, where funds are mostly available, and the local level, where funds are needed.

The fourth major challenge is to implement the planned water infrastructure project and to manage it wisely. Even if a good financial deal has been struck, and money is available, the project still has to be implemented and the infrastructure must be maintained over many years.

To meet these challenges, this chapter has proposed several actions that could be taken to channel money into the water sector in the most effective way:

- Encourage traditional lenders and existing actors in the water sector to finance water infrastructure projects.
- Increase the part of available equity that is dedicated to finance water infrastructure at the international or national level.
- Increase the availability of money to finance water projects at the local level.
- Develop the capacity of national staff to tackle the challenges at the national and local level.
- Develop country water partnerships to enhance the environmental and social sustainability of water infrastructure projects.
- Develop a trusting relationship between the financial world and the water sector.

These actions should be seen as a set of independent measures that have to be developed to improve the availability of money in the water sector. Implementing the different actions is possible in every country; but the effects will be more important if several countries, organizations and/or institutions work together. It is obvious that implementing these measures simultaneously would create a valuable synergy. In particular, the existence of regional partnerships will favour a better understanding of transboundary issues (see Chapters 9 and 10) and the development of regional cooperation (see Chapters 3 and 10).

What is needed, first and foremost, is to find the US$100 billion before it is too late for millions of people in the developing world. The water sector urgently requires money for infrastructure, and the people without access to water cannot wait until the foreign investors are prepared to accept the risk of investment. To improve the relationship between the financial world and the water sector, it is essential that today's world leaders reach an agreement on these water financial issues and decide to act in the short term. The Third World Water Forum in 2003 in Japan offers a unique opportunity to go from consensus (money is highly needed) to action (money is made available). In this context, the work of the new panel of financial experts could be effective in helping high executives from governments (ministers) and private organizations (chief executive officers) to find practical solutions that involve the global and the local level. We need to pump money into the water sector quickly, before it is too late for millions of men, women and children.

NOTES

1 The 1992 International Conference on Water and Environment in Dublin affirmed a set of principles for good water resources management, often referred to as the Dublin Principles. They were significant factors in Chapter 18 of the *Agenda 21*

recommendations adopted by the United Nations Conference on Environment and Development (UNCED) in Rio de Janeiro the same year.

REFERENCES

Alaerts G J, Hartvelt, F J A and Patorni, F M (eds) (1999) *Water Sector Capacity Building: Concepts and Instruments*, Proceedings of the Second UNDP Symposium on Water Sector Capacity Building, Delft, Balkema, Rotterdam/Brookfield

Allan, T (2003) *Millennial Water Management Paradigms: Making Integrated Water Resources Management (IWRM) Work*, in press

Blokland, M, Okke, B and Schwartz, K (eds) (1999) *Private Business, Public Owners: Government Shareholding in Water Enterprises*, Min VROM, The Netherlands, 90-802070-5-5

Blom, G (2000) 'Changing roles in private public partnerships', *Land and Water International*, vol 98, NEDECO, The Hague, pp4–6

Chauvin, S et al (2001) *Tobin Tax, Speculation and Poverty*, Background paper, ATTAC, Paris

Cosgrove, J W and Rijsberman, F R (2000) *World Water Vision: Making Water Everybody's Business*, Earthscan, London

Economist (The) (2000) *The Economist Pocket Book, Figures 2001*, The Economist Group, London

Figuères, C (2002) 'In search of integrating water managers', *New World Water*, March, pp65–68

Figuères, C (2001) 'True water partnership: A key to poverty alleviation and water development', Paper prepared for the Hamedabad Conference on Poverty Alleviation and Water Development, January

Figuères, C (2000) 'Are you ready to make the water switch?', *Land and Water International*, vol 97, NEDECO, The Hague, pp5–7

Finnerty, J D (1996) *Project Financing: Asset-Based Financial Engineering*, John Wiley and Sons, New York

Global Water Partnership (GWP) (2001) 'Toolbox water resources management: Sharing knowledge for equitable and sustainable water resources management', GWP, Stockholm

Global Water Partnership (GWP) (2000) *Towards Water Security: A Framework for Action*, No 91-630-9202-6, GWP, Stockholm,

Global Water Report (2001) 'Saur's miscalculation on the Dolphin Coast. Issue 123', *Financial Times*, 11 June 2001, pp4–5

Grusky, S (2000) 'The poverty reduction strategy papers: An initial NGP Assessment', Issue 3, April, Bread for the World Institute, Washington, DC

Haarmeyer, D and Mody, A (2000) *Tapping the Private Sector: Approaches to Managing Risk in Water and Sanitation*, RMC Discussion Paper Series 122, World Bank, Washington, DC

Hall, D (2001) 'Water in public hands', Paper commissioned by Public Services International (PSIRU), University of Greenwich, Greenwich

Herfkens, E (2001) 'The capacity issue in Africa: Building on your own strengths', Speech presented at the African Capacity Building Forum, Bamako, Mali, 22 October 2001, in *Land and Water International*, vol 101, NEDECO, The Hague

IHE (2000) 'Value of water: An interdisciplinary research program', IHE, Delft, The Netherlands

IMF et al (2000) *A Better World for All,* Joint report by the International Monetary Fund, the OECD, the UN and the World Bank

Kaul, I, Grunberg, I and Stern, M A (1999) *Global Public Goods: International Cooperation in the 21st Century,* Oxford University Press, New York

Leclerc, G and Raes, T (2001) *Water: A World Financial Issue,* Sustainable Development Series, PricewaterhouseCoopers, Paris

Lumby, S and Jones, C (1999) *Investment Appraisal and Financial Decisions,* Thomson International Business Press, London

Maksimovic, C and Tejada-Guibert, J A (eds) (2001) *Frontiers in Urban Water Management: Deadlock or Hope,* UNESCO, Paris

Miller, R and Lessard, D R (2001) *The Strategic Management of Large Engineering Projects: Shaping Institutions, Risks and Governance,* MIT Press, London

Ministry of Foreign Affairs, Sweden (2001) *Transboundary Water Management as an International Public Good,* Fritzes Kundservice, Stockholm

NEDECO (2001) 'Shinyanga water supply scheme', Unpublished internal report, NEDECO, The Hague

Perrot, J Y and Chatelus, G (eds) (2000) *Financing of Major Infrastructure and Public Service Projects: Public–Private Partnerships. Lessons from the French Experience throughout the World,* Presses de l'Ecole Nationale des Ponts et Chaussees, Paris

Richelle K (2001) 'Complementary assistance: The new idea', *Land and Water International,* vol 100, pp11–13

Schmidt, R H and Zeitinger, C-P (1997) 'Critical issues in microbusiness finance and the role of donors', Unpublished mimeo, Frankfurt, www.gdrc.org/icm/mfi-donor.pdf

SME Financing (2000) *Lessons from Micro-Finance: SME Issues,* vol 1, no 1, World Bank, Washington, DC

UNCHS (Habitat) (2001) *Water for African Cities (WAC): Building Capacity to Improve Water Management in African Cities,* UNCHS (Habitat) in collaboration with UNDP, Nairobi

UNESCO-IHE (2002) 'Training and capacity building component of the WAC-Program: Methodology', Unpublished internal document, UNESCO-IHE Partnership, Delft

van Dijk, M P and Schwarz (2002) 'Financing the water sector in The Netherlands: A first analysis', Invited paper by The Netherlands Water Partnership (NWP) to prepare the Financing Water Infrastructure Panel held in The Hague, 8 October

Van de Vijver, J J (2001) *Risks Allocation in BOT Projects,* Lecture for the FME-CWM Workshop BOO/BOT Projects, FME-CWM Zoetermeer

Vivendi Water (2001) *Environmental Report: For a Responsible, Measurable and Sustainable Commitment Towards the Environment,* Vivendi Water, Paris

World Bank (2001) *Global Development Finance: Building Coalitions for Effective Development Finance,* World Bank, Washington, DC

World Water Council (2000) *Making Water Everybody's Business,* Report from the Second World Water Forum, The Hague, March, World Water Council, Marseilles

Chapter 12

Conclusion: The way forward

Caroline M Figuères, Johan Rockström and
Cecilia Tortajada

ENTRY POINT TO SUSTAINABLE WATER MANAGEMENT

When the environmental state of our 'Blue Planet' is painted, it almost exclusively comes out dark and gloomy. What can be expected in a situation where 1 billion people are without proper drinking water and 3 billion people lack adequate sanitation? On top of this we are faced with large-scale impacts of human mismanagement, resulting in severe water-quality deterioration, groundwater decline, human-induced drying-up of rivers, and loss of immense ecological values from drained wetlands and regulated waterways. As if this was not enough, there will be 3 billion more mouths to feed in 2050, and an incredible 800 million currently undernourished people to raise from a life of nutritional misery to a minimum quality of life. Producing food is by far the world's largest direct water-consuming activity, where each human meal corresponds to between 1000 and 2000 litres of water just to sustain the plant growth forming the base for all human terrestrial caloric intakes. This enormous food-induced human pressure on water resources will occur, moreover, in developing, predominantly tropical, countries – 95 per cent of the population growth occurs here.

This is our gloomy reality. In an effort to find a sustainable water future, the tendency is, unfortunately, to start from this gloomy picture and take one of two dead-end paths to the future. The first one simply is dropping water out of the picture altogether. This was done in the United Nations Conference on Environment and Development (UNCED or Earth Summit) process in Rio de Janeiro in 1992, where water was discussed as a problem, but was never properly part of the solution (except water quality). This strategy may derive from a kind of human paralysis. The problem is so daunting that, relating to a common resource with little or no ownership, the steam of action evaporates at the same moment that solutions are sought. The second strategy is to linearly project business-as-usual scenarios into the future. This was largely done in the efforts during the Second World Water Forum in The Hague in 2000.

Conventional paradigms and water management strategies are projected to solve tomorrow's problems. This leads to arithmetic exercises that project increases in the numbers of dams, irrigation schemes and urban water supplies. This is just more of the same, combined with honest efforts to increase efficiency and reduce environmental side effects. All of these efforts are embedded in an integrated water resource management (IWRM) setting, and based on a sustainable development path. However, very little is said about how the integration will be carried out and what is actually meant by 'sustainable'. Fundamentally, integration within the business-as-usual scenarios are not truly integrated, as the conventional narrowness leads to the omission of many opportunities derived from new approaches to water resource management.

The reader has been led through diverse subjects in this book – from the existing paradigms to practical case studies – all having the underlying thread of examining the current situation and providing recommendations, and/or suggesting actions for the future. The different chapters confirm that the water crisis is primarily a water management crisis. However, it also shows that in certain arid environments with dense human populations, the challenges of livelihood security are strongly linked to coping with physical water scarcity.

CHANGE OF WATER PARADIGM IS REQUIRED

In this book we have argued that there is a need for a change of water paradigm, one that is not only truly integrated, but also brings with it the opportunities of innovations and new approaches to water resources management. The book has given a positive outlook on the possibilities at hand to embark on a sustainable path to the future. However, it has also shown that the challenges are huge, and, perhaps more importantly, that there is an urgent need for all professionals working with water-related management to realize their personal responsibilities in creating an accountable and conscious stewardship of water for present and future generations.

This said, it is also important to acknowledge that the authors in this book only tackle a limited set of water challenges for the future, and only cover a few possible avenues for solving them. The purpose has not been to make a catalogue of all areas where water, human and ecosystem interactions have resulted in environmental problems. Instead, it has been to highlight some of the major challenges and to show that there is reason to be optimistic.

An overarching question in the book is whether the challenges concerning water management give rise to a deadlock or to the human paralysis discussed above, or whether there are prospects of solving the water problems facing humankind now and in the future. The collective answer of the authors to this question has been unequivocal: Yes, the prospects are good.

The gloomy arithmetic of water is only one side of the coin. On the other we find ample evidence of large untapped water resources, good opportunities to improve water productivity and thereby reduce the risk of depleting water for ecosystems, and, perhaps most important, a very significant human knowledge base of how we could do things better. The picture that evolves is very different from the conventional gloom. For example, there is very little evidence to suggest that humankind is facing a physical scarcity of water, while there is ample evidence to suggest that where humans suffer from scarcity, it is caused by mismanagement. The light at the end of the tunnel must be found in fundamental human spheres concerning perceptions, awareness and feelings of accountability to future generation, rather than sought in technical and economic solutions and mitigation efforts.

One of the central concepts encountered time and again in the book is that new approaches, even new mental perceptions and concepts, are required to successfully face the current water challenge. A sense of urgency comes out clearly in the different chapters. We simply have to act now in order to address the alarming water resource challenges, especially in developing countries, and the water environment challenges facing both developing and developed countries.

SHARING COMMON WATER RESOURCES: PARADIGM SHIFTS IN THE LIGHT OF GLOBALIZATION

In Chapter 4, Faruqui shows that we are at a critical threshold in the juncture of water management and development. Increasing population, pollution and urbanization all threaten the per-capita availability and the quality of freshwater. Such a juncture requires new ways of thinking about and managing water resources. Economic globalization offers some opportunities for making the necessary changes, but also poses risks.

Just as the flow of water ignores political boundaries, its management strains the capabilities of institutional boundaries. Water managers tend to advocate the importance of managing water at catchment or river-basin scales, as it follows the natural boundaries of flowing water. Institutions have rarely followed these natural boundaries, instead acting according to administrative and political boundaries at the national and sub-national scale. As shown by Wolf in Chapter 9, water resource management necessarily crosses borders, changing the nature of the water source as well as the potential conflicts related to the sharing of a resource that does not respect national frontiers.

To complicate things, many of these sources – such as deep fossil aquifers, wastewater reclamation, and inter-basin transfers – are not restricted by the confines of watershed boundaries, our fundamental unit of analysis. Both the worlds of water and of conflict are undergoing slow and steady changes which may obviate much of the thinking. Conflict, too, is becoming less traditional, increasingly driven by internal or local pressures, or by more subtle issues of poverty and stability. The combination of changes, both in water resources and conflict, suggest that tomorrow's water disputes may look very different from today's.

The prospects of peaceful and wise sharing of common water resources are strongly influenced by the globalization of societies. In Chapter 3, Al-Jayyousi suggests that the emergence of a globalized economy can contribute to a rethinking of the conventional paradigms in water management. The crucial challenge for water professionals in the future is how to induce a paradigm shift in the conventional modes of water-sector planning to new modes of thinking that take into account the global and regional perspective as units of analysis, rather than the nation state. In another context, Ahmad, in Chapter 10, believes that the true spirit of regional cooperation lies in moving away from bilateralism towards multilateralism. The congeniality in the political atmosphere may lead to a visionary approach among the politicians of the regional countries to create an enabling environment of multilateralism. The message is straightforward. Water managers of the future: span your thinking across borders!

THE FUTURE WATER MANAGER

As stated in Chapter 1, past water management experiences have conclusively demonstrated that the future solutions of current and emerging water challenges must span regions, disciplines and stakeholders, and should be viewed within an inter-generational framework.

But what is wrong with water management? Not the water, of course, but the manager! Good water management will only become a reality once we recognize that water managers have complex duties. A fundamental reason for this is the complexity of water flowing through the landscape, and the multiple role of water in sustaining both the direct well-being of humans and the generation of ecosystem goods and services. It is becoming clearer that water is not only important to engineering and natural sciences, but to the social and economic sciences, law, policies and institutions, as well. Water is not only about supply management. It is also about human decisions about water demand. Water is not only shared between people of different regions and nations. It is shared between humans and nature. Water not only flows in liquid form. It changes state in the course of the water cycle between rain, soil moisture, liquid and vapour. This highlights the need for new water managers who cover a wider spectrum of disciplines and can communicate across vertical disciplinary structures.

In Chapter 11, Figuères shows that, even when dealing with the financing of water infrastructure, water managers have a huge role to play. They must participate in water partnerships to enhance the environmental and social sustainability of water infrastructure projects, and must encourage a trusting relationship between the financial world and the water sector.

SUSTAINABLE DEVELOPMENT: FROM RHETORIC TO ACTION

As shown by Tortajada in Chapter 2, sustainable development has become a powerful and all-embracing international slogan over the past 15 years. Every government is for it, as are all the major international organizations and all the environmental non-governmental organizations (NGOs). This is despite the fact that there is no consensus about what sustainable development means, whether it works and, if it does work, under what conditions and with what impacts on human lives. Overall, there is a disparity between the desired meaning of sustainable development and the reality of it in terms of translating desire to action and linking this action with appropriate development indicators.

Poor management of water resources will continue to have serious social, economic and environmental implications at the local and national levels over the short and long term. Often, such mismanagement has contributed to increasing poverty and a deteriorating quality of life. While insufficient funding is certainly a constraint, even bigger constraints have been the absence of leadership and managerial and technical capacities, the almost exclusive top-down, centralized approach, the absence of stakeholder participation, and the lack of any long-term vision in any field. We are thus faced with a critical conceptual 'growing pain' in development. While the thinking and conceptual development on environmental issues has grown impressively over the last couple of decades, the policies, practices and tools for translating that into sustainable management of natural resources are not keeping up with the pace of conceptual development.

RAIN IS WATER: BROADENING THE RESOURCE BASE

In Chapter 5, Rockström shows that there is a deep integration gap within the water community. This involves two broad areas that, once integrated, may open larger opportunities for improved environmental management and could secure human livelihoods in poverty-stricken tropical countries.

The first area is in the complex nexus of water for food and the environment. There is an urgent need to break management barriers and to develop common policies and new institutional arrangements for managing water from a landscape perspective, not a sector perspective.

The second area refers to the conventional, and largely prevailing, professional water focus on liquid ('blue water') resources, largely omitting the environmental and economic role that is played by the much larger vapour ('green water') flow. Blue water sustains irrigation, industry and domestic water usage. Traditionally, the accessible portion of blue water is the only one understood by water resource managers, policy-makers and economists as the resource contributing to social and economic development. However, because this resource only constitutes roughly 10 per cent of the total freshwater resources in the world, it means that we are focusing 100 per cent of our attention on one tenth of the resource base. The remaining 90 per cent comprise blue water flows sustaining ecosystem services and green water flows sustaining all plant growth on Earth. With a new water management approach that integrates blue and green water flows, and takes rainwater as the genuine starting point for water resource management, new opportunities in water management may arise. As shown in Chapters 5 and 6, small-scale management options focusing on the best use of local rainfall may not only improve local food production and water supply, but also reduce negative environmental side effects at the catchment scale.

The third area in need of water integration is between the traditionally isolated sectors of water for food and water for nature. This is a paradox. One may wonder how water flows that are completely entangled in interactions at all levels between food and ecosystems in the real landscape have become totally separated in management. But that was the reality, until recently. As Rockström has shown in Chapter 5, the Second World Water Forum, with the frustrations of isolating water for food and nature, has resulted in a turning point in this respect. Launched in 2001, the Dialogue on Water, Food and Environment carries much promise in seeking to bridge the gap between food and environmental sectors through open and transparent dialogues and knowledge sharing. The Dialogue process will end with the Fourth World Water Forum in 2006.

In conclusion, the starting point is to break the conventional 'blue water' bias in water resources policy and management in favour of a holistic approach that takes rainfall (precipitation) as the starting point for integrated catchment management. Water managers: think about managing rain for the future!

INNOVATIVE MANAGEMENT OPTIONS

In Chapter 5, Rockström suggests that if we can solve the water challenges facing poor communities in the most water-scarce regions, than we should be able to do so in the less water-scarce regions, as well. Interestingly, even for water-scarce, semi-arid tropical environments, opportunities to increase food production and improve water resource usage exist. However, these opportunities will only surface by shifting to a more holistic hydrological thinking, as discussed above, combined with a more optimistic view on semi-arid environments and an open mind towards novel technologies and innovations.

In Chapter 6, Scott presents an overview of prospects and challenges for the use of derivative or secondary sources of water. These are not really 'unconventional'; in fact, many derivative water sources are being used conventionally around the world, particularly in rainwater harvesting and effluent reuse. Together with desalination, they represent important examples of water resources that might otherwise not be used productively. As a result, they are important in addressing water scarcity. By adopting water recycling and water-saving management strategies, win–win solutions can be achieved.

More direct ecosystem goods, such as food, can be generated per drop of water, which in turn reduces the risk of depleting water to sustain critical ecosystem functions. Both humans and the environment gain. Water managers of the future: open your minds to the opportunities of using old water in new ways!

INVISIBLE WATER RESOURCES: THE NEED FOR NEW ACTION

Similar to green water or vapour, groundwater has often not been given proper attention in water resource management. In Chapter 7, Kemper shows that groundwater is shifting from an 'invisible resource' to a highly visible one in areas where groundwater overdraft and pollution are taking place and affecting different stakeholders. But, at the same time, a new institutional framework for groundwater management is on the horizon. There is a clear shift from the laissez-faire approach that focused on the exploitation of the resource, without consideration for long-term sustainability, toward an approach centred on providing incentives to the different stakeholders for better and more equitable resource management. But providing incentives is not enough. An enabling environment (including the government's regulatory role and capacity-building function) and a fine-tuned combination of top-down and bottom-up approaches are required. Thus, the new management tool package does not only focus on market-based instruments, such as water pricing and groundwater usage rights, but also on groundwater users themselves in decision-making structures. It may require a bigger step from 'business as usual' than many existing agencies can handle. Water managers of the future: take care of your groundwater!

WATER RIGHTS AND USER INVOLVEMENT

As presented by Shen in Chapter 8, the nation, state or public agency owns water resources. In the resources allocation process, water rights are the most critical issue. But there is no correct and unique method of assigning water rights. Because of the different water resources management systems worldwide, a considerable exploration is needed to effectively address the new water resources issues. A lot of work must be done, such as empowerment of water users and security of water rights tenure. Chapter 8 shows that user/stakeholder participation is fundamental to improving water management. This participation can present many challenges depending on the local conditions, the most extreme being water-user rights in the decentralization/democratization process. Water managers of the future: open your minds to the opportunities of involving your water users/ stakeholders/owners!

CAPACITY BUILDING AND KNOWLEDGE SHIFTS TOWARDS INTEGRATING WATER MANAGEMENT

Today's water managers are often hydrologists or engineers. If one were to characterize them, the same clichés would be heard: knowledge workers who follow the cult of technology and worship rationality, calculation and hierarchical structures and approaches.

Luckily, many of them have made a switch in thinking, becoming social and ecological engineers. They understand the importance of environmental and social aspects and take them into account in their work. This switch towards a new brand of professionals, defined by Ahmad in Chapter 10 as 'social engineers', is fundamental to addressing problems in a more integrated way. These engineers have not become sociologists or ecologists; but their background enables them to understand the ecologists and sociologists in their teams. The skills of such socio-/eco-engineers are useful for integrated water resource management.

They must develop communication skills to better understand the various stakeholders involved in the process, and ensure that the participation and consultation process is completed in a structured manner. Water managers are also at the interface of politics and must understand short-term political commitments, conciliating them with the long-term sustainable perspective on water resources management.

At present, stakeholder participation is commonly accepted and the multi-actor process appears quite normal (albeit, not yet put into practice), and the quest for a collective understanding of the problem in many river basins is no longer the limiting factor for integrated water resource management (IWRM). But if IWRM is seen as a result ('integrated') and not as a process ('integrating'), and is always addressed by a solution-oriented approach, there is no process management. Today's water managers continue looking for practical solutions and results in the short term. The gloomy conclusion is that many of today's water managers do not have the skills to implement IWRM properly.

There is a need to develop the skills of the integrating water managers. Several organizations, such as the United Nations Educational, Scientific and Cultural Organization–IHE Water Education Institute (UNESCO-IHE) partnership, have started developing courses that are adapted to these new managers. As indicated by Figuères in Chapter 11, US$75 million are required for water supply and sanitation, primarily for infrastructure. In conventional sanitary engineering practices, not less than 65 per cent of the required investments are in the water distribution and wastewater collection systems ('pipes'), with the remainder in abstraction, treatment and disposal. This implies that in the field of water supply and sanitation, a lot of the water managers'/engineers' work is in the operation of entire water and sanitation. It is obvious that we still need new water managers to deal more wisely with, for example, the operational management of infrastructure.

But, at the same time, a new curriculum is urgently needed for individuals looking at water from a more holistic point of view. They have to develop the capacities to comprehend a sustainable system that combines not only the technical, but also the financial, social and environmental aspects and their impacts. As requests for stakeholder participation increase, water managers have to become like spiders in a web: connected to all interests in the same way. They need to manage complex processes. But most water managers are not trained for the tasks ahead because they have received a mono-disciplinary education.

THE INTER-GENERATION CHALLENGE

We are in trouble. There is no doubt that our present lifestyle choices, in both developed and developing countries, will not carry us into the sustainable future that we all wish for – a future where our children and grandchildren inherit an Earth that can provide for all without jeopardizing the quality of future life.

We are also in trouble if there is truth to Albert Einstein's saying that 'No problem can be solved by the same consciousness that created it.' Is this correct? We prefer not to know. What we do know is that action is needed now, in terms of both perceptual and professional changes. This means that we have to urgently invest in three inter-generational segments of society: the present senior generation, the present young professionals, and the future professionals. The complex water problems highlighted in this book are making life difficult for humans and ecosystems today.

Today's water managers need to drop old-world views and embark on a path that embraces novel ideas about integrated water management. At the same time, we should build more platforms for young professionals that strengthen their voices in planning, policy-making, decisions and implementation. Finally, in the long term we need to invest in our own children and theirs. The roots of a new water conscience can grow only if future generations are watered early with thorough and integrated water knowledge. Together, this inter-generational water troika can do wonders, now and in the future. We simply cannot wait for the next generation. In this complex jungle of uncertainties, there is one thing that we know for sure. If we wait for the next generation of water managers to do something, it will be too late for too many people.

Index

Page references in *italics* refer to boxes, figures and tables